SALAD DAZE
WAYNE HUSSEY

OMNIBUS PRESS

London / New York / Paris / Sydney / Copenhagen / Berlin / Madrid / Tokyo

SALAD DAZE

For Cinthya – the one true love of my life, whilst all others have been merely pretenders. Only you and you alone know the truth of who I am.

"Tinkerbellies, Tinkerbellies… ♫♫ "

For Mum and Dad, without whom.

"In the end, it's not going to matter how many breaths you took, but how many moments took your breath away." – Shing Xiong.

Foreword by Gary Numan

It's very rare that I hear a song that is so perfect, so beautifully written, that listening to it becomes a genuinely bittersweet experience. The pleasure you feel from letting something truly exceptional wash over you battles against the painful realisation of knowing that you will never write anything that good. That's what I have to deal with every time I listen to 'Tower Of Strength'. It puts things into perspective that's for sure.

I know Wayne has a real issue with the 'Legend' label that comes his way so often but, to me, he deserves it. As the brightest star of an entire genre he could have packed his guitar away decades ago and retired, rightfully considering himself, a glorious success in a brutal and difficult business. But he has no interest in that, not in retiring or looking at himself too seriously. He just keeps working, delivering music of exceptional quality year after year and touring constantly, in one form or another. This is what separates the genuine career musician from everyone else. This is for life, not two albums and back to your day job. Wayne Hussey is the real thing.

So many artists come along, have some success, fade away, fuck it up, lose the drive, whatever. Only a few are able to navigate their way through the endless minefields of music business treachery and disaster and yet stay positive and enjoy a career that spans decades. It's incredibly difficult, and only those that have truly devoted their life to music, to being in a band, to being an artist, to living the life, can ever hope to achieve the longevity and gloriously high moments that Wayne Hussey has achieved, and he shows no signs of stopping.

I'm proud to call him a friend. I don't see him nearly as much as I would like but that's part of the sacrifice. We've had some seriously mad nights together, shared our deepest problems and bared our souls to each other more than once, and it is an honour to be given the opportunity to write this little piece for his book. He is one of a kind, and whether he likes it or not, he's an absolute legend, and I can't think of anyone on planet Earth who has a better story to tell.

Gary Numan
January 2019

Foreword by Iggy Pop

I toured a lot with The Mission in the 90s and Wayne was much too bright and nice a guy to be in the rock business. I suppose that's why he never really was. I mean, his voice was nothing short of commanding, and his grooves were more goth and operatic than the run of the mill. But Wayne always had a sense of humour, and that's where the rock kicked in, because sometimes it's just fucking fun. He's living in Brazil now, and his new album (*As Irmãs Siamesas*) is worlds away from his past. And that's a beautiful thing.

Iggy Pop
January 2019

Preface & Disclaimer

This book may be a pack of lies. Or the unmitigated truth. It really depends what you prefer to believe. I *have* dutifully researched, as well as trawled the memory banks of myself and others, but have written without being slavish to fact. These are *my* memories and I can't demand absolute accuracy of them, so neither should you. My story is certainly based on very true events but even the most honest of men and women are prone to exaggeration in the pursuit of self-mythology, wouldn't you agree?

My apologies for putting words into the mouths of others. Conversations are recorded here but I must confess that liberties may well have been taken in their recall. Who can remember verbatim a conversation that took place merely an hour ago let alone 40 years? It's the *gist* of the conversation that's important rather than the actual words. It's the *gist* that is remembered.

As a musician I don't consider myself a writer as such, I'm only in this position of *writing a book* because of my achievements whilst making music. But I've enjoyed the process of writing. The disciplines involved. The finding of words. And memories long forgotten. I've enjoyed the remembering, mostly.

Flaubert once wrote, 'our worth should be measured by our aspirations more than our works.' Well said, that man.

For each chapter in this book I have constructed a playlist that pertains to the content of that particular chapter, or were 'hits' in the time period I am writing about. Designed to enrich the reading experience, we have set up playlists for you with Spotify and YouTube (see instructions below). Where I was unable to find a particular song that's listed in the book I have substituted it with another that has some relevance, however tenuous.

I must add that a few of these choices are purely for context, but most are because I love the songs. Despite my eventual moral ruin, of which you shall soon be reading, my heart continues to beat fiercely, insanely, to the same incessant rhythm of love for music that propelled me to pick up a guitar in the first place. And in music there is redemption. Believe you me. It's because of music that this book exists. It's only right that there should be a soundtrack to its reading. You don't even need to read the book to enjoy the playlists!

For Spotify:
Open and log-in to the Spotify app, type husseysaladdaze into the search engine. Upon results go to the husseysaladdaze *Profile*. On *Overview* click on *All* and you will then have access to the playlists for all 20 chapters. Choose the corresponding number for the chapter you are currently reading.

For YouTube:
Type Wayne Hussey into the search engine, filter the search to *channel* and then click on the Wayne Hussey – Official icon. Once on the official channel page, highlight playlists, and, again, choose the corresponding chapter for the one you are currently reading.

Wayne Hussey
January 2019

Contents

Introducing...
The Star Of The Show

PLAYLIST:
1. Refrain – Lys Assia   2. Heartbreak Hotel – Elvis Presley
3. You Make Me Feel So Young – Frank Sinatra
4. Who's Sorry Now – Connie Francis   5. Blue Moon – Elvis Presley
6. Only The Lonely – Frank Sinatra

It was summer, 1956. Britain and her Tory prime minister, Anthony Eden, were embroiled in a developing ruckus over the Egyptian Suez Canal. Heroin had recently been criminalised in Britain, joining cocaine as a Class A. Elvis Presley had scored his first hit with 'Heartbreak Hotel' and Switzerland's Lys Assia, wearing a powder-blue ankle-length dress, had just won the inaugural Eurovision Song Contest with a charming ditty called 'Refrain'. It banes me to record that Manchester United were crowned league champions of England, while their more likeable neighbours, City, won the FA Cup by beating Birmingham 3-1 in a game best remembered for the courage of their goalkeeper, German Bert Trautmann, who played on to the end despite breaking his neck in the 75th minute. Liverpool were languishing in Division Two. Frank Sinatra topped the maiden UK album chart with *Songs For Swinging Lovers*. It was still a year away from John Lennon meeting Paul McCartney for the first time.

In Mangotsfield, Bristol, 17-year-old Wendy Lovelock, as is the wont of teenagers, found herself in conflict with her mum, Edith. To escape the restrictions imposed by her disciplinarian mater, she left the family home to live with her friend Beryl in Arlesey, Bedfordshire. Finding menial work in a local factory – "putting little wires into computer things" – Wendy's routine was like that of most young people of the time, before and since: work all week, count down the hours until the weekend, then let your hair down. Once a month Wendy and Beryl, two pretty young British girls, were invited to the dances at the local US Air Force base in Biggleswade where they met "quite a wild lot. They were always having parties, and there was always drink there, you know what it's like." Oh yes, I do.

Well, as it often does in these situations, one thing led to another and Wendy hooked up with a handsome native of Los Angeles named Tony. They knocked about together for more or less four months through the summer of 1957, but young hearts can be fickle and Wendy soon tired of her Angeleno paramour, her affections switching swiftly to another "really nice lad, but I can't remember his name now". Not long after the break-up, Wendy suspected she was pregnant. Only Tony could be the father. But she couldn't bring herself to tell him. "I was too proud for that. We'd finished, and he'd moved on and I'd moved on, it was just one of those things, really."*

Wendy went to see her local GP who confirmed her pregnancy and inquired what she was going to do. Remember, Wendy, Cardiff-born and Bristol-raised, was a long way from

---

* Tony, who a year or so later returned home to LA, never knew that Wendy was pregnant; never knew he had fathered a child while stationed in England.

home and her family; a young girl defiled and lost. Abortion, illegal until 1967, the same year that homosexuality was decriminalised, was not an option. Not that Wendy would've ever gone that route if it was available to her anyway. The late Fifties were still the moral dark ages, a time when unmarried mothers were deeply stigmatised, besmirching a family's good name and bringing shame on the community; when sex outside of marriage was still proscribed as sinful in the eyes of society and the church. "Well," Wendy informed her doctor, "under my current circumstances I'm going to have to give the baby up for adoption."

"Your best bet is to go into a church-run Mother & Baby Home," the GP suggested. "Leave it with me and I'll sort something out for you. I'll be in touch."

Wendy kept mum, not telling a living soul of her predicament apart from Beryl. The GP eventually got back in touch. "I've found you a place. It's in Bristol."

"Oh no," was Wendy's reaction, "not Bristol. I don't really want to go to Bristol, I might bump into someone I know."

But the doctor was shrewd, as well as kindly. "Ah, you're a young girl all on your own here. You have family in Bristol. I know what it's like, once they find out they'll rally around and support you."

Seven months into the pregnancy, Wendy returned to Bristol and joined 15 other young, unmarried, pregnant girls in a Church Of England Mother & Baby Home, a large Edwardian house on Ashley Road, not far from the city centre.

"It was horrendous," she recalls. "They worked us silly, scrubbing floors and wooden benches, doing all the cooking, and washing, right up to when we were about to give birth. It really wasn't very pleasant there. It was hard. Matron Turton was a real battle-axe. I remember one day we had beef for dinner and it was covered in little maggots and they made us eat it.

"And we all had to go up to the St Mary Redcliffe Church to be confirmed and forgiven for our sins," she adds, laughing.

On her arrival in Bristol, Wendy had contacted her best friend, Pauline, to let her know she was back in town. And pregnant. Not permitted visitors, Wendy was nevertheless allowed out a couple of hours a week, so she'd meet Pauline in the recently opened Lewis' department store on The Horsefair. Having not yet told her mum, or her younger sisters, Jean and Ruth, that she was with child and so close to home, Wendy was persuaded by Pauline to write a letter to her mum explaining her situation and hoping for a reconciliation. The letter arrived on Good Friday, and Edith Lovelock was horrified, her immediate reaction to proclaim, "She must've been raped." Still, Edith made no attempt to visit Wendy while she waited to give birth in the nearby Mother & Baby home. Nor was an invitation extended to Wendy to come home, the excuse being that the family abode was too small to accommodate a heavily pregnant daughter.

Seven or eight weeks later and it was time for Wendy to give birth. Admitted into Southmead Hospital at tea-time, 5pm–ish, on Monday, May 26, 1958, Wendy gave birth to a healthy baby boy at just after 9pm.

"It wasn't an easy birthing," she remembers. "They used forceps to help it along."

Connie Francis was at number one in the UK hit parade that day with 'Who's Sorry Now'.

With nowhere else to go after the birth and the Anglican Church unable to find anyone to immediately adopt her newborn, Wendy stayed on at the home, and was back to scrubbing floors and peeling buckets of spuds within days. A few weeks later the matron and social worker informed Wendy they'd found a nice American couple to adopt her little boy.

They'd already arrived from the USA and were scheduled to pick up the neonate the very next day. Wendy was handed the adoption documents to sign.

It was at this point that she had a dramatic change of heart. "I'm not doing it," she told the shocked matron. Having nursed the infant since its birth, a mother and child bond, a genuine attachment, had naturally developed. After spending these few weeks with him, Wendy couldn't now give up her little boy.

Matron Turton and the social worker did their very best to persuade Wendy otherwise. "How do you think you're gonna cope? There's no help out there for you, your family aren't supporting you, what're you going to do? You've got nowhere to live and nowhere to go."

But Wendy was resolute, "I don't know but I'll find something, I'll do something. I can't give up my little boy now."

Matron Turton wasn't happy. "Well, we can't have you staying here any longer with the baby, you have to leave and we'll have to put him in a nursery home until you either come to your senses or make suitable arrangements."

Later that day Wendy was notified that a place for her baby had been found in Salisbury. Since there were plenty of children's homes in Bristol, this was obviously a tactic to make life difficult for Wendy, an attempt to deter her from visiting regularly. With no access to a car, and with public transport in 1958 being what it was, it was a long, arduous bus journey of more than 60 miles each way with several changes en route every time she wanted to visit her baby son.

"I think they thought I'd give up after a couple of months and just sign the release papers," she says. "But I wouldn't give 'em the satisfaction. We visited a couple of times. I say we as I remember my mum and my sister, Jean, being with me one time, my mum now gradually coming around to me having had the baby. Like all grandmothers, once she held him in her arms she was a goner. But there still wasn't room in her tiny two-bedroomed cottage for me and the child. Jean and Ruth were sharing one small bedroom and my mum had the other. It would've been impossible. But bit by bit I turned my life around. I got a job in Durham's on Morley Road as a machinist, and eventually moved into Anne and Frank's, whom I knew from when my older brother, John, had once gone out with Anne's sister. They turned their front room into a bedsit for me, with a bed and a cot, and after about nine months of him living in that nursery home, when he was almost one year old, I was finally able to bring my little boy home to live with me."

Yep, that little boy, who was almost given up for adoption and taken off to America to live, was me. You know me as Wayne Hussey but I was christened Jerry Wayne Lovelock on July 18, 1958, by Anglican Father Hibbard.

There aren't words enough to tell you how thankful I am to my mum, Wendy, for her fortitude and strength of will in fighting to keep me despite the hardships and struggles she endured. It's too hypothetical to wonder who and how and where and what I might have become if she hadn't done so. It certainly would've been a very different story to the one you're about to read...

CHAPTER 1

Born Of The Sign Of Air & The Twins

Still, having to work every day meant that Mum had to rely on the kindness of friends, mostly her best friend who I came to know as Auntie Pauline, to look after me, now a toddling imp, during the daytime. When I was about two years old Nanny Lovelock, Edith, my mum's mum, was allocated a bigger three-bedroomed council house on James Road in Staple Hill. Mother and daughter now reconciled, Mum and I moved into one of the bedrooms, my nan had a room and the third bedroom was occupied by aunties Jean and Ruth, Mum's younger sisters. John, Mum's elder brother, had long since married and moved out of the family home so I was surrounded solely by females, most of them teenage, who no doubt mollycoddled and spoilt me rotten. They dressed me up as they would their dolls, in dresses, striped jackets and dickie-bows. I flourished within this matriarchal community. I was their little prince. Everybody *loved* me. The fact that I had grown from being a Mr Magoo lookalike at birth, a shrivelled up prune as Mum lovingly described me, to being an adorable cherub by the time I was just a few months old, certainly helped my cause. After all, I was Monday's child, fair of face. There is a justified argument that I was never again to be as beauteous as I was at two years old.

Auntie Pauline had by this time married Terry and had a daughter of her own. Just as my princely court would dote on me I doted on baby Deborah who was just over two years younger than me: my first girlfriend at two and a half years old. She was just a newborn so accusations of cradle-snatching are not without merit. At nappy-changing time I was fascinated by the fact that Deborah didn't have a little winkle like me.* In fact I was the only person I knew with a little winkle which, in my mind, set me apart from everybody else in my world. It came as great relief when Auntie Jean married Graham, who, for some reason, I came to know as Uncle Nobby, and together their union produced, in September 1961, a cousin for me, Mark, a boy. Mark had a winkle too but not as big as mine. Even at three years old I was already comparing dick sizes. Although there was a new princeling in my kingdom to contend with, it was nonetheless reassuring for me to learn that I was not so different after all. I was not the only person in the world to have a winkle.

One evening in the summer of 1961 Mum and her friend Hazel went to the Star Inn in Congresbury on the A370, the Weston

---

* I'm sure I don't really have to explain this but I feel I must, just to avoid any possible misunderstanding. Winkle was the substitute name for penis in our household. Winkle! I ask you. I would blush uncontrollably on holiday at the seaside as a kid when asked if I wanted a punnet of 'cockles and winkles'.

road, to see local rock'n'roll duo, Chantilly Lace. Featuring Slim Hendy on drums and Brian Gilbertson on piano, a precursor to acts like Chas & Dave, they played around the pubs, clubs, and holiday camps of the South West covering the hits of the day. Acting as their chauffeur and self-appointed bodyguard was a young scallywag from Winterbourne named Arthur Hussey. Three months younger than my mum and not long out of the army having been conscripted at 18, Arthur, a twin and eldest of six sons, liked a pint and was prone to letting his fists do the talking for him. Bristol born and bred and, to this day, speaking with a West Country brogue thicker than the trunk of a 2,000-year-old sequoia, Arthur met Wendy and immediately they fell in love.

The following summer, on Saturday, August 11, 1962, Arthur and Wendy married at St Stephens C of E Church, Soundwell. At number one in the UK hit parade that week was 'I Remember You' by the yodelling Frank Ifield. I was the page boy at the wedding with Deborah, 'Auntie' Pauline's daughter, and Vanessa the bridesmaids. Vanessa was new on the scene. Arthur's twin, Alfie, was married to Doreen and Vanessa was their daughter, 18 months my junior. She was my latest flame. Born of the sign of air and the twins I was already typically Geminian capricious.

My mum's wedding is my earliest memory. I have vague recollections of other occasions preceding this but they are shrouded in murk and I can't be certain it's a memory or… something else. After the marriage ceremony photographs were taken outside the doors of the church, including one of my mum being lifted off her feet by Arthur with me looking up at them, my hand in my mouth, as if to say, 'What're you doing with my mum? Put her down, she's *my* mum'. Then the newlyweds, me leading my flower girls on either side, made their way through the gathered confetti-throwing throng of family, friends, and well-wishers to a waiting car festooned with streamers, balloons and a couple of empty cans tied by string to the back bumper. Mum climbed into the back-seat and I tried to follow her but was held back by Auntie Pauline and *that man* took my place in the car next to Mum. Then they were driven off to God knows where while I was left behind screaming and bawling and kicking up a rumpus. That is my first *real* memory. A tantrum. Of course they were off on their honeymoon but I didn't understand what that meant. I was four years old and I'd just seen Mum waltz off with this Arthur bloke, a usurper in my mum's affections.

A week or so later and they were home from honeymooning in Cornwall and we became a family. I was encouraged to call Arthur *Dad*, something I gladly took to as my cousins all had dads and I wanted one too. From that day on I never considered Arthur anything less than *my dad*. As far as I'm concerned he is, and has always been, *my dad*. So from now on in this story Arthur'll be known as *my dad*. To make everything legal I was officially adopted by my dad and took his surname, just as my mum had also done. Despite everybody now calling me Wayne, ever since I had come back to Bristol from the children's home in Salisbury, I was still listed as Jerry Wayne on the adoption certificate, but I had now become a Hussey.

The first home I remember, and this would be just after Mum and Dad had married, was 43 Stonewalls, Down Road, in Winterbourne Down, seven miles north-east of Bristol. We rented the ground floor and a couple of first floor bedrooms from a pair of spinsters who lived upstairs – Nanny Matthews and Auntie Glad. Of course they weren't my real nanny and auntie but I called them that because that's what you did in those days with people who were close. Family was more extended then. Anyway, I say spinsters as I don't recall either of them ever having a man in their lives. Auntie Glad was definitely the one that wore the trousers in that relationship and was very good at fixing the car and taking out the dustbins while Nanny Matthews took on the then-more-traditional woman's role of cooking and cleaning.

Going down the hill the house was situated on the left-hand side just past the bend where there are two churches – the Church Of England on the right and the Methodist Church on the left – and opposite Henderson's The Hairdressers that was still serving heads as recently as 2016 although I suspect the original Mrs Henderson had long since retired her scissors by then. Mum used to go there to have her hair styled in the latest fashions of the day. Well, why not? It was only about ten yards from our front door. Mum and Dad used to send me 30 yards off up the road to Sunday School at the Methodist Church every Sunday morning. I suspect it was more to do with them being able to snatch a couple of hours alone rather than for my spiritual well-being.

It was the coldest winter in over 200 years in England. It started with a heavy, dense fog covering swathes of the country in early December 1962, with London perhaps hardest hit with its last great, 'old style' smog blanketing the capital. The first snows fell a week or so later, a short wintry outbreak of the white stuff that lasted just two days. As Elvis hit number one in the UK pop charts with 'Return To Sender', a little known Liverpool band had just crept into the Top 20 at number 19 with their first single release, 'Love Me Do'. It had taken ten weeks to reach this dizzying height, taking a further two weeks to peak at 17 and then begin its slow descent down and out of the Top 50.

Just before Christmas the temperatures dropped below freezing and the snow began falling again on Christmas Day – a rare white Christmas. And then it didn't *stop* snowing. The country froze, *the Big Freeze* it was called. A blizzard blew in just before New Year, drifting snow throughout Britain to over 20 feet deep in places, causing major disruptions to the roads, the railways, and the football season. Power lines were down. Telephones were out. Then two whole months of more snow, below zero temperatures, and freezing fog. Rivers and ponds froze over. Even parts of the sea up to a mile off the coastline of Kent, apparently. Milk delivered in glass bottles to our doorstep froze, with the milk expanding and breaking through the silver foil bottle tops. They looked like tall white candles in a bottle. Icicle spears hung like fangs from the gutters and trees, some as long as two or three feet.

The family car sat in the driveway engulfed in snow. Dad couldn't drive it anyway. A black 1936 Ford 8 for which he'd paid £10, it was so old it wouldn't even start in this weather. Furthermore, he couldn't go to work as he was a labourer on a building site and no one could be expected to work outside in these arctic conditions.

Mum would dress me in two pairs of trousers and socks, and make me wear two jumpers over two t-shirts in an attempt to stave off the cold. And don't forget the long johns and vest. I looked like the Michelin Man. It cost a lot of money to heat the house, money that we, and millions of others in this sceptred isle, didn't have. Better to wrap up as warm as we could. The country came to a standstill and for most people, mostly grown-ups, the situation became a scourge. But to me, a four-year-old boy, this was a winter wonderland.

Having my new dad at home all the time was brilliant as he helped me build a big snowman in the garden, played snowball fights with me, and, best of all, together we built a sledge from a couple of wooden crates and a plank that he found in the outhouse. It was probably a right old jalopy of a sledge but because my dad had made it for us, to my four-year-old eyes it was the most beautiful thing I'd ever seen. We trekked the quarter mile through the deep snow to the top of Harcombe Hill, next to the viaduct, where there was a field that ran down a steep slope to the frozen River Frome below. There were other dads there too, with their kids sledging down the hill. We took our turn, Dad sitting on the sledge first, keeping it steady with his feet planted either side while I clambered on and sat between his legs. He wrapped his arms around my waist and then lifted his feet onto the runners and, with a push on Dad's back from Mum, down that hill we flew. As we gathered speed on the downslope, with the cold air rushing past my ears and our sledge kicking up a snow flurry like schist and scree, I was thrilled. I had a dad just like everybody else who would play with me. The sledge came to a halt on the flat ground at the bottom of the hill, just a yard or two from the frozen-over river. "Can we do it again, Dad, please?", I begged. We made our ascent back up the hill and did it all again, over and over.

The thaw started at the beginning of March 1963. *The Big Freeze* was over. Sadly for me, Dad got the car started and went back to work. Coincidentally, those likeable young lads from Liverpool had just peaked at number two in the UK pop chart with their second single, 'Please Please Me'. The Beatles they were called. What a funny name that was. I was four years old and I loved The Beatles... and *Fireball XL5*.*

---

* A children's television show following the missions of spaceship Fireball XL5, commanded by Colonel Steve Zodiac of the World Space Patrol. Produced by the Andersons, Gerry & Sylvia, who went onto produce the fabulous and timeless *Stingray* and *Thunderbirds*, and other lesser shows, all filmed in Supermarionation, a form of puppetry.

Sometime in the late spring of 1963 Mum and Dad told me that they were expecting another baby. Where it was coming from I had no idea and was really none the wiser when Mum explained it was growing in her tummy and would be coming out from between her legs. "What, like a poo?" I asked, not unreasonably. "Yeah, a bit like a poo," Mum laughed.

Adam, my little brother, looking just a little bit like a poo, came along on June 13. Another winkle in the family. In fact, winkles were now abounding as Auntie Doreen and Uncle Alfie had given Vanessa a younger brother, Roderick; while Uncle John was married to Peggy and the fruits of their loins had yielded Richard; and Auntie Jean and Uncle Nobby had presented my cousin Mark with a baby brother, Paul, to fight with. Auntie Ruth would soon be *in the club* when she married Pete who sired Steven and Andrew in close succession. Both clans, the Lovelocks and the Husseys, were enthusiastic in their procreation and happily contributed to the over-population of the planet, although it was my mum and dad who took the crown as most productive with subsequent additions to our family of Westley in 1967, Amelia in 1968, and baby Adele in 1974. Of my generation I am the eldest of the more than 25 offspring from both sides of my lineage.

Not long after Adam was born The Beatles became even more popular with the release of 'She Loves You', their fourth single, on August 23. It took two weeks to ascend to the number one position, staying there for six, eventually amassing a mammoth 33 weeks in the charts. 'She Loves You' became the first single ever to sell a million copies in the UK. Beatles records were being played constantly on the coffin-sized radiogram in our front room and we were so taken with the lovable Scouse mop-tops, as were the rest of the country, that Mum bought a purple-and-white tea towel adorned with their pictures and their 'real' autographs! Dad made a lovely wooden frame for it, from wood left over from the sledge no doubt, and it was hung proudly on our living room wall. John was my favourite, closely followed by George. I got that right, even at the age of five. Sadly, the tea towel got taken down and used as a tea towel when John went weird and grew a beard.

I started at junior school in September 1963, aged five. My first school, the same school that my dad attended when he was a nipper, was Winterbourne C of E Primary on the High Street, a walk of a mile each way every day. We only had the one old car, the 1936 Ford 8 that Dad used to drive to work, so Mum, pushing the industrial-sized Silver Cross pram that held my baby brother Adam, had to walk me to school come rain or shine or sleet or snow. Apparently, I used to whine and moan all the way there and all the way home.

My favourite time of the week was Saturday tea time when Mum would toast some crumpets and slather them with *real* butter, not the margarine that we spread on our bread the rest of the week, and we would all sit down together to watch Troy Tempest captain *Stingray* through some great undersea adventure on our little black-and-white TV in front of a blazing real fire. This is when I first fell in love with the exquisite and enigmatic Marina. I mean no disrespect to Deborah or Vanessa but what could I have known of love at four years old? Now I was five I knew my heart. Marina didn't speak a word but she could hold her breath underwater forever, attributes I've been looking for in my women ever since but to no avail. (Now, now, no need for anyone to start erecting a soapbox... or a scaffold.)

I bought the DVD box set of *Stingray* a couple of years ago – all 39 episodes *and* extras – and fell in love with Marina all over again. It's remarkable how well it has aged, unlike other TV shows that I loved as a kid such as *The Man From U.N.C.L.E.* and *Joe 90*. I also bought the complete DVD box set of *Thunderbirds* around the same time and I have to say that the Tracy family and Lady Penelope and Parker are, for me, the quintessential Sixties icons, along with the luminescent Alexandra Bastedo who starred in *The Champions*, another TV show I loved. I also had a huge crush on Julie Andrews as Mary Poppins and, watching it today, I can quite imagine Mary Poppins as the dominatrix. Go on, just imagine *that*. Nanny Lovelock took me to the Van Dyck, now a pub, on Fishponds Road to see *Mary Poppins*, it being the first film I ever saw in the cinema.

Nanny Lovelock was a character. When her four kids were really young, the youngest, Ruth, being just a few months old at the time, her husband, Seriol, my grandad, did a runner back to Cardiff from whence he came, with a younger Eastern European woman with gold teeth, apparently. He left my nan with the four nippers and no financial support. Of course this was during the war in the early Forties and poor old Nanny Lovelock would have to work two, and sometimes three jobs to support herself and her young family. It wasn't an untypical scenario at the time because the war was making widows of many wives who were losing their husbands on the battlefields of Europe. Not many, though, had lost their husband to some European floozy with gold teeth. But karma was to wield its justice on my grandad a few years later. After he'd split up with his golden-toothed hussy who my nan always contended was a German spy, he got hitched to a young Welsh country girl with white teeth and with whom he had four more children. *She* left him with the four kids when *they* were all still very young to run off with, a-ha, a younger man. What goes around, eh?

I remember seeing my grandad only once when I was about eight or nine, mostly because he gave me £5 which was a veritable fortune then. Much to my chagrin, Mum made me deposit it in my Post Office savings account. He came to our home and there was a reconciliation of sorts with Mum. That was when we found out that she had two half-brothers and two half-sisters in Cardiff, the eldest boy just a year or so older than me. My grandad was dying of lung cancer at the time and it was, at first, assumed the reconciliation was an attempt on his part to put right the wrongs he had committed against Mum and her siblings before he departed this mortal coil. In reality the prime reason was to ingratiate himself with the family and to ask my nan if she would take his four new children after his death. Of course, she told him, quite rightly, to drop dead. Taking my nan at her word, Grandad died in 1967 and the four children were put into the childcare system. David, Peter, Wendy, and Pauline, for that is their names, had it pretty rough at times but, happily, they managed to stay together throughout their childhood and, in the last ten years or so, have got together for a meal in a pub once or twice a year with their half-brother and sisters, my uncle John, my mum, and aunties Jean & Ruth.

Nanny Lovelock never remarried although late in life she did find a boyfriend named Ted who would pamper her and, as she deserved, treat her like a princess, staying with her until she died in 1998 at the grand old age of 90. Maybe her longevity was down to the fact that she'd cycle everywhere. Never owned a car. I remember when I was a young teenager I'd see her cycling around the streets of Fishponds, Downend, and Staple Hill cutting quite the dashing, if not eccentric, figure; long flowing dark locks, long skirts and hobnail boots. And she was well into her sixties by then.

Her only vice was fondness for a little flutter on the horses. It was never huge amounts, just a couple of bob here and a shilling there. It must've raised a smile at her local bookies when she came in to place her meagre wager. A high roller, she wasn't. She did take me once or twice to the horse racing in Chepstow, just the other side of the Severn Bridge. It was in the school holidays and I was staying with my nan for a few days to give my poor beleaguered mum a respite from looking after me. As we boarded the bus home, my nan said, "Don't tell your mother where we've been today or she won't let you come and stay with me again."

As I used to love going to stay with my nan it was quite the threat so I never uttered a word until just a few years ago, many years after my nan had passed. My mum never had a clue. Nan also took me to the evening greyhound racing at Eastville Stadium a couple of times too. I used to love it there under the floodlights with grown men (and my nan) screaming at the dogs as they chased the little fake rabbit lure around the track. Again, she'd only bet pennies but she loved it and would get such a thrill out of winning, even though her prize money would always be just enough for the bus fare home.

Another little story about my nan that always raises a smile at family gatherings is when she went to stay with my uncle John who, by that time, was running a pub in Portskewett, near Chepstow funnily enough, in South Wales. Now, Uncle John had a Doberman named Duke that my nan used to take for afternoon walks while she was staying there. Once my nan had left to go back home to Bristol it fell to my uncle John to resume his dog walking responsibilities, and the first day he took Duke out for a walk the dog led him straight into the nearest bookies where all the staff knew Duke by name. Uncle John had never been in that betting shop before. Duke had.

I don't know whose brilliant idea it was, probably Dad's as he was out at work all day and wouldn't have to endure the noise, but, in an attempt to encourage some innate musical ability I may have possessed, for my sixth birthday Mum and Dad bought me a glittery blue toy drum kit. So, on sunny days, of which there seemed to be a lot more then than there are now, I used to set my little drum kit up in our front garden, just across the road from Henderson's, and imagine myself as Ringo and bash

away. On one of these sunny days, just after I had come out of hospital and was supposed to be taking it easy having had my tonsils ripped out, I set up my drum kit and was happily banging along to 'I Want To Hold Your Hand'. All of a sudden and without warning, like a scene from *The Exorcist*, this vile projectile vomiting of blood spewed from my mouth and all over my lovely little blue drum kit. I was haemorrhaging and an ambulance was called. I was rushed back into hospital for emergency surgery. I gave up the drums after that. How different my life could've been if I hadn't.

On May 1, 1965, Liverpool beat Leeds 2-1 with an Ian St John extra time winner at Wembley Stadium to win the FA Cup for the first time in the club's history. In the days preceding the final on the playground at my school, and most likely playgrounds all over England, kids were picking 'their' team for the match. My best friend at school was Clive Brewer, who along with his family actually hailed from Liverpool, so in a show of support that would ultimately shape my life in ways I could never have dreamed of, at the grand old age of six years and 340 days I chose Liverpool. To this day, over 50 years later, Liverpool are still my team, which has sometimes been a curse but mostly a blessing. We have enjoyed more than our fair share of triumphs over the last half-century as well as our dark days.

Just think, I could've chosen Leeds and how miserable would that have made my life? (Soz, Craig.)

When I was six or seven years old Mum was diagnosed with tuberculosis. TB can be contagious and a killer so the local health authority wanted to sequester Mum to a local sanitarium but she refused to go as Adam, my little brother, was still just a baby. Mum's weight dropped down to about seven stone (45 kgs) and a nurse would come to the house every day for nine months to administer a streptomycin injection, and once that treatment finished she had to take tablets as big as an old penny daily for the next five years. Gradually and eventually, and thankfully, she got better and the upside of Mum's illness was that it qualified us for a council house. So we moved to the Watley's End part of Winterbourne and 61 Star Barn Road.

Winterbourne was and still is a large village that is surrounded by green fields and hills. A short commute to the city, it was favoured by footballers and their managers and professionals with young families and sizeable incomes. It was and still is a predominantly middle-class village, as reflected in its house prices. But in among the homes of the affluent the local council built small areas, pockets really, of council housing. It's one of those idiosyncratic, well-intentioned and forward-looking planning schemes so characteristic of the Sixties in Britain but, because it was more rural than inner city, it was for the most part a very pleasant place to grow up and spend my childhood. I guess it was an attempt by the planning authorities to integrate us plebs with the toffs but it didn't really work out that way, of course. We generally kept to our own kind and were tolerated more than accepted. I'm sure my lifelong suspicion of the privileged classes was first engendered by the way I felt inferior to the nobs I lived amongst and with whom I went to school. I don't really have a problem with privilege per se, it's when I see a sense of entitlement being exhibited that gets my goat. And entitlement can be flaunted by anyone of any class, colour, creed and denomination, but in my experience when I've come across it it's generally been a behaviour of those with privileged backgrounds. Or of spoilt, indulged rock stars. That said, Winterbourne was a really good, safe place in which to grow up and even though we lived in a council house, while not idyllic, it was nowhere near as bad as living in inner city high rises or the council estates that were sprouting up just a few miles away in Bristol and in most other cities around Britain at that time.

CHAPTER 2

From One Jesus To Another

Not long after we had moved to Star Barn Road there was a knock at our front door and there stood two handsome, smart young Americans dressed in dark suits with name-tags attached to their lapels. They were Mormons or rather, to identify them fully, missionaries from The Church Of Jesus Christ Of Latter-Day Saints. Anyway, because Mum had just been perilously ill with her bout of TB and was maybe feeling a little sensitive about the value of life, she invited the young men into our home to listen to what they had to say. They'd come around on a Friday evening for discussion and, as they were coming in the front door, Dad would be sneaking off out the side door and down the pub for his weekly night out with the lads. Mum was impressed with the Mormon belief that a family could be bound together for all time and eternity in the hereafter and very soon became a convert, being baptised in early 1966. Now, I reckon that for some people the idea of being bound to their families forever is more like purgatory than heaven. But it's a concept that appealed to Mum and many others who are of the Mormon faith. And in its simplest and purest form amongst a family that is loving and close, it's easy to see its appeal.

Adam and I started going with Mum to the chapel in Downend every Sunday and when I turned eight years old later that same year I was baptised too, by Elder Brown, another missionary from the USA. Despite Dad enjoying the social activities that the church offered – he'd attend the dances and sporting activities but nip down the pub for a quick pint or two during the prayer intervals – he resisted the doctrine and wouldn't go to church on a Sunday for a good few years. Amongst other self-disciplines the Mormon's Word Of Wisdom advocates no alcohol or smoking but Dad couldn't be doing with that, he liked his tipple too much. Eventually though, when the hangovers started getting more severe, he *saw the light* and gave up his drinking. When I was 13, he was baptised too.

Being members of the LDS faith became all-consuming, the biggest thing in our lives, and as well as Sundays we would spend most evenings of the week at church. Since I knew no different, being raised as a Mormon seemed quite natural to me. Now, in hindsight, I believe that the way I was raised and the basic precepts and values I was taught have held me in good stead throughout my life. I'm not religious, and I certainly have no faith in any organised religion, but I do consider myself a decent human being, albeit one that is deeply flawed, and I'm convinced that my church upbringing has contributed to me being that way. On the other hand, being raised religiously was to cast a shadow over my life for many moons to come.

Every time I did something that went against the church's teachings, even just masturbation, then the guilt, like Catholic but Mormon, would stay with me for years, all through my late teens and most of my early adulthood. I think I'm okay now at 60. The only guilt I feel is for the way I have treated and hurt particular people in my life, though I'm sure I've condemned myself through sin to be a son of perdition in the eyes of the church. Mormonism preaches *free will*, our divine right to choose between right and wrong, and I know that I've deliberately chosen 'wrong' many times according to the values of the church. Nevertheless, try as I might to be ex-communicated I am still a baptised Mormon and as long as I remain inactive in the church I will remain a member no matter what sins I commit. How ass about tit is that? Mum and Dad are still very active in the church and even served an 18-month long mission in Manila in the Philippines when they were both 70 years old. And while I don't agree with them about many things, theology being principal in our disagreements, I can't resent, and if I'm honest I'm even a little bit envious of, the surety and certainty of their beliefs. I'm sure, if such a place does really exist, they'll be going to the Celestial Kingdom. Not sure where I'll be off to though.

I was an average height, slight child but good at football, which, all through my school years, held the bullies in abeyance. Good at art or music, you'd get a good ribbing and more often than not a thumping for your artistic bent. Good at football then you were 'one of the lads' and mostly safe. At seven I was playing with and against boys aged ten and 11; the youngest boy on record up to that point to play for the school when I was picked at centre-forward against our big local rivals, Elm Park. I remember early in the match, imagining myself as Roger Hunt at the Kop End, being through on goal one-on-one with just their goalkeeper to beat. At that moment between the sticks he loomed up as seemingly big as King Kong and, in my nervousness, I tripped over the ball and fell flat on my face. Not for the last time would I fall flat on my face but as the years progressed balls had less and less to do with the mishap. From then on my performance went from bad to worse and was so abject that for another three years I wasn't picked to represent the school again – a demoralising and humiliating experience for a young boy that lived and breathed football.

Around this same time it was established by my teacher, Mrs Snailum, that maybe young Wayne might have a problem with his eyesight. I was falling behind in maths as I was copying the numbers down wrongly from the blackboard. Mum and I went to the opticians and, yes, indeed I had an eyesight deficiency and needed glasses. Absolutely traumatic for a kid of my tender years. All of a sudden, being the only kid in my class that had to wear glasses, I was the school freak and, football skills notwithstanding, was referred to as 'four eyes' and 'goggles' and other similar insults. I tell you this because it was one of those events, much like my choosing to support Liverpool in the 1965 FA Cup final, that is pivotal in my life. I went from being a carefree little boy who loved football to a diffident and taciturn wallflower that barely spoke even when spoken to. It's evidenced by the fact that in the family photograph albums there are plenty of photos of me pre-glasses and, with a newly developed aversion to having my photograph taken, just a handful after I started wearing them. It wasn't until many years later when I realised I could actually wear prescription sunglasses that I started to feel 'normal' again.

The Great British Summer holiday. Most years we holidayed with Doreen and Alfie and their family and Jean and Nobby and their kids, and sometimes Pauline and Terry with Deborah and her little sister Louise. All family together. A week spent in a rented caravan on a freezing cold beach somewhere in Devon or Cornwall. We'd be lucky to get a couple of days where the sun would occasionally peek through the clouds and, by damn, we'd make the most of it. Even in drizzle and wind we'd be on the beach in our bathing costumes, our skin pimpled with goosebumps, building castles with the cold, wet sand, and insisting on totally burying, from head to toe, one of the more game grown-ups.

At dinner time the dads would trundle off over the street – a quick half pint in the pub en route – to the beach-front chippie and come back with a pile of chips, salted & vinegar'd and wrapped in yesterday's *Daily Mirror*. Maybe, if one of the dads had gotten lucky on the horses, we were treated to some battered cod or a sausage as well, which we'd all sit around in a large circle in the sand and share. The mums would have bought some buttered baps which we would load up with chips and have ourselves a lovely chip butty, replete with sand grit. Chip butties just don't taste the same without a dash of sand. All washed down with a tumbler full of R. White's lemonade. I still think of chips and R. White's as a special treat but these days more for dietary consideration rather than my pocket. Only if there were gale force winds and thunderstorms would we not go on the beach, either spending an hour or two in the amusement arcade trying to make our 20p last for the duration, or sit in the caravan playing cards or monopoly while looking out the window at the typical British dismal summer day. Or, donning our rain-macs, we'd play a round of crazy golf in the downpour. We were hardy stock who took our pleasures where we found 'em. Our holidays were fantastic and I write this with no implied sarcasm or irony. Not that I'd want to holiday like that now, mind.

Butlin's was the best though, I used to love Butlin's. Affordable all-inclusive holiday camps scattered around the coastline of Britain, Butlin's was the perfect holiday for working-class families. If you had a bit more money then you might go to Pontins instead. So it was always a week at Butlin's for us. We'd be housed in chalets with our breakfast and tea, evening meal to the posh, served in a huge canteen with all the other families from the camp. During the daytime us kids between the ages of three and eight would join The Beaver Club and be involved in activities – scavenger and treasure hunts, games, shows, talent competitions, and, best of all, the Captain Blood hunt where us bloodthirsty kids would pursue a pirate around the camp and, on capture, force him to walk the plank, the diving board of the swimming pool – all organised by the famous Redcoats. It was great for the grown-ups to be able to shunt the kids off for the day so they could laze on the beach if there was sun, or even if there wasn't; or, if it was raining, the women would play bingo (I love bingo!) while the men would down a few pints in the bar.

In the evenings those same Redcoats that had earlier entertained us kids would then entertain the adults as singers, comedians, dancers, and members of the band. While the parents frolicked, chaperones were provided who would regularly check up on the younger ones asleep in the chalets. It was a long working day for the Redcoat.

In The Beaver Club – yeah, that was *really* what it was called – competitions were run daily. One day a fancy dress competition, where my cousin Mark and I dressed up as Bonnie & Clyde. I wanted to be Bonnie and to wear the wig, dress, and lipstick, but because I was taller than Mark, being three years older, I ended up having to be Clyde, despite the tantrums and sulks. We looked like extras from the Seventies kiddie gangster film, *Bugsy Malone*. Another competition Mark and I entered was *Tarzan*. It would probably be construed as being a little suspect these days; a line of young boys dressed just in their swimming trunks flexing their muscles aping Ron Ely. It was all innocent fun. Of course I didn't win, I was the archetypal skinny little runt with a pigeon chest. I did have the best Tarzan call though, always did have the gob.

One year we went to glamorous Minehead, another year to the exotic sounding Bognor Regis, and the last time to the unpronounceable Pwllheli in north-west Wales. I remember Mum moaning because the camp was full of families from Liverpool. "We have to watch those Scousers, they're a bit rough, they are," she'd say. Little did she know that within ten years her first born would be living amongst those ruffians. I befriended a Redcoat, Kai, in Pwllheli, who became a pen-pal of mine for a few months. Fleetingly I wanted to be a Redcoat when I grew up and was after an easy way in. Another pen-pal I met on holiday was a girl named Lynn from Galashiels. Again, exchanging letters lasted only a few months. Funnily enough I did hear from Lynn again many years later once The Mission had gained some notoriety and we once again exchanged a flurry of letters.

Summer holiday as a kid was the biggest event of the year, whether it was a week in Butlin's or a week in a caravan on a cold beach on the south coast. It was something we all looked forward to all year round. As the family got bigger though, it became more expensive for us to go to Butlin's and more difficult to find caravans that could birth six of us. Mum and Dad ended up buying a family tent and from thence on it was camping for us.

It was around the age of eight or nine that I had my first sexual frisson, shall we say. My dad's twin brother, Alfie, and his wife, my auntie Doreen, lived just across the road from us and so I used to play with my cousins, Vanessa & Roderick, fairly frequently. One day I was playing Kings & Queens with Vanessa in our front room in Star Barn Road and I had been a *bad* King so I had to be executed. I was sentenced to having my head chopped off. So, there I kneeled in front of Vanessa with my head bowed and down she brought the toy sword onto the back of my neck. Instead of decapitation I got an erection. For the first time that I was aware of my little winkle got all hard and stiff in my underpants. I didn't know what was happening to me but I did know it felt really good. I spent the rest of the afternoon asking to be decollated over and over again. Mock execution is not a peccadillo that I particularly carried with me into later life but I do still feel a little butterfly in my stomach whenever I hear about a beheading. That is weird, right?

I made the local paper when the school arranged a coach trip on December 5, 1967, to Wembley Stadium to see England, who were then the world champions lest we forget, take on the might of Lev Yashin's Russia. The result was 2-2 with Bobby Charlton and Alan Ball both scoring for the Three Lions. Anyway, on the coach trip up to London I was taken ill with travel sickness and was throwing up on the bus, something that would become quite habitual in later years (the throwing up, not the travel sickness), so Mr Dunn, the very same headmaster that used to cane my dad when he was a misbehaving tike, took it upon himself to take me under his wing and look after me. His last words to the throng of over-excited schoolboys itching to exit the bus and get into the stadium was, "Now, don't be late back to the bus after the match. If you are we'll leave you behind." Remember, this was in the days before 'political correctness' became au fait. Guess what? Mr Dunn, with yours truly in tow, got completely lost after the match and made it back to the bus more than two hours late. That made the *Bristol Evening Post*, the first time I ever saw my name in a newspaper, something I would become so blasé about in later years.

The Winterbourne C of E school still exists although it is now at a different location in the village. The building that celebrated its centenary in 1967 remains on the High Street but it is now an old people's home. Maybe some of the current residents once went to school there and lived, as we all did, in fear of Mr Dunn and the wielding of his cane. Bless him. Don't make 'em like that anymore. Thank God. A fellow alumni of the C of E, albeit just a few short years younger than I, was Joanne Rowling, perhaps you'll know her as J.K., and it has been suggested that Mr Alfred Dunn, he of the cane and headmaster to us both, was the inspiration for the character of Albus Dumbledore in her Harry Potter books. I don't wish to make any spurious claims but when you see photos of me from the same time that J.K. lived in Winterbourne and we went to school together, it does make me wonder who her visual inspiration was for the Harry Potter character.

A highlight of Christmas for me was the annual showing on TV of the Beatles film, *A Hard Day's Night*. I still love that film. I loved the idea of being in a band with my best mates, being cheeky and having a laugh, playing music on trains, and being chased everywhere by screaming girls. Still sounds like quite a good deal to me. I remember there was always music playing in the house, either the radio or the singles that Mum and Dad regularly bought – alongside The Beatles there were early classics from, among many others, The Kinks, Rolling Stones, Animals, Small Faces, Dave Clark Five, the Brothers Walker and Righteous and, one of my favourites, 'Excerpt From A Teenage Opera', perhaps more widely remembered as 'Grocer Jack', by Keith West.

Sometime later Dad acquired an upright piano that found its home in our front room. I guess it was another effort to encourage at least one of us kids to be musical. Well, as the eldest the onus fell to me and I was packed off for piano lessons to a little old lady that lived on the edge of the village, right next to the entrance to the Hilly Fields. With tall trees overhanging her bungalow it was very dark inside and out, even during the day. She also liked taxidermy and had loads of stuffed animals, a rabbit, a badger, a rat, a mole, and other smaller creatures, adorning the walls and pretty much every surface of her home. I think it would terrify me now so imagine how scary it was for a 10-year-old boy. And she used to whack me over the knuckles with a heavy wooden ruler every time I made a mistake in my playing. And I made a lot. Still do but I've learned how to bluff it now. Anyway, I hated those piano lessons with a passion and so I celebrated like I'd scored the winning goal in a cup final when, after a few months of this weekly hell, we received a phone call to say that the little old lady had died and my piano lessons were cancelled forthwith.

I performed at the Colston Hall in Bristol for the first time when I was in my last year at junior school. I was part of the school's modern dance troupe. Rather than choreographed dance we practiced what was called Movement Of Free Expression. Come on, it was the late Sixties after all. Anyway, there we were, a group of eight or nine of us, in our little leotards cavorting around the stage in some random fashion to the 'Age Of Aquarius'. It must've made riveting entertainment. Thank God there's no YouTube clip of *that* performance.

That same night I also 'played' violin in the Bristol Schools Orchestra. I say played but really I faked it. I couldn't play, couldn't sight-read music, and the noise I elicited from the violin was akin to a cat screeching in pain. So I held the bow just above the strings and pretended to be playing along with everyone else. No one ever noticed. It was another exercise in the art of bluff that would come in very handy later on in life.

I'm telling you about the piano lessons and the 'fake' violin playing because, as an adult, I regret not pursuing both activities as a kid. It would've added, ahem, more strings to my bow, so to speak, as a musician. I can now play the piano, albeit basically. I'm more John Lennon than Elton John, and learnt by transposing guitar chords to notes on the piano rather than learning to play 'properly'. I have a piano in the house and sit at it and work out chords and melodies and it's become an essential writing tool for me but I do wish I could sit there and play the classics and, particularly, jazz. Unfortunately my attempts at violin playing in adulthood pretty much sound like the strangled cat it did when I was a kid.

But it was football that was my abiding passion as a youngster. Playing, watching, dreaming of playing for Liverpool and England. Being Bristol born and bred I'm sorry to say that we've never really had a football team to be proud of. I've always kept an eye out for both Rovers and City's results and do feel a flicker of local pride when I hear they're doing well or they go on a cup run, but the occasional successes of both clubs are far exceeded by the many years of yoyoing between the lower leagues, and disappointment that Bristol doesn't have a football club commensurate with its size.

Before we move on let me just reiterate and make it absolutely clear that my childhood was generally a good, happy one and I was brought up by parents who, while not overly demonstrative, did raise me with love and the very best intentions. Judging by many of the books I've read about the lives of rock stars, it seems to me that the path they follow in life is determined by the deprived, neglected or even abused childhood they suffered within a dysfunctional family. They are propelled by anger, loss, pain, instability, frustration, disruption and rebellion. This informs (or perhaps excuses) their art, their behaviour and personalities. And this may well be the case for some people, Christ knows we do all accrue our own demons to varying degrees as we grow up, but my childhood was a perfectly regular upbringing, with no great traumas that emotionally disfigured me. In fact, I would go as far to say that I have grown up to be the most well-balanced, normal, foible-free adult I know. As I made this claim to Simon Hinkler recently, he stopped and pondered for a moment, then replied, "You're right, but how the hell did that happen?"

In the summer of 1969 at age 11 I left the C of E school and started at the secondary modern, The Ridings High School, just a couple of hundred yards further up the High Street.

CHAPTER 3

These Salad Days...

PLAYLIST:
1. Space Oddity – David Bowie
2. He Ain't Heavy, He's My Brother – The Hollies
3. (If Paradise Is) Half As Nice – Amen Corner
4. The Ballad Of John & Yoko – The Beatles   5. Albatross – Fleetwood Mac
6. Where Do You Go To My Lovely – Peter Sarstedt
7. Woodstock – Matthews Southern Comfort   8. Lola – The Kinks
9. I Hear You Knocking – Dave Edmunds   10. Maggie May – Rod Stewart
11. My Sweet Lord – George Harrison   12. Jeepster – T. Rex

One bright sunny Monday morning in early September 1969, aged 11, I was packed off for my first day at the Ridings High School on the High Street in Winterbourne. The school, a secondary comprehensive opened in 1957 by the Rt Hon Labour politician Tony Benn, served the surrounding villages of Frampton Cotterall, Coalpit Heath, Iron Acton, Rangeworthy, Hambrook, and, of course, Winterbourne itself.

On arrival all of us first year kids were herded onto a large concrete playground hemmed in on all sides by a tall wire fence, the only thing missing to make it feel even more like a concentration camp was the barbed wire. Oh, and the sentry towers and the Nazis armed with machine guns. The school, however, did employ Nazis armed with clipboards, more commonly referred to as teachers, assigning us to our respective houses.

The headmaster, Mr Martin, was a fearsome fellow with a reputation as hard and grey as the granite from the quarries of Cornwall. Addressing us in his own stern fashion he welcomed us to our new academic home for the next five years by instilling in us the fear of God and the devil both if we were to contravene any of the school rules. Corporal punishment was still rife and widely exercised at this time and some of the teachers came with tremlable* reputations that travelled well beyond the school gates.

We arrived on our first day at the school already well versed in the terrifying legend that Mr Martin and his deputy, Mr Douglas, preferred the use of the cane in the administration of their disciplines. Mr Hatfield, Art, and Mr McEldon, Physical Education, wielded the 'dap', the tennis shoe as we now know it; while Mr 'Peg-Leg' Johnstone, History, and Mr Gliddon, Maths and my house master, dispensed their punishments with the wooden ruler. Funnily enough none of the female teachers delivered their correction physically, preferring after-school and lunch-break detentions. We really should elect and promote more women to positions of power and leadership in the world; it would definitely cut down on armed conflict.

Every September the first-year pupils were assigned to one of the eight houses with which you would stay for the duration of the five years you were legally obliged to attend high school. Let me explain something here before we go any further in an attempt to avoid any further confusion. When I say 'year' in the context of school I mean the pupils in a particular age group, as in first year, second year, third year and so on. Comprendez vous? Yeah, I took French.

---

* Causing dread or horror; dreadful.

In each house there were around 150 kids, divided into approximately 30 each of the five-year age groups; 30 first years, 30 second years and ad nauseum. No, I didn't take Latin. Some of the fifth years that weren't designated school prefects would, with their little chips on their shoulders, serve as elected house prefects (I would become a house prefect myself in my fifth year), a system that encouraged rampant bullying by some of the more cruelly inclined.

I was assigned to the house named after Sir Humphry Davy, a Cornish chemist who invented the Davy Lamp. History lesson over. As previously stated our housemaster was Mr Gliddon, a dour man whom I never once saw smile in the six years I attended the school. Our daily routine was unwavering. We'd congregate in our houses at 9am for the recital of the Lord's Prayer, a hymn, falling just short of pledging allegiance to the flag, the taking of the register, and the reading of any school news, and then we'd disperse to our classes.

The classes were structured thus: each year was divided into nine classes, with pupils from all eight houses in each class. It's getting confusing this, isn't it? Well, I've started so… please, bear with me. The nine classes were then divided into three bands, the first band being the highest, and the third being the lowest. So, in our first year we had classes ranging from the highest in prestige, 111, through to the lowest of the dullards, 133. The first digit indicating the year, the second digit signifying the band, and the third denoting the class. Which class we were assigned to was dictated by the reports on each pupil that the teachers at our previous junior schools had submitted to the Ridings High. The more intelligent kids were put in the first band and then, depending on precisely *how* clever you were, you were then designated a specific class. So the really bright kids were put in 111, while the slower, shall we say, found themselves all the way down in 133. The idea was that through hard work, diligence, and positive attitude, you could work your way up into higher classes over the course of the academic year. And conversely you could fall down the rankings if you turned out to be a nincompoop and not as smart as they first thought you were. I was put into 122. Slap bang in the middle, Mr bloody average. And despite my very best, and worst, efforts I never moved up or down in the five years that I was part of the band-class scheme.

Our compulsory school uniform was a dark navy blue blazer with grey pants, white shirt, and the tie was a striped navy blue and red affair. School caps were optional while black shoes were mandatory. So, there I was, first day at big school and I was one of only two boys in the entire student body wearing shorts. I was mortified. I couldn't wait for the day to end, rush home and censure Mum for sending me to school in shorts. Shorts! Obviously I was complicit in their purchase without ever realising that no other bugger would be wearing 'em at school. Fortunately Mum had the foresight to also buy me a pair of long-legged trousers which I henceforth wore every day, relegating the shorts to the bottom of my wardrobe. The other poor blighter that wore shorts on that first day at the Ridings, whose name I remember was Edward Parkinson, was sent to school throughout the seasons, even in the freezing dead of winter, in shorts for a couple of years and the poor sod was mercilessly picked on by all and sundry. In fact he was downright bullied, cruelly and viciously every day at school. He was a quiet, shy boy, slightly plump and ginger, kept himself to himself, and would blush whenever anyone even said hello to him. Even the teachers picked on him in class. I felt sorry for him. He was a train-spotter and in an attempt to foster friendship I even joined him on the platforms at Bristol Temple

Meads once or twice. It was true he was maybe a little strange and later in life I would say that could be a positive attribute but at 11, 12 years old you really don't want to stand out from the crowd, do you?

Academically I was distinctly average throughout my school life. As I said earlier I was assigned to class 122, stayed there for 222, and through onto 522. My school reports make interesting reading but only in as much as it confirms my contention that, as a student, I was only ever as good as the teacher. For example, my English teacher throughout my first five years at school was Mr Holness and I always enjoyed his classes. He made them fun, we talked about literature but also pop music of the day. He was a big Neil Young fan, and while we had our required reading – *Cider With Rosie*, *Animal Farm* and *The Importance Of Being Earnest* being just three I remember – we would also go off curriculum. And the fact I enjoyed English classes was evidenced by my school reports, consistently As and Bs for English Literature and Language.

Religious Education was another subject I did well in but being an active Mormon helped. I was studying the Bible and the Book of Mormon concurrently with my school studies so I had a bit of a head start on that one. Again, I had a good teacher, Miss Houselander, and although she was religious she didn't use the class to espouse her own beliefs and dogma. Neither was she particularly judgmental of my Mormon upbringing, although we did have some good classroom theological debates. Again, my results were mostly As throughout.

My first year music report was a C, average. Yeah, I can just hear some of my detractors agreeing with that one and they'd be tickled pink to learn that for my second year report I received a D. And then in my third year a new music teacher arrived, and guess what? I made an A. So stuff ya, oh ye of little faith.

French, I was useless throughout apart from a couple of terms when we had a very pretty, young mini-skirted Miss Barker teaching us and, for some inexplicable reason, I made more of an effort and received an A for my troubles. She left too soon and the following year I reverted to type and received a D.

I am one of the few musicians that doesn't claim to be good at art, Cs most of the time if I was lucky, with my skills in metalwork, woodwork, and technical drawing being even more dismal. I hated the sciences, Bunsen burners and test tubes, and dissecting mice, and all that nonsense − not for me. I loved history when we were studying kings and queens and beheadings and imprisonments in towers but as soon as we got into the industrial revolution it became a snooze fest.

Geography, again, I loved learning about places but not rock formations. Boring. Maths, I never understood it but somehow wangled myself an O-level pass. We were always expected to show our workings in the margins as to how we arrived at our answers, and the concept was that even if we got the answer wrong but the workings right we'd be given a positive mark. I always got the answers right but my workings were always wrong. I never understood the process but somehow always got the right answer... so how could they fail me?

Physical education, or PE as we knew it, I only ever really liked football and cross-country running. I regularly came second in the school cross-country runs, beaten by Graham bloody McIntyre every time. And he also went out with Barbara Salter for a while, a girl on whom I had a huge crush for ages and who didn't even know I existed. Anyway, I became a rock star, what happened to Graham bloody McIntyre, eh? And football, you already know of my deep and long-abiding passion for the beautiful game. I remember one time playing football on a cold blustery day and I was playing okay, I thought, and then

I got tackled and the PE teacher, Mr McEldon, he of the swinging 'dap', exclaimed, "Oh, Hussey. You could be the best player in this school if only you made the effort!" I was trying my bloody hardest, honest, but felt strangely exhilarated at his admonishment, simultaneously frustrated that he didn't recognise my endeavour. For PE? B for standard and D for effort.

A new sports teacher arrived as I was going into my fourth year and he introduced rugby to the school. Mr Keith Lowe was his name and he came with an enviable reputation as he had once played rugby for Wales, apparently, at some schoolboy level or other. I hated it, too physical for me and it gave the bigger bullyboys license, much like pheasant shooting, to trample all over us little 'uns in the name of sport. However, because of my speed and nippiness down the wings, mostly in the vain attempt to avoid getting clattered, I was invited to join the school team but begged off by claiming that I had Bible classes at church on the same afternoons that rugby practice was held after school. Luckily for me, my Bible classes didn't clash with football practice. Strange that.

I wasn't and am not an academic. I was never destined for the stuffy rarified air of the corridors of higher learning at Oxford or Cambridge, or any university if it comes to that. I consider my real education came later when I left home for Liverpool. But anyway, I finished school with the equivalent of five O-levels – English literature, English language, history, religious education and maths – and that was after an additional year spent in the sixth form. And before you scoff let me qualify that by telling you that I left school with more qualifications than any of my four younger brothers and sisters. So, runt of the litter I may be, black sheep I could be, but I'm not the dunce of the family, okay? I'll let my siblings squabble over who is most deserving of that dubious accolade.

I played football for the school occasionally but wasn't a regular first choice, no matter how hard I tried. I did enjoy the inter-house football tournament though, as Davy had a pretty decent side and we'd usually get to the final only to be beaten by Southey. And that was even with Graham bloody McIntyre in our team. I also played for the local Fromeside Youth Club in the Bristol Junior league and we travelled as far as Hartcliffe and Bedminster for away games. Playing away in Hartcliffe was always fraught with danger as, along with Knowle West, it was the hardest, as in deprived, area of Bristol. Their teams were made up of boys from council estates and high rises who thought nothing of giving you a good thumping off the ball while the ref was looking the other way. We usually beat them with cunning, guile, and skill though. And then had to run for our lives at the final whistle to our waiting minibus and posthaste get the hell out of there before the kids, and their dads, caught up with us for a bout of Hartcliffe retribution.

We never won the league although we did finish in the top four which by premier league standards would mean a place in Europe but not so with the Bristol Junior league. There were some good teams in that league, one particular team I remember featuring a certain Gary Mabbutt who went on to play for Bristol Rovers before joining Tottenham and playing for England and earning himself an MBE in the process. We lost 15-0 against them. Couldn't touch the ball. Despite our capitulation against Mabbutt's Mangotsfield side I shared the Fromeside player of the season award with our captain, Colin Oakley, that year. There was a photo of the two of us receiving our trophies in the sports section of the *Bristol Evening Post*. Mum kept my trophy on her mantelpiece for years but it's now long since been replaced, and quite rightly so, by photos of her grandchildren.

It was during my time playing for Fromeside that Walsall FC sent a scout to watch a couple of us play. The scout watched one match and didn't return. I also played with Bill Dodgin, the Bristol Rovers manager at the time, on Winterbourne Rec on Sunday afternoons. He was impressed enough to comment kindly about my passing of the football but not enough to invite me to have a trial with the Rovers.

I made friends with the Rovers dashing right-winger, Ray Graydon. He was my favourite player at the time after Liverpool's Roger Hunt and I found out that he lived only about half a mile from us at 30 Court Road, Watleys End. As an 11-year-old shameless football maniac I one day just knocked on his front door to ask for his autograph. He and his wife, Sue, very kindly invited me into their home and Ray signed my programmes and autograph book. I then began regularly to go and see Ray and Sue and, as much as an 11 year old can, became friends with them both to the extent that they would take me to the Rovers home games at Eastville Stadium. As we'd drive through the player's entrance I would be praying that school friends of mine would see me sat in the back of the Graydon's car, with Ray himself driving, and be riven with jealousy. Sadly, none of my friends ever admitted to seeing me so my Monday morning school stories about going to the match with one of the players were always believed to be tall.

It was one afternoon towards the end of the 1970–71 season after I'd I ridden my bike to Ray and Sue's that they invited me into their living room and asked me to sit down as they had some news to break to me. Ray was being transferred to Aston Villa. Aston Villa was in Birmingham, like a million miles away to a 12 year old with just a bicycle. I was heartbroken, devastated, felt betrayed even.

"Please, Ray, tell me it's not so."

"It is, Wayne. I'm sorry but it's a good move for Sue and I. Aston Villa are a big club and going places."

And it was true. Although languishing in the old third division at the time, Aston Villa soon won promotion back up to the second and within four years were winners of the League Cup at Wembley Stadium, my mate Ray scoring the only goal in a 1-0 win against Norwich.

Although almost 13, I cried like a three year old over the crushing news of Ray's imminent transfer. To comfort me Ray and Sue promised they would keep in touch and, once they were settled, would invite me up to Birmingham and their new home. As a 12 year old I hadn't yet developed cynicism as a reflex reaction to promises like this and so I believed them. And do you know what? Ray was as good as his word. Early in the season, end of August, he phoned and invited me to visit. He spoke with Mum and Dad to quell any concerns they might have had and I travelled alone by train from Temple Meads to Birmingham New Street where, as arranged, Ray and Sue met me.

It was a wonderful, magical couple of days apart from one horrendous booboo I made that I will regale you with shortly.

The first afternoon Ray took me to Villa Park, Aston Villa's famous old stadium, and showed me around the changing rooms and from there we walked out onto the pitch just as the players would on a Saturday afternoon. I could just imagine the adrenaline that would surge through them as they ran out to the roar of the crowd. Not unlike going on stage in front of an audience which I would come to know and love myself in years to come. It doesn't matter whether there's 50, 500, 5,000, or 50,000 people out there, the rush is always the same.

I was shown around the newly built luxury directors' boxes, and we finished our tour of the stadium with a visit to the manager Vic Crowe's office. Mr Crowe very graciously signed the scrapbook that I had been compiling for the last few months, since Ray had signed for Villa, with clippings from the newspapers and my weekly *Shoot* magazine. He asked me what I wanted to be when I grew up and I instantly replied, "A footballer, of course."

Mr Crowe asked me which team I preferred, Bristol Rovers or City. I still blush with embarrassment at the memory of my reply. With Ray, being a Bristol born lad and a Rovers supporter since he first kicked a football and, lest we forget, the man who used to take me to Rovers home games as his guest, standing next to me I uttered the cringeworthy reply, "Neither, I like Villa now."

Ray's disappointment was palpable. I could feel it as he turned his head to look at me in disbelief. I refused to meet his eye as I knew the instant the words left my mouth it was a despicable betrayal that only served to illustrate how fickle I was with my allegiances. Not for the first and certainly not for the last time would I be so capricious. It's not one of my more admirable traits, I must admit.

We bade our farewells to the inadvertent troublemaking Mr Crowe and made our way silently to Ray's car. On the journey home Ray started to make light, polite conversation and by the time we reached his home I was seemingly forgiven for my unforgivable aberration and was nattering away like any other 13 year old without a care in the world or a single pang of guilt. Kids, eh?

When we arrived home Sue had prepared tea of fish fingers, chips, and peas. I'm not sure footballers of today with their sport nutritionists and recovery metrics diet would even know what Birds Eye fish fingers are but back in the early Seventies it was a different culture, different game, and it was not unusual to see more rotund players gracing the playing fields of the great British stadiums. It wasn't unheard of for players to go out for a meat pie and a couple of pints the night before a big game. After tea Ray and Sue took me to the cinema to see *Willie Wonka And The Chocolate Factory*. That was a big treat for me as I'd only been to the cinema a handful of occasions previously; *Mary Poppins*, *The Great Escape*, *The Battle Of Britain* and *Chitty Chitty Bang Bang*. And then back home to sleep the night in the Graydon's guest bedroom with the promise of another exciting day to come tomorrow.

The next morning I was woken early and after breakfast I travelled with Ray to the Villa training ground. When we arrived I was introduced to some of the other players and busied myself collecting autographs. Look, there's Bruce Rioch! And Andy Lochead! Brian Little! Wow! Those names won't mean anything to anyone in Germany or Brazil or wherever, or maybe even Birmingham these days, but at the time these were big players if not quite household renowned. I sat pitch-side and watched enthralled as Vic Crowe put the team through their paces with warming up and training exercises, ball work, the practice of set plays, free kicks, corners, and then finished the session with a couple of five-a-side games. I was exhilarated, enraptured, energised. This was the life for me. Watching footballers at work like this just re-enforced my (pipe) dream of one day becoming a professional myself.

After showering and changing Ray then drove me to Birmingham New Street station and I caught the train back to Bristol and real life.

I was in the Scouts for a couple of years. The church had a troop and one evening a week we'd get together to practise our reef knots and sing 'Ging Gang Goolie'. Every summer from the age of 11 to 14 we'd go off to the Gower Coast or the Wye Valley for a week's camping, overseen by overzealous Scout leaders, one of whom, sadly but predictably, would be had up on pedophile offences a few years later. Not that I was ever a victim of any abuse myself, I hasten to add, the vast majority of Scout leaders being straight up, decent men, even if they are strangely evangelical about potholing and caving. Up with the lark to raise and salute the flag, on with your Scout shirt, neckerchief and woggle, bathing and peeing in rivers, and burning breakfast sausages on the campfire. Baden Powell has a lot to answer for.

One of the four boys in my patrol who shared the tent with me was Jon Klein who, years later as a lapsed Mormon like myself, would play guitar in the Specimen and Siouxsie & The Banshees. Us ex-Mormons get everywhere, I tell you.

In August of 1971 on Scout camp in the Wye Valley, a Primus stove blew up and burnt my right hand really badly. Screaming in agony I scurried off to the nearby river intending to immerse my smouldering hand in the cool, healing water. Except I was stopped en route by one of the Scout masters and told to sit down while he administered butter to my burns. Butter! It was a widely adhered to old wives' tale that butter was a good healant. Is it heck. Butter is for toast and crumpets, not bloody burns.

"Ah, be a man, Wayne, stop your squalling. It's just a few little burns. They'll be gone in a few days," was the sage advice of the adult charged with my temporary care. I'll tell you what, this soddin' nonce of a Scout master should've had his First Aid badge ceremoniously ripped from his Scout shirt and strangled with his own bloody woggle. My hand came up in huge blisters – Jon remembers them as the biggest he's ever seen – which were duly bandaged. Not for one instant, though, was it considered that maybe I should be taken to the nearest hospital.

The following weekend when I arrived home Mum was apoplectic when she saw the state of my hand. "You stupid man. You should've taken him straight to hospital," she bellowed at the cowering Scout master. Mum and Dad drove me straight to the A&E at nearby Frenchay Hospital where, on examining the burns, a doctor proffered the prognosis that because I hadn't been attended to promptly there would undoubtedly be some scarring for life. All we could do, he continued, was apply a healing ointment regularly and keep the hand bandaged for a few weeks, and pray for the best.

On the weekend of August 28 the first ever Mormon general conference in the UK was held in Manchester. The prophet, Joseph Fielding Smith, was scheduled to attend and to speak to the gathered faithful. We, like thousands of other Mormons from around the UK, made the pilgrimage to Lancashire. We travelled with fellow church members and family friends, the Yulls Steve and Lynn and their young daughters, Becky and Joanne. As there were no such things as Premier Inns or Travelodges – cheaper budget hotels – at that time, we took our tents and camped in the hills outside of Manchester. Just think about that for a moment. Who goes camping in Manchester? And it rained. Of course it did, it was Manchester. And the thing is, we weren't alone. The campsite was full of Mormons, all there for the privilege of being in the presence of our prophet. I bet he wasn't bloody camping though, no doubt lording it up at the best hotel in town. Would Jesus have camped or checked into the nearest Holiday Inn? In fairness to the prophet, though, he was 95 years old at the time so we couldn't really expect him to bunk down in a sleeping bag on the cold, damp Greater Manchester earth.

The highlight of the weekend for me was going to Maine Road, home at the time to Manchester City, with my dad and

Steve. They were playing Tottenham Hotspur in a Division One (now the Premier League) league match. The City team included such legends as Colin Bell, Frannie Lee, Mike Summerbee, Joe Corrigan, and Wynn Davies. Lining up for Spurs were even more legends – Martin Peters, Alan Mullery, the Welshman Mike England, Pat Jennings, Joe Kinnear, Ralph Coates, Martin Chivers, Steve Perryman, and an old army team mate of my dad's, Alan Gilzean. All players that *were* household names and featured regularly as pin-ups in my *Football Monthly* and *Shoot* magazines.

Of course, being a football mad 13 year old, it was thrilling to get to watch these illustrious players in real life when, apart from the excursion in December 1967 to Wembley to see England, my staple diet of mediocrity was Rovers and City of Bristol. Manchester City ran out 4-0 winners that day – all the legends scored, Bell, Summerbee, Davies, and Lee – and looked every inch the challengers to the title, eventually won by Derby County (alright, Jez), that they proved to be that season. Three teams, City, Liverpool, and Leeds, finished on 57 points; Derby had accrued 58. It's because of my excursion to Maine Road as a kid that I have always had a soft spot for City and I am chuffed to bits that they are currently the top dogs in Manchester. And England, if it comes to that. In the absence of Liverpool winning everything, or even anything, I really don't mind when City do. It's a far more preferable scenario for me than United or Chelsea winning.

On the Sunday after the match we went to the Mormon conference and heard, amongst seemingly interminable others, the prophet Joseph Fielding Smith talk. Well before the end of the conference I'd slunk out and gone around to the back door hoping for a close-up glimpse of the prophet as he left. I wasn't the only one with the same idea. Gathered was a small excited crowd, all waiting as I was. A lifelong desire for proximity to the stars was probably fostered in me that day. The metallic hydraulic back gate was raised and out drove a big black car. As it slowly passed through the waiting throng, the back window on my side was wound down and there sat the prophet. Everybody put their hands forward to hopefully be shaken by the great man, my heavily bandaged right hand amongst them. The prophet reached out and shook only two or three of the tendered hands, but mine, maybe because of the grubby dirty bandage making it *stand out*, was one of them. Now, I don't know if I believe in miracles of the biblical kind; the prosaic, yes, like Liverpool winning the Champions League or The Mission having a hit single. But when I went back to hospital on our return to Bristol a few days later, the doctor and nurses were astonished at how well my hand had healed and with absolutely no scarring. They claimed it a miracle. Was I healed by the hand of God? Some certainly thought so including Mum. And who am I to disagree?

CHAPTER 4

I'm Born Once Again, For You

PLAYLIST:

1. Telegram Sam – T. Rex   2. What Is Life – George Harrison
3. Get It On – T. Rex   4. Mr Pleasant – The Kinks
5. Horse With No Name – America   6. Without You – Nilsson
7. Coz I Luv You – Slade   8. Stay With Me – Rod Stewart & The Faces
9. Starman – David Bowie 10. School's Out – Alice Cooper
11. Virginia Plain – Roxy Music   12. All The Young Dudes – Mott The Hoople
13. Moonage Daydream – David Bowie

I was reborn. It was a Thursday evening, early January 1972, getting on for 8pm. I was 13 going on 14 years old. That evening the course of my life was changed irrevocably forever. I saw my destiny in a blinding flash of glitter, a touch of mascara and dark curls. From that moment I knew I was pre-ordained. I was gonna be a rock star. Well, somebody has to be, don't they, so why not me?

I had just watched Marc Bolan and T. Rex dazzle the nation on the institutional British TV show, *Top Of The Pops*. Miming to 'Telegram Sam', the new number one single in the charts, Bolan pranced and preened across our TV screens and straight into the hearts of teens, dividing the generations for perhaps the first time since The Beatles had done so almost ten years before.

That was it for me. In one fell swoop I no longer wanted to be Kevin Keegan, I wanted to be Marc Bolan. Bolan had better hair than Keegan and was far prettier. It looked like a really good job to me, playing guitar and singing, being on TV and being screamed at by girls. And even some boys. And a darn sight more agreeable and easier than all the dedication, training and physical exercise required to become a professional footballer.

I think it was beginning to dawn on me that I wasn't gonna make the grade as a footballer, I couldn't even establish myself as a regular in the school team and, to be frank, girls liked rock stars more than they liked footballers and I was getting to the age where that began to matter to a boy. What I didn't realise at the time, though, was the deal I had to make with the devil. And just how much tenacity, perseverance, single-mindedness and sacrifice would be needed, how much humble pie I'd have to eat, and dignity I'd have to subsume along the way to achieve my dream. Worth it? You bet.

If you're one of the lucky ones, and I have been, one of the upsides to becoming a musician over a footballer is that being a musician can be a job for life while for most footballers their careers are over by the time they are 35. It's commonplace today to read of players earning upwards of £150,000 a week but that is really just the superstars that reach the top echelons of the game. The majority of professionals earn far less and can't retire in splendid luxury when their time is up. It's the same for musicians. Those at the top earn untold wealth but most of us are hard-working folk who don't always know when our next pay-cheque is coming or where from. It can be fraught and there have been times in my life when I have been very close to if not destitution then bankruptcy at least. But we muddle through, don't we, and somehow survive.

Anyway, switching allegiances as easy as finding sand in a desert, down came my posters of Keegan, Ray Clemence, Tommy Smith (!) et al and up went centre page pull-outs from *Jackie* and *Disco 45* of dear beloved Marc. Marc Bolan was my first and, still to this day, an enduring love.

For Christmas just past I had received a little blue Dansette record player from Mum and Dad. And record tokens enough from my uncles and aunts to go out and buy myself three 7-inch singles. As soon as the shops were open after Christmas I nagged Dad to drive me to Kays Record store in Fishponds and there, with my record tokens, the first records I bought were 'Jeepster' by T. Rex, George Harrison's 'My Sweet Lord', and 'Ernie' by Benny Hill. I still have the first two but Ernie long ago drove his fastest milk-cart in the west straight into the dustbin. I'd play those records over and over for hours every night when I came home from school. And their B-sides: 'Life's A Gas' to A-side 'Jeepster' and Harrison's brilliant 'What Is Life'.

I was T. Rex crazy and, like a million other kids, I would pose in front of the mirror with a tennis racket, pretending to play guitar while singing along to Bolan. The first LP I ever bought was *Electric Warrior*, maybe a month or two later after saving up enough money from my paper round wages. *Electric Warrior* is a fantastic album and it's still high on my list of best albums ever. I love the earthiness of its sound, the funkiness, the otherworldly mystical lyrics, the simplicity of the songs, the instrumentation, the guitar playing, the backing vocals of Howard Kaylan and Mark Volman (better known as The Turtles), but most of all, it's that voice, that extraordinarily fey, quivering, tactile Bolan voice that just oozes sexual exuberance.

To a young boy that was starting to lose control of my hormones *Electric Warrior* was the soundtrack to the burgeoning confusion I was feeling about my teenage sexual identity. The intro guitar riff to 'Get It On' is perhaps the simplest and easiest guitar riff in the whole world to play but no matter how many guitars and amps and effect pedals I have owned and used over the years I have never been able to make a guitar sound as sexual as Bolan did with that riff. Even now when I hear that song it stirs some kind of latent feeling in me and all the memories of doubt, excitement, and anticipation, of adolescent sexuality come roaring back. It's said that smell is the most provocative trigger of memories. I politely disagree and would say it is music, at least for me it is. 'Get It On' is pure sex.

And then I started raiding Mum and Dad's record collection and found some real goodies there too. Among them was 'Mr Pleasant', an early fave that we would cover with The Mission many years later, the B-side to The Kinks 'Autumn Almanac', a great example of where the B-side was better than the A. Rod Stewart's 'Maggie May' was another.

I'd listen religiously every week to the chart rundown on Radio One, making lists of my favourite records and predicting next week's chart based solely on nothing more than my preferences. I changed my weekly *Shoot* subscription to *Disco 45*, a comic that boasted the lyrics to the top pop hits as well as posters and stories about the top pop stars. In those early months of 1972 I came to love Slade, Rod Stewart & The Faces, America's 'Horse With No Name', Nilsson's 'Without You', and many, many others but no one came remotely close to that place in my affections where Bolan and T. Rex resided. That is until early July of that same year when David Bowie performed 'Starman' on *Top Of The Pops* and, swiftly following on Bolan's Anello & Davide tap shoe heels, a bigger and more abiding lifelong love affair commenced.

The Rise And Fall Of Ziggy Stardust And The Spiders From Mars, wow, what a mouthful that was, was the second album I bought.

I had some birthday money, my birthday being May 26 lest you forget, that Mum was making me save for a new pair of school shoes. But I wanted to buy *Ziggy Stardust* and she forbade me to do so. I decided I just had to have it and so one day, in defiance, when she was out I raided my piggy bank and walked the mile or so to the local record store, Kays, and spent £2 on the album. I took it home and played it over and over on my Dansette in the bedroom I shared with my two brothers, hiding the cover under the bed whenever Mum walked into the room. When she asked, "What's that rubbish you're listening to?" I told her it was David Bowie and I had borrowed it from a friend.

I was hoping to be able to replenish my depleted funds with earnings from my paper round before Mum found out but, as fate would have it, a few days later Mum decided it was time to take me to buy my new shoes. Seeing that my piggy bank was light she quickly ascertained my misdemeanour and, eliciting a confession, demanded that I return the *Ziggy* album to Kays and ask for my money back. Of course I argued my side but she insisted on coming with me much to my embarrassment. In we walked to Kays and the kindly lady behind the counter listened to my rueful request to return the album. Handing it over to her she took the record out of its sleeve and gave it the once over.

"I'm sorry, young man, but you've played this record and it looks like you've played it many times so I can't take it back." Looking at Mum she reiterated her position. "I'm sorry but we just can't do it."

I suppressed the urge to leap up and punch the air and shout 'hallelujah' but instead confined myself to a silent sigh of relief while feigning disappointment and contrition to Mum. She was furious and as a punishment I had to wash the dishes every night for the next three months. It was a small price to pay to own what became and remains such a much-loved album.

Later that same summer along came other venerable favourites in Roxy Music with 'Virginia Plain', Mott The Hoople with the Bowie-penned 'All The Young Dudes', and, with 'School's Out', the shock-meister Alice Cooper, who coincidentally The Mission supported for a handful of shows in the arenas of Britain in November 2017. For me 1972 was an incredibly exciting time for pop singles that hasn't been matched since in terms of quality. Just look at the Top 30 for any week during the first half of that year and there are loads of classic singles, far too many to list here.

But by the end of that year and going into 1973 Bowie and Bolan were more and more being seen as the spearhead to a glam rock movement that was beginning to spawn such opportunistic pale imitators as Gary Glitter, Alvin Stardust and Mud. The Sweet could also be bracketed in that same group but, for some reason, I liked Brian Connolly and his boys who looked like camped up dockers on *TOTP*, and they had a great run of singles with 'Blockbuster', 'Ballroom Blitz', 'Hellraiser' and 'Teenage Rampage'; 'Little Willy' not so much. For a £1 membership fee I even joined the official Sweet fan club and received a membership card along with a signed poster that immediately went up on the wall next to Bolan and Bowie. Slade were another fave and another fan club I joined and, of course, many years later The Mission would get to work with Noddy Holder and Jim Lea on the Metal Gurus project.

By early 1973 Bolan's star was sadly starting to wane, his records beginning to sound samey, and with drugs and ego taking over Marc was beginning to look bloated, cruelly nicknamed 'the glittering chipolata' in the music press; while Bowie went from strength to strength, initially confounding and eventually exceeding our expectations of him with each album release. Only Bowie and, to a far lesser degree, Roxy Music managed to transcend the glam rock tag and survive the Seventies with their reputations not only intact but enhanced. Slade enjoyed a brief renaissance in the early Eighties as a heavy metal festival favourite and, of course, Bolan was dead by the end of 1977.

Interviewers often ask about my musical influences. The truth is pretty much everything I've ever listened to is assimilated, even music I don't like, but it was Bolan, particularly, and Bowie who were the early inspiration for me to want to make music, to want to be a rock star, to want to pick up a guitar and write my own songs. They were the ones that made me believe.

But I had a problem that prevented me from pursuing my dream. I didn't have a guitar – until we went to Spain on our family holiday that summer.

It was the first time any of us had ever been outside of Britain. We drove down through France in the family Ford Escort Estate and stopped off en route in a lay-by somewhere outside of Clermont-Ferrand and the six of us, my little sister yet to be born, all slept in the car. On arrival the next afternoon we erected our tent on a campsite just outside of Barcelona. Two things I remember from this holiday. The first was that I was stung on my foot by something unseen under the surface while paddling offshore in the Mediterranean. I hobbled screaming blue murder from the water convinced that my big toe was sliced in half only to find it intact but with a blazing red sting mark throbbing in the Spanish sun. I presume it was a jellyfish. Beautiful creatures, I can watch 'em for hours, but, as I can vouch, they sting like a mofo.

The second was that we were ejected from our campsite because I had 'accidentally' set one of the rubbish bins on fire. Well, it wasn't really accidental but that's what I was claiming to my parents. We were instructed to pack up our tent and leave forthwith as the evening sun was setting. I wasn't usually a misbehaving blighter but, to be honest, I was led astray by a lad from Macclesfield I had befriended who was also on holiday with his family on this particular campsite. He thought it would cause great mirth to set the rubbish bins alight and in yet another example of my weak-willed kowtowing to mindless peer pressure, I went along with it. *We* were asked to leave and *he* got away with it. I'd love to claim that I learnt my lesson but later evidence would prove that a lie time and time again. After packing the car with our tent and the family, we drove off the campsite with my mate from Macclesfield waving us off. We found another campsite a few miles up the coast and had to set up the tent that night in the dark. Mum and Dad were less than happy with me, shall we say.

With no more campsite evictions our holiday eventually came to an end and we set off for home early one morning, driving up through the Pyrenees on our way to the south of France. Wow! What a spectacular drive that is. I have done it many times since on tour buses and its beauty never ceases to amaze me. It's also one of the most precarious roads to negotiate with its endless steep bends and no barriers to speak of to stop you from toppling over the edge and down sheer mountainsides. One moment of misjudgement at the wheel and that's it.

In the eastern Pyrenees en route to France is the principality of Andorra and its capital Andorra La Vella where we stopped for a break to munch on our sandwiches and drink orange squash that Mum had thoughtfully prepared before we'd set off. There were some souvenir shops and we had one last browse before getting back into the car and heading down the mountain and into France. In one of the shops I spotted this beautiful Spanish guitar hanging on the wall. It was love at first sight. It was on sale for the currency equivalent of roughly £10. Well, I didn't have £10 or anything remotely close to that amount. It was a veritable King's ransom in 1972, but Mum and Dad, possibly in an attempt to discourage a potential new interest in arson, bought it for me. I almost wept tears of joy. I certainly vowed, short lived though it was, never to do a naughty thing ever again and be the perfect son. I lovingly cradled that baby in my arms, drinking in the aroma of the wood and the nylon strings stopping just short of actually licking her, all the way through France and on the ferry from Le Havre to Portsmouth and on into Bristol, forbidding any of my siblings to even breathe near her, let alone touch her. I've just thought, why do I think of guitars as being feminine? Are they? Is it because when you play a guitar you hold it close to your body, as in an intimate dance? And through the dexterity of your fingers you can elicit magical sounds? I'm going too far now, right? Okay.

Once home I started playing that guitar every day. Every spare moment I would be strumming away, my fingers bleeding, learning the basic major and minor chords from a chord sheet and making up my own when I couldn't find a chord that sounded right. I started writing my own songs straight away because I couldn't play anybody else's, a fortuitous habit that has held me in good stead ever since. With no facility to record the songs back then and my lyric notebooks long gone the way of Ernie, I only now have memory to rely on and at best that is suspect, but some of the song titles I remember are 'When I Look', 'The Hitchhiker', 'First Night With You', and the very first song I ever wrote with a title totally cribbed from a T. Rex song, 'Seagull Woman'. I would sometimes write three or four songs a day. And while I can't now attest to their quality I do wish I could still be that prolific.

Within a week of beginning to play the guitar I had enough songs for an album. Not a very good album in all probability but nonetheless it's an achievement that I'm proud of and wish I was still capable of now.

I started taking the guitar to school so that I could practise in the breaks between classes and was amazed to find that girls who previously hadn't even acknowledged my existence were surrounding me, listening while I sang and played my songs and becoming confidantes and friends as a result. I also found that because there were girls around I was attracting a new set of friends among the boys too. Gone was the talk of Peter Osgood and Georgie Best, replaced by discourse on the merits of *The Slider* and Roxy's first album. And, boys being boys, I was starting to hear of groups with names like Led Zeppelin, Black Sabbath and Wishbone Ash.

Within three weeks of starting to play the guitar I had put my first band together and played my first ever gig. Gig is such an ugly little word, isn't it, but I don't know what else to call it. Show, concert, recital, performance? All a bit highbrow for the undoubtedly cacophonous noise we made at my first gig. Amongst my new friends I'd met a lad named Pete Brunt who claimed to be a drummer and owned an Olympic drum kit, Premier's budget line. He had a friend named Steve Smith who played bass. I'd found my first rhythm section without having to look too hard. We called ourselves Blueprint and I was the singer and guitarist. The only problem was I only had an acoustic guitar. Somehow, between us, we managed to borrow an electric guitar and a small amp and we practised after school every night for a week in the front room of Pete's house close to the Ridings High that we all attended.

I don't recall what the occasion was but the gig was at the Mormon chapel that I was still attending in Downend. I do recall, however, loving every single second of being on that stage. We played four or five of my songs and a cover of Bowie's 'Soul Love'. There must've been 20-25 people there, mostly Mormon kids between the ages of 12 and 18, and I thought we were fantastic, lapping up the applause and exhilarated at the fact that some of them even attempted to dance to us. I felt like a star. But that didn't last long. After we'd finished and I was basking in the afterglow of the adulation from my Mormon friends, the Bishop came up and, in front of my *fans*, informed us in no uncertain terms that we played too loud and banned us from playing in the chapel ever again. Ah well, it was a start. Just a few short years later the Sex Pistols launched a career on being banned. As has often happened in my long career in music I was ahead of my time. Snigger all you like.

Mum and Dad were in the audience the evening of my first ever gig and it's a habit they've persisted with ever since having seen pretty much every band I've ever played with. Even today, aged almost 80 years old, they still come along to Mission and solo shows when I'm playing in the UK. I'm not sure they've always enjoyed the music, I know for a fact they didn't like The Sisters Of Mercy very much, but they do seem to genuinely like The Mission. I'm not sure if that's a recommendation or not. Dad's favourite song is 'Beyond The Pale' while Mum's is 'You Make Me Breathe' from the *Masque* album.

The reason I'm telling you this is because from the very beginning they have always supported and encouraged me in my musical endeavours. After seeing me play with Blueprint and realising my passion for it was real and not just a passing fad, they went out and bought me my own electric guitar and amp. Remember, they didn't have much money and they had four kids, with another one on the way, to feed and clothe, so to do so was a big sacrifice on their part that I've come to appreciate more with each passing year. The guitar was from Woolworth's, an Audition six-string electric guitar, a kind of cherry sunburst colour, that came with its very own small ten-watt Audition amp, a guitar lead to connect the guitar to the amp, a strap and a plectrum. It was cheap but I loved it and thought it was the bees knees and spent even more hours in my bedroom practising and writing songs.

When I was in the third year at school I had to decide what subjects I was going to continue with for my exam courses. The courses would be spread over the fourth and fifth years of schooling and at the end of the fifth we had to take exams. What courses we chose to pursue were largely dictated by what career path we wanted to follow. But what kid at 13 or 14 years old realistically knows what they want to do with their lives? There are a few that do and a few that have parents that decide for them but most kids have an idealistic view if any at all at that age. I remember meeting with the careers adviser whose job it was to visit all the schools in the area and speak with all the students in the third year to help them determine what exam courses they should choose.

My interview went something like this:

"So, Wayne, what job would you like to do when you leave school?"

Me: "Be a footballer."

Him: "No, Wayne, be realistic."

Me: "Well, a rock star then."

Him: "Hmm, I think I need to have a word with your parents, Wayne."

As it happens what he suggested, attempting to extinguish my dreams by pissing on my parade, was to become a trainee manager at the local Co-op. Which is what I did when I first left school. But the point to raise here is that none of us were encouraged to pursue any lofty ideals or ambitions, none of us encouraged to chase our dreams. All of us were advised against taking any risks. What was suggested was to conform, play it safe and take the easier option and be trainee managers, or hairdressers, or estate agents, or work in a bank. We are taught to be realistic but who the hell wants to be realistic at 13, 14, 15 and 16 years old? We have plenty of time for that when we get older. Who leaves school at 16 thinking of their retirement pension? I'm almost 60 as I write, and it's maybe a bit late, but I'm just starting to think about mine now. I have enjoyed a life pursuing my dream rather than being trapped in the humdrum doing something for the last 40-odd years that I wasn't really happy doing. I'm not knocking it, each to their own, with circumstances being different for all of us that dictate the way our lives go. I know I've been lucky in my life to have done what I've been able to do but I also know that to do it I had to make hard choices early on not to blindly accept what my elders considered to be the safer and seemingly easier options for me.

During my fourth year at the Ridings High School we moved from Winterbourne to 48 Celestine Road in Yate, about five or six miles away. It was a council house swap with a family originally from Winterbourne that wanted to move back to the area, having been unable to settle well in the new town of Yate. The house in Celestine Road was bigger and with another baby on the way Mum and Dad felt we could do with the extra room. There were two secondary comprehensive schools nearer our new home, one in Yate and one in Chipping Sodbury, than the Ridings High but because I had already commenced my CSE and O-level courses it was felt that it would be less disruptive for me to continue attending the Winterbourne school.

The only problem was the only way I could get back and forth to school every day was by bus and the nearest bus stop for this particular route was about a mile walk from our house across open fields and muddy lanes. There was only one bus in the morning and one bus back after school and it served all the outlying hamlets, picking up children that attended the Ridings. My stop, the top of North Road, was where the route commenced so I was always the first on the bus in the morning and the last to get off in the afternoon. So, that's what I had to do, catch the bus. If, perchance, I'd miss it, which did happen on occasion, I'd then have to walk another mile or so to the village of Iron Acton to catch a bus on what was a more regular route to Winterbourne. And I'd have to do this in all weathers, all seasons, and quite often would arrive at school soaked through to the skin because of the pouring rain. And doing this most days with the guitar on my back. But it never seemed a hardship or an inconvenience at that age. Isn't life simpler when you're younger?

One of the outcomes of moving to Yate but still attending school in Winterbourne was that I had no friends or opportunity to make new friends in the area of our new home. All my friends lived miles away and with no direct bus routes to get back and forth I began to become more reliant on my own good company. With no one to play with or hang out with in the evenings or at weekends I basically spent every moment at home with my guitar, filling up notebook after notebook with the songs I was writing.

Blueprint had split up as I lived too far away now to rehearse after school and so I was also without a band for a while. But I still took my guitar to school and continued to make new friends with both boys and girls as a result of our mutual love for music. I even started to have a girlfriend or two. Of course, at that age every romantic relationship was life-or-death serious and one errant word or look could send me spiralling downwards into the depths of despair. It didn't take much, still doesn't really, just ask my wife, Cinthya, sensitive soul that I am. I was so desperate for attention, even just acknowledgement, that I'd fall in tragic and unrequited love with someone new every few days.

Just a smile, a small kindness, or a "Can I borrow your slide-rule?", or "What're you staring at, four eyes", and I'd be pledging undying love for time and eternity. My young fickle, brittle heart would concoct scenarios whereby I'd already have our lives mapped out − kissing first, then marriage and kids − before we'd even said more than two words to each other.

It was all innocent enough, furtive looks across a classroom, holding hands in the playground, a peck on the cheek at the end of the school day as we climbed onto our separate buses home. Some of the other kids were talking about kissing and how they kissed with their mouths open and with their tongues down each other's throats. French kissing it was called. I'd never heard of such things and went home and told Mum. Her reply, "Oh, Wayne, you don't wanna fraternise with girls like that, they're hussies," confused me. Oh yes I bloody well do, I thought, and, anyway, aren't I a hussy too?

Rosalind was my first teenage love. The first time we were boyfriend and girlfriend was when I was in the third year and she was in the first. I was hopelessly besotted. We only wrote little love letters to each other that we got friends to pass on for us. We never kissed, we never touched, never held hands, we never even spoke to each other preferring to just blush and nod as we'd pass each other in the corridors at school. She chucked me after three weeks for another boy. I had heard a rumour that she was exchanging love notes with someone else as well as me but I preferred to deny the evidence until it was too late. In an attempt to win back Rosalind's affections I surreptitiously and cunningly befriended her elder brother, Chris, who was in the same year as me and shared a few of the same classes. I must admit I didn't really like him too much to start with and he wasn't popular at all as all the other lads thought he was queer. Like hussy, I didn't really know what queer meant either, I just thought it meant he was a little strange. But I could put up with that in the pursuit of true love.

I would sometimes go to their home, a lovely picturesque cottage on Woodend Road, Frampton Cotterall, on a weekend playing records with Chris hoping for just a brief hello from Rosalind, stealing glances at the family photos that adorned the walls and the mantelpiece over the fireplace, and praying that I would be sat next to her at the dinner table at lunch time. She was very rarely there, as it happens, apparently attending ballet or horse riding classes, but it didn't discourage me from going in the vain hope of convening our great love affair. In retrospect, it was tantamount to stalking really and pretty creepy behaviour on my part, to be honest, and I'm surprised when I think about it now how welcomed I was into their family home. I'm sure it was only because Chris was so unpopular that, as a consequence, he was so easy to befriend and I was able to get so close. I also think his parents were very relieved to see that he had finally made a friend. They were a lovely, close family actually and I would remain friends with them even after I left school and moved to Liverpool. And we did become very good friends, as it happens, over time, Chris and I, sharing a mutual love for Pink Floyd's *Wish You Were Here*, Dylan's *Desire*, and Lennon's *Walls & Bridges*, and I grew to like him very much. And I did get to go out with Rosalind again a couple more times for very short periods over the next couple of years, progressing eventually to the kissing that Mum had warned me against. And each time she broke my heart by chucking me for Steve Smith, the bass player who played in Blueprint with me. Gotta watch those bloody bass players, dark horses, they are.

I would see Rosalind a couple more times a few years later when The Mission played in Rome. She was living there and working as an English teacher and would come along to the show with her handsome Italian boyfriend that I was always very jealous of. Somehow she could always make my heart beat that little faster. Sadly, I lost touch with all the family many years ago, they'd moved away and left no forwarding address.

Another girlfriend I had around this time was Jackie from church. She used to attend the Wells Road branch on the other side of Bristol so I would only ever see her when there were Stake (the area) activities or meetings. I was so shy and diffident I could never even say hello to her when I saw her but we would send love letters to each other courtesy of the Royal Mail. It was only just a few years ago that I found out that she had never actually written any of the letters that I received in her name. It was her elder brother, Tony, who had written them. Hmm.

There were a few other girls who, I guess, could be considered girlfriends through this period – Suzy Valentine, and Judy Bunce (what great names they are) from school, and Diane, another girl at church, but none of these relationships progressed beyond the occasional snog. And while you could call it puppy love it certainly wasn't the teenage amour fou that I'd felt for Rosalind.

As I mentioned earlier while the girls were generally fans of the poppier, lighter music some of my friends, boys, were into the heavier bands and so I started borrowing their albums and listening to Led Zeppelin, Deep Purple and Black Sabbath. I liked Zeppelin because they had some lighter stuff like 'Stairway To Heaven' and pretty much all of their third album, and Purple had one or two good tunes – 'Smoke On The Water', 'Woman From Tokyo' spring to mind – but I didn't like Sabbath very much, too heavy and masculine for me. In fact, most rock music is too macho for me. And I'm not a big fan of twiddly-widdly guitar solos, never have been. I always liked Jimmy Page's playing of chords and arpeggios and riffs but I always skipped the tracks that had big long guitar solos.

Mick Ronson, who was raised as a Mormon as I was and with whom I shared my birthday, albeit 12 years apart, was a fave of mine for the work he did with Bowie and then with Mott The Hoople and Ian Hunter, his solo on 'Moonage Daydream' being one of the best ever. Wishbone Ash's *Argus* was another album I liked a lot for the guitar playing because, while there were solos, it wasn't all speedy notes with an over-driven sound, it was actually very melodic and employed guitar sounds that were cleaner than the Sabbaths and the Purples. Peter Green and Fleetwood Mac remains another fave of mine. The guy from Mud could play but I didn't like their songs while Dave Hill of Slade was rubbish but I loved theirs. And going back further, Harrison with The Beatles, the guitars of The Rolling Stones, some great playing in amongst all of that but in the end it all comes down to the song. The song is what is important. Without the song you have nothing.

Amongst my peers I was the only kid that spanned the bridge between pop music and the heavy bands – liking Led Zeppelin and Stevie Wonder, Wishbone Ash and Al Green, Deep Purple and The Partridge Family.

One day I came home from school and Mum had ripped down all my posters from my bedroom wall. Bolan, Bowie, Rod

Stewart, Alice Cooper, Roxy Music were all servants of Satan, she declared, making devil's music to corrupt the youth. She never did that with my Kevin Keegan posters. I think she must've had a bad day and decided to take it out on yours truly.

Just a couple of years ago I was with Mum and Dad and we stopped off in a pub for lunch somewhere and the music playing *quietly* over the sound system was Bowie's greatest hits and 'Life On Mars' came on. Mum said, "Aw, this is such a lovely song, isn't it?" She's right of course but nonetheless it goes to show you how, with time, something that was once perceived as outrageous and flouting convention has become institutionalised. I mean, *Sir* Mick Jagger, *Sir* Elton John, *Sir* Paul McCartney, *Sir* Rod Stewart, *Sir* Ringo Starr? These were all counterculture heroes in decades past and look at them now. Whatever next, *Sir* Liam Gallagher? *Sir* John Lydon? *Dame* Siouxsie Sioux? It's not beyond the realm of possibility, I tell you. I also found out that my parents had bought tickets to see Rod Stewart at the Birmingham NEC a couple of years ago. I took great delight in reminding Mum that when I used to play his records as a kid she would say, "Get that rubbish off, he can't sing."

Back at school and towards the end of the fifth year, one of my friends, Mark Richardson, was putting a new band together. He was gonna be the singer, Brian 'Fee' Powell was the lead guitarist, John Ashton was the bass player, and Kevin 'Jam' Jarvis was the drummer and they were called Stockdove. I was asked if I would like to join as the rhythm guitarist.

CHAPTER 5

As Sweet As Sin, Sweeter Still The Taste

PLAYLIST:

1. Badge – Cream   2. If – Telly Savalas
3. House Of The Rising Sun – The Animals
4. Brown Sugar – The Rolling Stones   5. Can't Get Enough – Bad Company
6. Guitar Man – Bread   7. Time – Pink Floyd   8. Bohemian Rhapsody – Queen
9. Once Bitten Twice Shy – Hunter/Ronson
10. Ships In The Night – Be Bop Deluxe
11. This Town Ain't Big For The Both Of Us – Sparks   12. In The Flesh – Blondie

In 1974, as we were nearing the summer holidays at the tail end of my fifth year at the Ridings High School, I accepted the invitation to join Stockdove as their rhythm guitarist. I had already decided to stay on at school for an extra year in an attempt to up my CSE Grades to O-Level equivalents. Well, that was the idea but if truth be known, it was more to do with procrastination on my part as regards joining the adult workforce. I just couldn't admit that to my parents. I wasn't quite ready to grow up just yet, and I'm not sure that I really ever have been. Being a musician is for the Peter Pans of the world, eh…?

Stockdove were the 'school' band inasmuch as they'd play lunchtime concerts for fellow students every now and then in the main or music hall. Mark Richardson, who was the same age as me, and also staying on for sixth form, was the singer. I'd known Mark since junior school at Winterbourne C of E and had once thrown up in his living room. It was his eighth birthday party and I'd eaten a Bounty* or two too many and had suffered a bad reaction. Even then I was already disgracing myself in public and I wasn't invited back for his ninth. I'm convinced I was deeply traumatised by this incident and, as a result, to this day I have a pathological aversion to coconut. Just the smell of it makes me want to heave, and I can always taste it if it's used in anything as an ingredient. Cinthya, my wife, tries to slip it in sometimes in cakes or cooking.

"Is there any coconut in this, my love?" I ask.

"No, baby," she replies, lying straight-faced as I bite into whatever she has made, and then laughing uproariously as I retch and splutter and spit out whatever is in my mouth into the nearest receptacle. She thinks it's funny. And the thing is, I always fall for it, so I suppose it is.

On lead guitar in Stockdove was Brian 'Fee' Powell. Brian was the hotshot guitarist in school. He was a year younger than me and, as his dad had recently lost his job, his parents had gone out and bought him a guitar and amp with the redundancy money. Hence, at 15 years old Brian was already playing a black-and-white vintage, 1963 to be precise, Fender Stratocaster through a Vox AC30. Not for Brian a cheap copy or an Audition guitar like mine. But boy, could he play guitar, making love with his ego... He could rattle off all the guitar riffs from all the great rock records of the day and before. Eric Clapton was his favourite (I always thought Eric was a bit boring myself, a bit too earnest, although I did like 'Badge' by Cream) but Brian

---

* Bounty – a chocolate covered coconut bar.

was equally at ease aping Jimmy Page or Jimi Hendrix. I really looked up to him and learnt a great deal from Brian in the two or three years I played with him. He acquired the nickname Fee because whenever you asked him for a favour – "Can I borrow a plectrum?" or "Can you show me how to play Layla?" – he'd say, "Yeah, sure, for a small fee."

A good few years later Craig and I were putting together what was to become The Mission, and we were auditioning for another guitarist. By that time, we'd decided I was going to be the singer as well as playing guitar and we needed someone to take some of the guitar playing responsibility off my shoulders. I thought of Brian and remembered how much better he was than me at school. So I tracked him down to Brighton where he'd moved to in the interim and phoned him to ask if he fancied auditioning for us.

"I'd love to," he replied and caught the train up from Brighton to Leeds a day or two later.

Well, we auditioned him and it quickly became apparent to Craig and myself that in the intervening years I had become a better player than Brian; certainly more creative with a distinctive style of my own while Brian was still reeling off the old-hat Clapton guitar solos like punk had never happened. He could certainly play but it really wasn't what we were looking for. So, I had to let him down gently before he caught his train back to Brighton.

I thought he took the rejection quite well. That is until The Mission played in Brighton at the Centre on the sea front a couple of years later by which time we were enjoying hit singles and albums and selling out big venues and all that malarkey. Brian came down to the soundcheck and, seemingly bearing no grievance, it was lovely to see him and so we put him on the guest list for that night's show. He came backstage afterwards and we invited him back to the hotel for a bit of a booze as was our wont in those days.

All was fine for a while, everybody was happy, and laughing, and drinking, and then all of a sudden and without warning Brian started spouting all this venomous vitriol, shouting abuse at myself and Craig, saying how crap we were, how rubbish our songs were, and how he was a much better guitarist than both Simon (Hinkler) and myself. He may well have had a point but there's a time and a place and it certainly wasn't there in the hotel bar while we were celebrating a successful show with friends and our crew. He was very aggressive and verging on getting physical to the extent that our tour manager and security guy, Dave Kentish, had to wrestle Brian to the floor and then, with the help of a roadie or two, carry him outside and eject him from the hotel.

The turnaround in Brian's demeanour within just a few seconds was astonishing. I guess he'd been bottling that resentment up since his failed audition and, with a few drinks inside him, couldn't hold it back any longer. I didn't see or hear from Brian again for many, many years but we made contact with each other in the last five or six years and have become good friends again, so much so that the last time I played a solo show in Brighton I invited him up on stage with me to play a few songs together. It was great fun as well as being quite emotional.

So that's Brian 'Fee' Powell on lead guitar. On drums in Stockdove was Kevin 'Jam' Jarvis. Two years younger than me, Kev earned his nickname from, yeah, you've guessed I'm sure, his predilection for jamming. Jamming, if you're not aware what it means, is when musicians get together with no prepared programme to play and just improvise. Most of the time jamming is self-indulgent rubbish, a bit like freeform jazz, that is largely unlistenable and no fun for anyone except the musicians involved, and sometimes not even for them.* We, the bands I play with, sometimes jam as it can occasionally be a good way to alight upon new ideas for songs but equally it can be a total waste of time. Kevin liked to jam.

John Ashton was our bass player, the kind of bloke that steps out of the shower to take a pee; and he liked Bread, the band. I remember when TV's Kojak, Telly Savalas, had a number one hit in the UK in early 1975 with an hilariously cheesy-as-gorgonzola spoken word version of their song 'If (A Picture Paints A Thousand Words)', I used to tell John that it was much better than the insipid version by Bread. He, not seeing my tongue planted firmly in my cheek, used to get really angry at me, and threaten to duff me up, which he could've done quite easily. Silly boy. Anyway, fancy calling your band 'Bread', it's a rubbish name, although, in truth, Stockdove was little better.

---

* I do like most forms of music, jazz being one of them, but freeform jazz I just don't understand. Well, I understand it in principle; I just don't understand how anyone can get any real pleasure from listening to it. It was explained to me by Steve Spring who was the drummer in The Mission for a few years in the Noughties. Steve was a fan of the genre; he certainly liked to play it as evidenced by some of his playing with the band. He described it thus: freeform jazz is when a group of musicians all play at the same time and they all play different tunes in different keys in different time signatures. Mmmm, not for me.

There have been and still are some great exponents of improvised music, the German band Can springs readily to mind. Tago Mago is one of my fave albums but I do know that each track on that album had been edited down from much longer jams. For jamming to work it does need, at least for me, the musicians to have a certain level of technical ability, empathy with their fellow musicians and, most importantly, to be able to listen to the other players in the group as they are playing. In my experience many musicians *don't* listen to what is going on around them, egocentric guitarists being the worst offenders. The best musicians are not the ones that can play the most notes per beat but the ones who are not afraid to play the simplest thing, or even play nothing at all if that is what works best for the music they're performing. As someone once said, 'music is the space between notes.'

John was an inveterate snob both in his musical tastes and in his attitude to my songwriting. "Your songs aren't as good as David Gates' songs," he'd claim, "and your music taste is rubbish. How can you like T. Rex and The Sweet?" Well, hello, I was 16 years old and barely knew my E minor from my E major and you're comparing me to an American superstar that's been making records for donkeys (as in years not asses, although on second thoughts)?

"Well, you write a bloody song then."

And of course he couldn't because he had his head so far up his bottom. And he liked Bread. My case rests.

That was the band I was joining.

As it was school holidays we had adjourned for the summer. They were all going off somewhere nice with their families. I'd be lucky to get a day trip to Weston-super-Mare. But I didn't care. That summer I was gonna work to earn some money to buy myself a new guitar. I got a job in a small rubber factory on the industrial estate in Yate. The fastest way to get to work was to nip over the fence and walk half a mile along the railway line, avoiding the trains speeding their way en route to London from Bristol Parkway. When a train did come I'd have to huddle down in the bushes that ran alongside the track and wait for it to pass, sometimes a little too closely for comfort. The safer alternative was to take the long way around which was a walk of almost two miles each way. What would you have done? Nah, I was young and foolhardy and getting to work this way allowed me an extra half an hour in bed of a morning. I'd do the same now, I'm sure.

I earned £13 a week for six weeks working from 8am to 5pm, with an hour for lunch, dipping rubber products into heavy duty detergent liquids to clean 'em when they had just come off the production line. I managed to save £70 which means, employing my failsafe method of doing sums, that I only spent £8 of my earnings during that period. Now that's what you call self-discipline. On the Saturday of the sixth week, the day after I had finished the job and just a couple of days before going back to school, I caught the bus from the end of Cranleigh Court Road into Bristol city centre and walked to one of the guitar shops on Gloucester Road. There I spent my hard earned £70 on a spiffing new sunburst Les Paul copy, the brand name escaping me now, that looked a lot like the one that Bolan sometimes played.

Walking back towards the bus station carrying my exquisite new guitar in the hard shell case that it came with (I'd never had one of those before, my Audition used to get carried around in a cardboard box) I felt immeasurable pride in the fact that I had gone out and spent six weeks doing something I hated doing to earn the money to pay for this myself. It was the first thing of any real value that I had bought with my own money in my life and it was a crucial lesson in appreciating the value of working for what you want. Excuse the cliché but it means so much more than having it handed to you on a plate.

John, our bass player, liked my new guitar but he still whinged about my little ten-watt Audition amp. Early in the new school year we played a lunch break show in the big music hall for the rest of the school. It wasn't mandatory for pupils to attend but it was free for those that wanted to spend half an hour indoors rather than outside in the cold on the playgrounds. The place was packed and would've been considered a sell-out if we'd sold tickets. We played such venerable staples as 'House Of The Rising Sun', 'Brown Sugar' and Bad Company's 'Can't Get Enough' but there was no place yet in the set for any of my self-penned ditties,

John the bass player proving immovable in his resistance to what I thought was their obvious quality and charm.

Of course I still loved every second and hammed it up as much as I could as rhythm guitarist. I even spied Rosalind in the audience beaming at me with her huge Cheshire cat grin. It's amazing how being on a stage with a guitar and/or microphone can transform the way people look at you. From being a skinny, spotty, four-eyed, Harry Potter* lookalike I was conferred with a coolness and an attractiveness that hitherto I had never felt before. It's a well observed theory that the most interesting rock stars are the ones that were the wallflowers when they were young, the ones that were bullied, the ones that were weird, the more sensitive ones, the weak, skinny boys on whom the the alphas looked down their noses, the ones that grew up with the biggest chips on their shoulders and with the most to prove to themselves and the world. Where once a physical or mental quirk would be construed as a defect and something to hide away, when you reach a certain age it's perceived as a unique and lauded trait and a characteristic to flaunt. It makes you different from the rest of the crowd. The ugly ducklings that grow up to be beautiful, graceful swans that can make hordes swoon with just a turn of their head or of poetic phrase.

In the days following Stockdove's first lunchtime show Mark Richardson surprised us all and quit the band. Quite why I can't remember now, maybe he was gently pushed, or maybe his parents insisted that he give up this band nonsense and concentrate on his A levels. It matters not what the reason was, the result was the same. I became the singer.

---

* Even though he hadn't yet been imagined or maybe he had but not yet been realised – it was still more than 20 years away from the publication of the first Harry Potter book in 1997.

And Brian, being the leader of the band, decided that with a new singer we should also have a new name and so we were re-christened Humph. Yeah, I know, no better than Stockdove or Bread really, is it? Apparently, Brian had seen it in *The Dandy*, a popular weekly comic of the day, in a Desperate Dan strip. Humph was an exclamation that Desperate Dan would make in the speech bubble above his head whenever he was expressing anger or befell some calamity or other.

So, as Humph we continued to rehearse at school during the week and even at weekends at John's parents' spacious family home on Down Road, Winterbourne Down, further on down the hill from where I lived when I was a tiddler. But now I was the singer as well as the rhythm guitarist I was able to throw my weight around a little, much to John's chagrin, and get a few of my own songs played by the band as well as the covers we continued to learn. I think we even had a go at 'Guitar Man' by Bread to pacify the ever-grumbling bass player. What is it about bass players, eh? And as well as the occasional lunch time show at school we also started to play at local youth clubs, discos, and pubs in the area establishing ourselves, still being cheap, as the band to call for any and every public function.

In November of 1974, along with a few friends from school, I went to see Pink Floyd at the Bristol Hippodrome on their *Dark Side Of The Moon* tour. It was my first ever 'proper' show. Tickets were only £1 and we had to apply for them by post. The shows attracted a lot more applications than there were actual tickets so we were lucky. We had front row balcony seats. There was no support band. Floyd played a first set of new songs that ended up being the basis for their next album, *Wish You Were Here*, then they went offstage and, I presume, had a fag break before coming back and playing the whole of *Dark Side Of The*

Moon from start to finish as their second set. They were using a quadraphonic sound system already by this stage and so for songs like 'On The Run' the sound was travelling around the old theatre; surround sound 25 or 30 years before it became more commonplace. And then they finished with a 30-minute version of 'Echoes' as an encore. I bloody well loved it. I have since seen many, many shows and I suspect that I'd maybe find the Floyd quite dull now but at the time I was overwhelmed, blown away. I soaked up every last minute detail.

For the record, the best shows I have ever seen were Queen at Bristol Colston Hall, almost exactly a year after the Floyd show, on their *Night At The Opera* tour just as 'Bohemian Rhapsody' was hitting number one in the singles chart. I was in the second or third row from the front and it was stunning, pandemonium, and Freddie was every inch the best performer I have ever been lucky enough to see. The other best show has been every time I've seen Radiohead. I've seen them maybe a dozen times and every time they are amazing. The first time was in June 1997 when I was living out in California, having just packed in The Mission for the first time. They played a show at the famous Troubadour club in Hollywood just as *OK Computer* was being released. I have a friend, Andi Watson, who works for Radiohead as their light designer, and he invited me to the show. It was rammed and full of celebrities, even the reclusive Axl Rose was in attendance. Lulu stood on my foot as she was pushing by but, bless her, she did apologise. I met Thom Yorke that night, Andi introducing us after the show, with Thom saying, "Yeah, I know who you are. I saw you once in Oxford."

Just a month later and Radiohead were back in LA at The Wiltern Theatre in Hollywood, a bigger venue than the Troubadour. *OK Computer* was selling by the truckload and Radiohead were getting very popular. Again, I went to the show, and again they were brilliant. And again I was stood with Andi after the show backstage and Thom came over and spoke with him and completely blanked me after he'd been so sociable the first time we had met just a few weeks earlier. Ah well, singers, eh? We all now know Thom can be a contrary, grumpy git. Still has the voice of an angel though. And then on April 1 the following year, 1998, they came back yet again and played the Universal Amphitheatre in LA. This time they had two backstage areas, one for the general riff-raff celebrities and Hollywood hangers-on and one far smaller and more exclusive area for which I had a guest pass courtesy of Andi. I was in there after the show, which again was fantastic, and stood at the tiny bar waiting to get a drink when I felt somebody come up and stand next to me. I turned my head to see who it was and stared straight into the face of Brad Pitt.

"Alright, mate. D'you enjoy that?"

"Yeah, it was great. Here, don't I recognise you?"

"Ah, I dunno. My name is Wayne and I used to sing in a band called The Mission."

"Yeah, that's right, I came to see you play in London a couple of years ago when I was over there filming *Interview With A Vampire*. I bought a couple of your t-shirts that night, actually."

"Aw, right. D'you still have 'em?"

"Nah, Jen and I used 'em for dusters ages ago."

"Yeah, that's all they're good for, eh?"

We both laughed, me sarcastically.

"See you later."

And with that he toddled off, drinks in hand to the waiting Jennifer Aniston. Talk about rubbing shoulders. By the way, Thom came and said hello to me that night. Funny bugger, he is.

I love Christmas. It's wonderful and magical. Christmas morning in our house always went like this: we'd wake up, usually very early, to find on our beds a Christmas stocking that contained a few small gifts like a pen, an orange, a chocolate bar, or even a chocolate orange, maybe a book, maybe a small toy, but nothing 'big'. All the big presents, from Mum and Dad and uncles and aunts, were piled up around the Christmas tree in the living room. They weren't there the night before when we'd gone to bed. During the night Santa had been and, as we didn't have a chimney, had somehow let himself into the house and had scoffed the digestive biscuits and drank the milk we'd left for him. And in return he'd left a huge pile of presents by the tree and stockings on our beds. Obviously, and sadly, by 1974 and being 16 years old I now saw through this charade and knew the truth, but because I had younger siblings we kept up this masquerade and I quite happily played along.

On Christmas morning we weren't allowed downstairs and certainly not into the living room where the presents were until Mum and Dad were up and awake. And then we had to have our breakfast. Always the bloody breakfast first. It was cruel to make us wait and eat our Weetabix or Shreddies first before opening the presents. But it did make us savour the anticipation all the more. Once breakfast was finished Dad would lead us into the living room and he would sit by the tree while we would all find a spot nearby. After a quick family prayer Dad would pick up the presents one by one and, reading the labels out aloud, hand them to the correct recipient. "Ah, this is for Adam from Auntie Jean & Uncle Nobby!" And then we'd all cheer and Adam would open the present in front of us all and show us what he had been given. "And this next one is for Wayne from Nanny Lovelock!" You could always tell Nanny Lovelock's presents because she couldn't really wrap them properly and so a bit of the present was usually hanging out before you'd even picked it up. It's a deficiency I have inherited from my nan, my presents are pretty much wrapped like that too.

This particular Christmas, 1974, Dad had handed out all the presents from under the tree and I'd carried my pile back to my bedroom thinking to myself that I'd made a pretty good haul this year – a few record tokens, a fake Ben Sherman, a box of Turkish Delight, an LFC annual, a diary, some new pants and socks, a Brut deodorant, and a Hai Karate gift pack. Yeah, I was lucky, some people get nothing. Then, maybe five minutes later, Dad called us kids from the bottom of the stairs, "Come back down 'ere, I've just found a present I missed behind the settee."

We, all four of us, my siblings and I, traipsed back down the stairs and into the living room again and resumed our positions. When we were comfortable Dad wheeled out from behind the couch a Marshall 50-watt combo amp! "Santa hid this one away, it's for Wayne."

And as my family cheered I burst into tears. I know, 16 years old and crying like a baby. They were tears of ecstatic joy just in case you are wondering, big bloody softie that I am. Wow, bloody wow. My first coherent thought though was, "This'll shut up that bass player John, well good and proper."

After giving Mum and Dad a huge big thank-you hug they explained to me that after seeing me work so hard and saving all the money I earned from my summer holiday job to buy my new guitar they thought it only fair to buy me an amp to go with it. What brilliant parents to have, eh? It's a shame, and a regret, I haven't always appreciated that.

Dad helped me carry the amp upstairs and, of course, I spent the rest of the day playing electric guitar really loudly and driving the whole house and possibly the neighbourhood crazy. I had to give it a rest for the Queen's speech though, my family, me excepted, being staunch royalists. I couldn't wait for the next band rehearsal to show off my new Marshall amp* and I swear even John the bass player was at least a little impressed.

Not long into the new year and already sick of the noise from my constant practising in the house, Dad cleared his garden shed out for me, storing the lawn mower and all his tools in the garage and, installing a bit of soundproofing, a small heater, and a chair and a desk, banished me to the garden and my own small rehearsal/writing space.

The following summer, 1975, I left school and got a job as a trainee manager at the Co-op. At the same time, in a fit of inspired pique, John the bass player left Humph in protest at us playing more and more of my songs. It was my first experience of 'musical differences'. I was to use that phrase again several times in the future but merely as cover for actually meaning, "I can't stand the twat and the twat can't stand me."

We soon found a replacement, a curly haired redhead by the name of Simon Heathfield. Simon lived not too far from me in Yate. His dad was the headmaster of St Mary's C of E Primary School which proved to be a godsend as it meant we could rehearse in the school hall a couple of evenings a week. A bit of nepotism never hurt anybody, eh? Again, with the change of line-up it was decided to change our name and this time to Rough Justice. Yeah, I know, it doesn't get any better, does it? Quite whose bright idea it was I can't now say so we'll blame Brian again, shall we?

We continued playing our sporadic local gigs and even started to get a few in the pubs in the city centre, once even getting our name in *NME*'s gig guide when we played the

---

* I eventually sold the Marshall 50-watt combo to my mate, Jon Klein, he of future Batcave, Specimen, and Banshees fame.

Naval Volunteer. I thought we'd made it, seeing our name in print in the *NME*! That put a spring in my step for all of a couple of days.

I had contracted the gig-going bug after my Pink Floyd experience and went to see a whole host of bands play at the Bristol Colston Hall and other smaller venues such as the Granary over the next few years. The highlights I remember, aside from Queen, were Ian Hunter with Mick Ronson, Rory Gallagher, Dr Feelgood, Be Bop Deluxe, Television supported by Blondie, Iggy Pop and Sparks. I did see T. Rex in April 1977, supported by The Damned. And while it wasn't the crazy screaming fandom of the early Seventies, the Colston Hall being embarrassingly undersold, the charisma of Marc Bolan was still potent and very evident. That same year, on my birthday, I went to see the White Riot Tour with The Clash (great energy and excitement), Buzzcocks (some great songs), Subway Sect (didn't get it) and The Slits (an interesting din). In years to come I would come back to Bristol and play the Colston Hall with The Mission a fair few times to sold-out crowds. It was always a great thrill for me, playing my home town, remembering the great shows I had seen there as a youngster in my formative musical years, and dreaming of one day being up on that stage myself. See, dreams *can* come true.

When I first left school I decided I wasn't going to church anymore. Over the course of the previous year or so I had spent the occasional Sunday morning in chapels of other denominations, observing what they had to offer compared to Mormonism. It's all very well being a believer but how much can you really believe in something if you know nothing else? I figured that by learning about other churches and their doctrine I could make up my own mind about what I believed, rather than just blindly accept the dogma I'd been subjected to since I was a nipper. I was happy to believe in God and the Mormon faith, but I believed because I'd been taught to believe. Church of England, Methodist, Jehovah's Witnesses, Presbyterian, and Roman Catholic all received investigation in my quest for divine enlightenment. I didn't receive a visitation or any dazzling revelation but what I did come to realise was that, while I believed in the spiritual, I did not believe in religion. Any religion, including Mormonism. And as a new member of the workforce and able to now pay my way within the Hussey household I thought I had every right to exert my independence by not going to church anymore.

Mum and Dad's response was the age old response of parents everywhere: "if you live under our roof then you abide by our rules, you either come to church on a Sunday or you can move out."

So move out I did. I went to live with Nanny and Grampy Hussey, my dad's mum and dad. Despite being unrelated by blood but by legal document only, they always treated me as one of their own. Nanny used to dote on us all but her arcane art was to make each of us feel as if we were her favourite. That's a special talent that most grandmothers seem to possess. They lived in Watley's End, not too far from the Winterbourne Co-op where I was currently working, so getting to and from work was easier for me.

Nan would fuss whenever I walked through the door. "Do you want some beans on toast, love?" she'd ask, and be offended when I declined her offer. "Well, how about a nice custard cream and a cuppa then?" she'd persist.

Gramps would be sat in his favourite armchair in the corner of the living room watching the horse racing on TV and puffing away at one of the 40 un-tipped Woodbines he'd smoke every day. Lovely folk, they were, and from a generation that was highly principled with a ferocious work ethic. I could come and go as I pleased without ever having to explain where I was going and with whom. And, best of all, I could lie in on a Sunday morning without being roused from my bed to go to priesthood at some ungodly hour. Actually, I guess some of the devout might claim it to be the *godly* hour. Either way, I didn't have to see it and get up and go to church.

Mum would call every few days or so and ask when I was coming home. "Not until you say I don't have to go to church anymore. I'm an adult now, I'm 17, and earning my own wage and paying rent. I'm agnostic, I don't believe in the church anymore," was my well-rehearsed litany.

The impasse was breached a couple of months later when Mum waved her white flag and decreed I could move back home and not be obliged to attend church. A victory for the obstinacy of youth. As much as I loved staying with my nan and gramps it wasn't home. And so I moved back into the bedroom I shared with my two brothers, Adam and Westley. Of course, come Sunday morning the house was in such an uproar. With everybody rushing around getting dressed in their Sunday best for church, sleep was impossible. Adam would be up first and out for seminary at seven, followed by Dad for priesthood at nine while the girls and Westley could take their time to get ready for Sunday School which commenced at 11. And all the time not one jot of consideration for the beauty sleep that I needed.

Without fail every Sunday just before she left for church Mum would poke her head around the bedroom door. "So, you're not coming to church with us today then, Wayne?"

"No, Mum, I'm not."

"Well, you can make yourself useful and get up and peel the potatoes and carrots and pod the peas and broad beans for Sunday dinner, okay?"

Bugger.

Obviously, being 17, 18 years old, full of testosterone and raging hormones, and being in a gigging band there were girls around. And interested. My sexual experience up to that point had been very limited, what with my church upbringing, shyness, fear, lack of opportunity, and guilt all factors in my abstinence. The occasional fondle here, a dry hump there, but mostly it was just a lot of heavy petting and frustration. I do remember the first time a girl, Anne was her name, put her hand down my pants and I came instantly, the shock of it making me lose all control. It was great. With Anne's help and a little more coaxing and practice over the next few weeks I ended up being able to last 30 seconds at least. Mind you, she wouldn't let me put *my* hand down *her* pants. That was a no-no, so I could never reciprocate the pleasure, not that I'd have known how to. Still, it would've been courteous to try.

Brian from Rough Justice knew two sisters, Carol and Julie, who used to attend the posh Clifton Girls School in Bristol. Quite how Brian came to know them I have no idea because they were definitely a little out of our league. Maybe they just liked to slum it a bit. Carol was Brian's girlfriend so I messed around with Julie for a little while. They used to live at the end of a cul-de-sac, Manor Close in Coalpit Heath. One evening when her parents were out, Julie and I were in her bedroom and, having removed our shoes and socks and outer garments, were enjoying a heavy snogging session on the bed. Oblivious to everything but the promise of impending carnal pleasure we didn't hear her mum and dad arrive home early.

"Julie, are you up there?" shouted her mum from the bottom of the stairs.

"Shit, it's my mum and dad. You can't be here, Dad'll kill me after he's killed you. You're gonna have to climb out the window," Julie hissed.

"What? But we're upstairs," was my panicked reply.

"Julie, you okay?" The voice getting nearer as her mum was coming up the stairs.

Raising her voice Julie answered, 'Yes, Mum, just dressing, I've just had a bath. Give me a minute," and lowering it for me, "Get the fuck out, quick. Grab your stuff and get out on the roof."

With that she ran to the window and flung it open. I gathered up my strewn clothes from around the room and, with her mum's voice getting ever nearer, climbed out onto the roof in my underpants and a t-shirt just as her mum knocked on the door.

"You okay, love?" asked Mum, as I ducked down beneath the window ledge.

"Yes, Mum, I'm fine. I'm just getting dressed, I'll be down in a minute, okay?"

"Okay, pet. Do you wanna cuppa?"

"Yeah, a hot choc would be lovely Mum, thanks."

Mum retreated back downstairs. Julie came to the open window and, after giving me a quick peck goodnight, closed it on me. Cheers.

Fortunately it was dark outside so the neighbours wouldn't have been able to witness my escape across the rooftop. But in the darkness it was hard for me to see how I could escape. I quickly and as quietly as I could got dressed and, carrying my shoes and socks in my hands, carefully tiptoed to the edge of the sloped roof to see how I could get down to ground level without breaking my neck. On the side of the house there was a small shed, a lean-to, that I could climb down onto and from there it was a short drop onto the pathway that led from the back garden to the front... and freedom. I ran like the clappers up Manor Close once I reached the street.

Julie and I were short lived, that last Benny Hill-like escapade the death knell in our fledgling relationship.

In the early winter of 1976 Carol, Julie's elder sister and Brian's paramour, brought a friend from school to our gigs. Bev and I hit it off and we started seeing each other. She was an only child and lived with her mum and dad on Clarence Avenue, Staple Hill. I would ride over there after work on my moped – yes, moped, more of that in a bit – and we would spend the evening in the front room playing records, snogging and feeling each other up. Her mum and dad would watch TV in the back room and occasionally her mum would knock on the door to ask if we wanted anything, a biscuit or a cup of tea. I'm sure it was just a ploy on her part to douse any fervent arousal that might have been getting out of hand. She wasn't wrong. It was certainly heating up between Bev and I, our physical relations becoming ever more passionate with each subsequent visit. We were getting proper het up and I would be leaving Bev's at the end of the evening feeling very frustrated, and, despite my very best efforts, *still* an 18-year-old virgin.

And so it was, after we'd been seeing each other for a couple of months, building up to the point of no return, one weekend in early 1977, Bev called me to say that her parents were going out that Sunday evening and would I like to come over? Would I ever. Making sure I arrived after her parents had left I nervously rang the doorbell. As soon as she opened the door Bev took me by the hand, pulled me into the house and straight upstairs to her lilac themed bedroom where we proceeded to get all hot and steamy. Within a couple of minutes it was all over. I can't claim that I heard trumpets, or angels singing, or that the earth moved but I'm damn sure I was trembling ferociously throughout the whole 120 seconds it took for me to lose my virginity.

Once the deed was done a huge wave of guilt, not remorse I hasten to add, just fucking horrible, religious guilt, came crashing down upon me. I was damned, I was going to hell, and no amount of contritional prayer could save me. How stupid it was, is, to feel that way? With absolutely zero consideration for Bev or how she was feeling I quickly got dressed, made my excuses and left. I didn't call Bev for weeks and like the coward I was I wouldn't take her calls when she called me. She came to one or two more Rough Justice gigs with Carol and, reprehensibly, I avoided her as best I could.

Bev did absolutely nothing to deserve being treated in such an appallingly offhand manner. The poor girl had no idea why, after a couple of months of us getting closer and closer, I wanted nothing more to do with her now that we had consummated our relationship. And to be truthful I'm not sure I knew either, I certainly don't think I would've been able to articulate why at that point.

Only much later, with the benefit of hindsight, could I rationalise my deplorable behaviour. It was religious guilt, a guilt that plagued me for years every time I did something that went against that which the church had taught me was right as I was growing up. If there is a God then he's got a lot of shit to answer for. In fact, I don't think God is to blame. It's men that have interpreted the Holy Scriptures to suit their own warped agendas, making the church, any church, an instrument of population control for their congregations ever since Christ was crucified on the cross – if that even happened at all. All through the ages, so much evil has been perpetrated in the name of God, not least the fear and guilt that gets foisted upon us that is so emotionally disfiguring throughout our lives. It's evil. That's not what God is really about.

None of this argument though makes up for the wretched way I treated Bev. Coincidentally, many years later Bev and I were in touch and through the course of our conversation she confessed that on that Sunday evening in the winter of 1976 she lost her virginity at the same time I lost mine. Which made my post-coital behaviour all the more abhorrent and hurtful. I made sure I apologised to Bev but, amazingly, her memory of me was a lot fonder than it deserved to be.

August 16, 1977, the news came over on the car radio that Elvis Presley had died. My mum cried. I didn't really understand why she was crying over the death of a fat, old rock star. Exactly a month later Marc Bolan was killed in a car accident. I cried my eyes out and totally got why Mum had cried for Elvis. For me at 19 years old, Bolan's death felt like the end of my childhood.

By late summer 1977 I was getting ready to leave home. I wasn't yet sure where I was going to go, maybe London, but I knew I had to get away from Bristol. First things first, I handed in my notice at the Co-op. The staff, I was led to believe, were sad to see me go although the same, I'm positive, couldn't be said of management. I'd worked at the Co-op for more than two years, commencing my employment as trainee manager fresh from school. I'd been shunted between three or four of their local stores before they settled me in at their Winterbourne location just a couple of hundred yards up the road from the Ridings High School, the school that I had left just a few months previously. I hadn't gotten far, certainly not as far as I would've liked. And to be totally frank I didn't see my future as one day being the manager of my own Co-op. I harboured bigger dreams than that.

As part of my managerial training I was sent to Soundwell Technical College one day a week, a journey by moped of about nine miles and 40 minutes. Yes, I had a moped. Not for me a big roaring mechanical beast between my legs. I paid the paltry sum of £5 for my moped. It may or may not have been a bargain. My little blue two-wheeler 50cc had no brakes to speak of and as it really didn't shift any faster than about 15 miles per hour – joggers would overtake me – it wasn't really a problem. I always had my feet to stop me in an emergency. It didn't have gears; it was just stop and go. I did get a good year or so out of that machine and, being ever the entrepreneur, I sold it for the same amount I'd bought it for, £5. Well, I got bored of college very quickly and just stopped going. But didn't tell anyone. I just took the day off every week. Management believed I was furthering my education in commerce. Eventually, of course, with the end of term results and reports, management found out that I'd been skiving, and I was called into the office where Mr Wilson, my store manager, and Mr Haskins, the area manager were seated.

"Wayne, we're very disappointed in you," one of them said. "We had high hopes for you to become an area manager one day, maybe even regional if you'd only knuckle down and show the same initiative that Malcolm shows."

Malcolm had left the Ridings at the same time as I had with very similar academic qualifications. In fact, we'd been in the same house and same class all through high school but Malcolm seemingly had more gumption than I, as evidenced by the fact that he rode a 750cc Suzuki to work and would undoubtedly go on to make a great area or even regional manager if it wasn't for the fact that a year or two later Malcolm was killed in a motor-cycle accident on the Iron Acton bypass.

Anyway, the upshot of my dressing down from management was that I was demoted from trainee manager to just being a store assistant with responsibilities such as receiving deliveries into the stockroom, replenishing the shelves when they were looking bare, and taking over the checkout so the ladies could have their tea breaks. I was no longer in charge of ordering stock or balancing stock sheets. And with my demotion came a £2.50 drop in my weekly wage. I was still earning about £18 per week, enough to run my £5 moped, give my mum £8 for house keeping with a bit left over for an occasional new set of guitar strings and a bottle of Woodpecker at the weekend. After a year or so in Winterbourne I was moved to a far smaller branch on Woodend Road, Coalpit Heath. My responsibilities were pretty much the same as before but, I was told, if I applied myself and showed initiative I might just be able to get back to the position of trainee manager again. Lucky me.

So, I left the Co-op and took temporary employment at Jacksons in Yate. My job this time was to load up cages with Russell Hobb kettles, all covered in greasy gunk, fresh off the production line. Wearing protective clothing, a face-mask, and heavy duty gloves to protect my increasingly valuable hands, when the cage was full I would then mechanically lower it into a large vat of heavy duty cleaning acid and soak the kettles for a few minutes before raising the cage and emptying it of its cargo onto waiting trolleys to be taken to the packing area and eventually on into the kitchens of Britain and beyond. I currently use a Russell Hobbs kettle in my kitchen at home in Brazil.

The pay was a lot better than the Co-op and the reason I took the job was so I could save up money to leave home. I had decided I was going to move to Liverpool just after Christmas coming.

Why Liverpool? As well as my continuing adventures with Rough Justice I had been asked to join a band set-up at church. The previously mentioned Steve Yull had found a troupe of five girls from Liverpool that sang together, accompanied by a piano player named Alan Webb. Steve had the novel idea of putting them together with a band and asked me to play guitar along with a couple of brothers from Bristol, Simon and Nick Bridgewater, on bass and drums respectively. The idea was that we'd play cabaret dances and social evenings at the weekends in Mormon chapels across Britain.

One weekend the girls and Alan came down to Bristol to meet with us, the band, and to rehearse to see if it could work. Of course, I got friendly with one of the girls, Pat, and soon we were sneaking off around the back of the chapel for a quick snog although she still had a boyfriend, unbeknownst to me, back in Liverpool. These Mormon girls, I tell ya… His name was Dave Wibberley and when I eventually met Dave he would prove pivotal in my life. But not just yet.

In the meantime Gibson, for that is what we were named – a dreadful name that I had nothing to do with in its choosing and nor did Brian from Rough Justice for a change – were playing a repertoire of mostly Abba and Carpenters songs, not that I had any say in that either. Now, I do like a bit of Abba and the Carps but when we performed at a couple of church dances and realised how truly atrocious it was we quickly, and mercifully, called it a day. But Pat and I, by this time, had become an item and so when it came to making the decision to leave home it was Liverpool that became my destination, not London as I'd first considered.

After all, as well as Pat, the city boasted Liverpool FC, my team, and was the birthplace of my favourite ever band, The Beatles. Of course it was Liverpool, it was always going to be, wasn't it?

'The Lovelock Girls.' Ruth, Wendy, Edith and Jean, Barry Island, circa 1952.

Wendy Lovelock, before she absconded. With her best friend, Pauline, 1956.

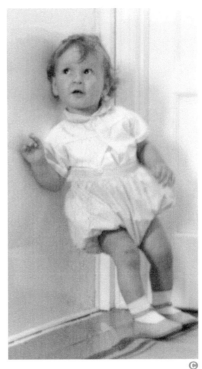

Ⓐ 'Mr MaGoo.' Me at 11 weeks old, 1958.
Ⓑ Wendy Lovelock rockin' the beatnik look at 20 years old, 1959.
Ⓒ 'Pretty Boy Wayne.' Me at one year old, 1959.

The scallywag Arthur Hussey, aged 18, 1957.

D Mum and Dad's wedding with me as pageboy with my two flowergirls, Deborah and Vanessa, August 1962.

E "Hey, you, put my mum down." August 1962.

F "I've got a dad!"
Me and Dad, Down Road, 1962.
G Snowballs, winter 1963.

H Me and 'the little poo' Adam, circa 1966.

I Nanny Lovelock and her gambling partner, Duke.

J Harry Potter or a young Wayne Hussey? (Credit: Steve Power)

K Bonnie & Clyde. Me as Clyde whilst my cousin
Mark got the more coveted role of Bonnie, Butlin's, 1967.
L Eyes centre, No.6. Butlin's, 1964.
M Me as 'the skinny little runt with a pigeon chest'
on the end (No.4) with cousin Mark (Bonnie) to my right,
Butlin's, 1967.
N Winterbourne C of E school team, 1968.
Me, back row, far left. Mark Richardson
(later singer in Stockdove), back row, far right.
Thanks to Phil Cardwell for the image, back row,
second right.
Below: Sartorial inelegance. Hussey family, circa 1971 (L)
and 1974 (R).

CHAPTER 6

Don't Confuse Ambition With Wishful Thinking

PLAYLIST:

1. Darlin' – The Beach Boys   2. China Grove – The Doobie Brothers
3. Wuthering Heights – Kate Bush   4. Big In Japan – Big In Japan
5. The Pictures On My Wall – Echo & The Funnymen
6. Better Scream – Wah Heat   7. Sleeping Gas – The Teardrop Explodes
8. Electricity – OMD   9. Black Leather – Nightmares In Wax
10. Beep Beep Love – Gruppo Sportivo   11. The Big Country – Talking Heads
12. Marquee Moon – Television

New Year 1978 had just come and gone when I left the familial
snugness of my parents' home in Bristol. With a self-belief that
possibly bordered on arrogance but patently fuelled by naiveté,
I'd decided it was time for me to venture out into the world on
my own and make my mark.

I packed my paltry belongings in a battered suitcase and a
couple of cardboard boxes and, along with my Gibson Les Paul
Recording guitar and my Music Man combo*, loaded it all into

---

* At some point over the previous two or three years I had traded in my Les Paul
copy for a white Fender Telecaster that I had gotten cheap as it had a hairline
fracture in the neck. This defect caused constant problems with its intonation so
I traded in the Tele for a Gibson Les Paul Recording guitar. What a monstrosity
that was but I wish I still owned it. Also, not long before I left for Liverpool I

the ancient family Vauxhall Cresta Estate. Mum and Dad drove me up to the port city of Liverpool on a wet, freezing, grim and grey early January day.

I was excited at the prospect of independence, a new chapter beginning in my life, and I can't remember feeling any nerves or trepidation although I surely must have. Ah, the bravado of youth, eh? Mum was a little tearful, proffering the sage wisdom, "Now, whatever you do, don't forget to eat your oranges. They're really good for you." Advice I still heed to this day. Dad, I think, on the other hand was quite happy to get the use of his garden shed back after I'd commandeered it as a practice room for the previous year or more.

I'd arranged to stay the first week or two with a Mormon family, the Nugents, who lived in a big rambling house on Church Road in the Huyton area of the city. The Nugents had a spare attic room that they very kindly let me have gratis while I looked for a job and my own accommodation. I registered with the local dole office so I could at least start collecting benefit while looking for gainful employment. I'd traipse to the job centre daily and after a week or so I was sent to an interview for a clerical job down at the Pier Head, close to the iconic Liver building. I got the job but it was mind numbing in its mundanity. Filing, copying, and making cups of tea – that was about it. I'd left the comforts and security of home in Bristol for this? This wasn't what I'd anticipated. This wasn't *living the dream*. And the wage I was earning was barely more than what I could collect on the dole. But, with a job I could secure my own lodgings, and I duly found another garret, a very

---

had sold my Marshall combo to Jon Klein, much to my parents' disappointment, and with the proceeds bought a Music Man 210-65 combo. I was beginning to favour a clean, jangly sound rather than the more overdriven sound for which Marshalls are famous.

cheap one-room partly furnished aerie atop a house with a shared bathroom at 23 Rawlins Street, next to Newsham Park, within walking distance of Anfield, home of my beloved Liverpool FC. Not that I could afford to go to the match that often. The occasional visit was a luxury. If memory serves my first game was a 3-0 home win against Norwich.

I had no hot water and no heat but I was happy. I felt that the world was about to reveal all its myriad, murky and enlightening secrets to me. I fancied myself as an *artist*, albeit one with a guitar rather than an easel or a quill. My new living conditions totally suited my idealised bohemian aspirations.

First of all I needed to change my job; being an office clerk really wasn't serving my ambition. On lunch breaks at work I would wander down into the Williamson Square area of the city centre, sometimes having lunch at the long-gone Kardomah Café on the corner of Stanley Street and Whitechapel. Just a couple of steps up on Stanley Street was Hessy's, the music shop where, legend has it, John Lennon bought his first guitar.* Next door was Curly Music, another music shop with not quite the same illustrious history but a celebrated history nonetheless. I'd stare in awe and lust at the guitars in their windows and imagined the day that I would be able to afford the glittering jewels on show. One day I spied a handwritten note in the window of Curly Music – Shop assistant required, apply within. I entered the shop, asked at the counter and was given a very informal interview there and then. "The job is yours if you can start next week." Could I? Damn right I could. I went back to the dismal office where I'd been licking stamps and envelopes all morning, handed in my notice and worked out the rest of the week.

---

* On the internet there's a picture of John and George buying their first Gibson J45s at Hessey's, probably with Brian Epstein's money.

The following Monday morning I caught the bus into town and started work at Curly Music. My first job was to tidy up the leads and tune the guitars hanging on the walls. This was it. I was in. Fraternising with the local musicians that would come into the shop for a few plectrums or a new set of strings and I'd tell 'em, "Yeah, I can play guitar and I'm looking for a band." Funnily enough, there were no immediate takers.

Taking advantage of staff discount, during that first week at Curly I traded in my Gibson guitar for a lovely black Fender Telecaster. Now... opening the case of a guitar and being intoxicated by the smell of the wood and the lacquer is one of the best olfactory experiences one can have, in my humble... And gently lifting that baby out of its plushly lined bed and cradling it in my arms, stroking the strings, fingering the chords, eliciting the promise of magic to be conjured... well, there ain't much better in Wayne's world, I can tell you. Still, to this day, I get that same thrill. And that's just how I felt when I got that *beauty* home to my flat that evening. You know how you can buy air fresheners for cars with fragrances such as 'new car smell' or 'ocean waves' or 'jasmine nights', well, I reckon there should be an 'opening a guitar case' fragrance. I'd buy it for my car, for sure.

On the Saturday afternoon of that same first week at Curly Music I was showing off a disco unit at the back of the shop to a potential mobile Tony Blackburn wannabe. "Just listen to this, this'll blow your head off," I boasted, and with that there was a huge pop, a bang and a big flash of electric blue at the wall where the disco was plugged in. Thick plumes of acrid smoke snaked up towards the ceiling. I'd just blown the bugger up. No sale and no job. I was sacked on the spot and told in no uncertain terms not to bother coming back to work the next week. I was gutted. But at least I'd got to use my staff discount.

So, I was back on the dole but not for long. One evening soon after I saw an ad in the *Liverpool Echo* for a guitarist wanted by a 'professional band'. Straightaway I went to the phone box at the end of my street and gave the number listed a call. I spoke to a bloke named Peter who told me they were holding auditions in a bar on Dale Street over the next few days. I caught the bus into town and with my guitar in one hand and my amp in the other waltzed into the bar just as the previous auditionee was leaving, each of us giving the other the evil glare as we passed on the stairs.

Peter was the vocalist, guitarist, and keyboard player. Les, the bass player, would later go onto be a bit part actor in Brookside and the drummer was called Cosy, more as in tea rather than Powell. The band was called Foxglove. Never heard of 'em? Nope, I hadn't either. They explained that their previous guitarist, Colin, had left to form his own band, Eat At Joe's, as he wrote his own songs and wanted to play 'em rather than the covers that Foxglove seemingly excelled at.

They played Working Men's clubs, social clubs and pubs throughout the north west and sometimes even further afield. They were indeed 'professional' inasmuch as they earned a weekly wage from their toils rather than the government stipend I collected every week from the dole office on Green Lane where, coincidentally, Pete Best, The Beatles' original drummer who was fired to make way for Ringo, apparently worked in the back office. I set up my amp, plugged in my recently acquired black Telecaster and joined in on a few songs – 'Darlin'' by The Beach Boys, I seem to remember, a Doobie Brothers song, maybe an Eagles song as well, and an extraordinary version of the then-current number one, 'Wuthering Heights' by Kate Bush. Apart from the Doobies I hadn't played any of these songs previously so I was, as is still my wont, bluffing it a bit but felt

I was doing okay. More than okay it transpired as I was, again, offered the job on the spot.

After back slaps and handshakes all round they explained they had a run of gigs coming up and we had two days to rehearse the set. The first gig was at the Bolton Nevada Ballroom before we went on to spend a week in Newcastle and then Cumbria for a few days before heading back to Liverpool to support Ken Dodd at the Philharmonic. Heady days.

When I first arrived in Liverpool I struggled to understand the accent. It felt like everybody was swearing at me and being overly aggressive but I soon came to understand that it was just colloquial and everybody spoke that way. But my perplexity at Scouse was nothing compared to Geordie speak. Blimey. For a West Country bumpkin with an accent to match, it proved impossible to have a conversation in Newcastle with a local other than a few grunts, groans and growls. I loved it.

Generally we were playing working men's social clubs and taking breaks for the bingo and the raffle. Oh, *this* was the dream. They were difficult audiences to please, these men who worked hard all week in factories and the like, out for a few beers with the missus and their mates. They wanted to hear songs they knew, The Beatles, of course, the Stones, other pub faves, and the hits of the day. There was no chance of being able to play any of our own songs, not that any of the other three in the band actually wrote. I quickly came to see why Colin had left Foxglove. As a songwriter I wanted to play *my* songs but I was willing to bide my time if only for the experience and, for the first time in my life, earning a living from playing music. We played five or six nights a week, one of which was a regular gig playing for the dancers in a strip club.

Not quite The Beatles on the Reeperbahn but for an innocent young boy up from the sticks, fresh to the ways of the world, this was an eye-opener in more ways than one. We, of course, had to share the same dressing rooms as the dancers so we sat there watching the girls in various states of undress getting ready for their performance. It felt rude to avert your eyes when some large breasted honey was talking to you about the price of Brussels sprouts while she rouged her nipples. I really didn't know where else to look.

I remember this one girl to whom I took a particular fancy, and she *knew* it. Each week she'd cavort in front of us while we played behind her on stage and as I concentrated studiously on my change from G minor to diminished D chord I tried not to gawk too hard at her ungodly body contortions. One week, as she reached the climax of her act, she turned her back to the audience and sauntered over to stand right in front of me. Looking me straight in the eye, her legs akimbo, she rubbed her crotch and, with a big wink and a knowing smirk, undid her bra and exposed her breasts to me, pulling my head into her bosom, steaming up my glasses and leaving them askew on my face, before turning around to delight the audience with her ample charms. She knew what she was doing, that girl. Of course the rest of the band, the punters, and the other girls were all in hysterics at my blushing discomfort. I must've *stank* of provincialism.

At this point in my life I'd only ever had sex twice previously, my shameful experience with Bev and a quick youthful fumble in the dark while parents were out at church. With such limited experience, I deposited some of the images that confronted me in my memory bank for later use back at home.

On the nights off, Peter, my boss lest we forget, started turning up at my flat with his paramour, Pauline, in tow. Peter was married at the time so he asked if he could use my flat for his extra-marital dalliance. Now, you could surmise that I was spineless for doing so, and you'd be pretty close to the mark, but I'd trundle off to feed the ducks in nearby Newsham Park for an hour or so while the illicit lovers indulged in carnal pleasures in my flat. Just like the Jack Lemmon character in the film *The Apartment*. Even on a couple of nights after getting back late from gigs they would stop over and be shagging on the bed that I'd meekly let them purloin whilst I pretended to sleep on the couch. This couldn't go on and, indeed, it didn't. Somehow Peter's wife found out about his affair and kicked him out of the flat they shared. Peter came to mine claiming he had nowhere else to go which I thought was strange as we'd only known each other a matter of weeks and were hardly bessie mates, but I'm guessing it was because he didn't want anyone else to know about the sticky situation he had gotten himself into. I sat up with Peter into the dark hours and, having zilch experience in matters such as these, I could offer no words of advice or comfort. I simply sat and listened as the silly boy poured his heart out, crying with remorse and regret. We eventually managed to get some sleep and he left early in the morning before I awoke. I never saw or heard from Peter ever again.

That very evening Pauline came around and I had *her* crying on my shoulder too. Apparently, Peter had called her that day and told her that it was all off between them and he was going back to his wife with the promise of giving up the band and settling down to a 'proper' job and a life of marital bliss. That was how I found out that Foxglove were no more. I was out of a job once again. Pauline, probably more through pity than any feelings of amour, offered to recompense me for the use of my flat and the loss of my job in the way she knew best but being the chaste young thing that I was, and terrified of a woman so forward and forthright, I politely demurred the invitation. Ever the gentleman, that night I slept on the couch again.

Without a job and no way to pay the next rent due on my flat it was with a heavy heart I had to call Mum and Dad to ask them to come and pick me up and take me, with my tail between my legs, back to Bristol. My first sojourn to Liverpool had lasted just four months.

During those four months I had still been attending the Mormon chapel, more for the social aspect rather than for the salvation of my soul, at the top of Millbank just up from the roundabout in Tuebrook. And it was there that I met two people that were to unwittingly change the course of my life.

The first was Dave Wibberley. Wibbs was someone who had graciously befriended me when I had first moved to Liverpool despite the fact that his girlfriend had chucked him to become mine. There was nothing underhand about this on my part. I had no knowledge of his existence until after Pat and I had got together. In fact, among the reasons for coming to Liverpool, being a Liverpool FC supporter, a Beatles lover, and feeling it was time to leave home anyway, Pat being my girlfriend was a principal factor in my decision to move there. It was ironic that she chucked *me* not too long after I had moved there. A heartbreaker was our Pat. But I quickly got over her, young love breaking hard and fast and moving swiftly onwards.

Anyway, Wibbs started telling me about this club in town, a punk club called Eric's where every Thursday night was a local bands night and entrance was free with a membership card. "Fancy it?" he asked.

"Yeah, sure," I replied, "Despite owning *Rumours* by Fleetwood Mac I can be a punk, I've seen The Clash and The Damned."

And so yet another freezing Thursday evening we caught the bus into town and went to Eric's. My life was never to be the same. For me, along with a host of other tawdry characters,

Eric's was to become the epicentre of my life for the next couple of years.

Eric's was situated on Mathew Street, not 50 yards up from the legendary Grapes pub where The Beatles used to down a pre-gig pint before their shows at the Cavern, which was opposite Eric's but – criminally – had been land filled and was now just a piece of wasteland used as a makeshift car park. We entered Eric's through a recessed door and on the right-hand side was the ticket desk behind which stood a very helpful young lady. Her name was Doreen and we would become very good friends in the ensuing years. This being my first night at Eric's I had to become a member so after coughing up the princely fee of £1.10 I received my membership card and was allowed to pass through the dark portal to this strange new netherworld. Making my first tentative steps down the stairs into what the Mormon Elders would surely declare to be a seething pit of iniquity, every nerve and every sense of my body was pulsing with delicious anticipation and trepidacious curiosity.

Maybe a dozen steps down and I was confronted by the bar on the left. To the right was an area with a few red tables and stools and a red ripped and beaten-up padded plastic bench that ran the length of the wall painted jet black, I seem to remember. Eric's was black and red, the colours of the devil. Straight on ahead through an arched entrance and on the right was the low stage where a band of spikey haired punks were making a spirited, cacophonous noise with drums and guitars. In front was a dance floor about three-quarters the size of a football penalty area. The official capacity for the place was 700 but I'm damn sure I was there some nights when almost twice as many were in attendance, with punters spilling out onto Mathew Street. And many more nights when it was almost empty.

There were maybe 50 people there at the most that first night I visited Eric's. Of course I'd been in *some* pubs and clubs before but nothing quite like this Sodom now before me. If my mother could've seen me she'd have been straight down on her knees in less time than it takes to say hallelujah, praying for my soon to be damned soul.

Obviously I'd seen punks around the streets of both Bristol and Liverpool. I even slightly considered myself one when I'd stuck a safety pin through the lapel of my old school blazer and took to wearing that around the village for a few days; a direct result of the furore in the tabloids after the Pistols' appearance on Bill Grundy's *Today* show. But I felt like a fuddy-duddy compared to the colourful cast of characters and delinquents I found in Eric's that night.

One of the bands I do remember that first evening was fronted by this strange-looking round-headed character with short bright orange hair and red tartan Rupert Bear trousers with braces over a cool white blouse. He played bass and sang the Velvet's 'Waiting For The Man'. Wibbers informed me that this was Holly Johnson moonlighting from his day job as bass player with up and coming local heroes Big In Japan. Wibbers also introduced me to a few acquaintances he had made on previous visits.

There was this motormouth rapier rapid fire wit by the name of Pete Wylie; a taller blond, handsome young man called Julian with, unlike the broad scouse of most of Eric's other patrons, a bit of a plummy accent, Copey as I came to know him; a short bespectacled chap with a big nose, it was like looking in a mirror, who happened to be the lead guitarist in Big In Japan, by the name of Ian Broudie; and after he had exited the stage Holly Johnson himself. Holly was the first openly fey gay person I had ever met, his slightly lispy scouse drawl accompanied by a handshake I can only liken to holding a dead fish. I immediately liked him. As I did all the people I met that night. There was a sullen, sulky chap, again bespectacled, sat in the corner nursing a pint of something brown who seemed to me to have few friends and brook no approach, pointed out as a member of a band called The Crucial Three. Going by the name of Mac, you may know him better as Ian McCulloch.

There was also the most outrageously flamboyant flouncer I had ever seen with his small coterie of hangers-on who I was told worked in the provocatively named nearby Probe. It was my first sighting of Pete Burns. Was I staring? I hope not. I was *scared* of him. There were others, Jayne Casey, Paul Rutherford, Bill Drummond, Budgie, Will & Les, Dave C., Hilary, Mick Aslanian, Boxhead, Hambi, Jamie and Yorkie amongst the many I came to meet over the next few weeks and months. I also got to meet the two owners of the club; the giant, in every sense of the word, Roger Eagle, and the more taciturn Pete Fulwell, both of whom always showed great interest in, and offered encouragement to, their younger clientele. A more hospitable crowd I couldn't have wished for despite their merriment at this newly arrived hick from the sticks who stuck with his orange juice rather than sinking a bevvy like the rest of 'em. Sod the Mormon Church, I immediately knew that I had found my 'true' spiritual home and Eric's was our temple.

Something else I noticed on my first few visits to Eric's was groups of people going into the toilet cubicles in twos, threes and fours and more, sometimes all boys, sometimes all girls, and sometimes boys *and* girls. What nefarious acts were going on behind those closed doors, I wondered? In my provincial gaucheness I didn't dare ask but could only speculate and fantasise. Of course in the years to come I would be among those that brazenly entered toilet cubicles with others to do things other than to use the stalls for the purpose they were built, but my first witness of this strange behaviour did leave me a little nonplussed, I must confess. It certainly didn't go on at the Mormon Church dances that I used to attend, no sir-ee.

Eric's became the social hub for this new generation of aspiring musicians, I being one of them, and acolytes, and Thursday nights couldn't come around soon enough for me. I just prayed that Foxglove didn't have a gig that night. Playing 'Hotel California' yet again had lost its sheen.

The first flush of punk had just come and gone in a storm of safety pins, shocking tabloid headlines and spittle. Although for me the more interesting first wave of punk music came out of NYC – Television, Talking Heads, Blondie and more – the UK punk scene certainly acted as a catalyst for thousands of kids to feel like they could pick up an instrument, learn some rudimentary chords, get up on stage and perform. We no longer felt that we had to be virtuosos aspiring to a diet of tedious dinosaur-like antiquated bands like Yes, Genesis, Barclay James Harvest and ELP. I can't claim there is scientific evidence to back up my theory but, in my opinion, at least 90% of bands that came after 1977 wouldn't or couldn't have existed without the advent of punk. But no matter how Mark 'slap (as in deserving of)' King may dress it up, there's no way you can put Level bloody 42 in that 90%.

And this was what I was witnessing week in week out at Eric's. Young kids ineptly fumbling with their instruments but fused with a passion, energy, fresh ideas and attitude, a music predicated on good, simple songs rather than instrumental wankery masquerading as virtuosity, and a new language in song that spoke to its audience rather than the vacuous airy-fairy pontification of the prog-rock generation.

As well as very early gigs by local bands Echo & The Bunnymen, The Teardrop Explodes, Wah Heat, Orchestral

Manoeuvres In The Dark, Pete Burns in Nightmares In Wax, I did get to see loads of national and international bands perform at Eric's over the next couple of years: Iggy Pop, The Clash, B52's, The Cramps, The Pretenders, a very young U2, Simon Gallup's first gig as a member of The Cure, XTC, The Only Ones, Wire, Siouxsie & The Banshees, and, one of my personal faves, the soon-to-be-forgotten Dutch band Gruppo Sportivo, to name just a few, before its untimely demise in early 1980. Some of those in the audiences with me went onto forge their own place in what would later be endearingly termed by the slothful British music press as 'POST-PUNK'.

It was an incredibly exciting and creative period that has left an indelible impression on the landscape of rock music and all the music that has come since. The best records from this period that were bequeathed to us are a part of the rich tapestry of rock music that, while some of them weren't the 'big hits' they deserved to be, simultaneously gave indication and instruction as to how rock music could move forward after the empty posturing and blind alleys of the mid-Seventies.

I was in a minority at Eric's. I'd been playing guitar for a few years by this time and could play to a reasonable standard; so for me it was almost a process of de-learning, simplifying and emphasising uniqueness and energy rather than practising my scales and minor 7^{ths}. I loved it. Inspired as I was, spending hours playing my guitar along to *Marquee Moon* and *More Songs About Buildings & Food*, new tunes were pouring out of me but, frustratingly, I could find no immediate outlet. Things had to and would change. But first the prodigal son had to limp back to the family domicile in Bristol and lick my wounds and face the jibes of my old school mates who snickered at my ignominious failure to take the world by storm. I'd show them though, plenty of time for that.

Providence soon intervened in the form of Wibbs who once again proved to be my inadvertent saviour. Phoning me a week or so later he told me about a new band that he had just joined, a punky art-school type of band charmingly named Ded Byrds, and they needed a lead guitarist, a job for which he had recommended me. He also told me that another part-time Mormon friend of ours, Steve Power, had suggested I move back to Liverpool and share his one room flat with him just off the Tuebrook roundabout. I was soon persuading my folks to let me load up the Vauxhall Cresta Estate again.

Without the intervention of Wibbs and Steve Power I may well have ended up staying in Bristol and my life would have taken an altogether different route. Who knows where I'd be today if it hadn't have been for their fortuitous intervention. But isn't that what the journey of life is all about – fortuitous interventions?

CHAPTER 7

Gasping For Colour, This Perfect Heart

PLAYLIST:
1. Cavatina (theme from *The Deer Hunter*) – John Williams
2. The Man With The Child In His Eyes – Kate Bush   3. Denis – Blondie
4. What A Way To End It All – Deaf School   5. Warszawa – David Bowie
6. 1/1 Music For Airports – Brian Eno   7. Slow Motion – Ultravox
8. She's Lost Control – Joy Division 9. Ever Fallen In Love – The Buzzcocks
10. Teenage Kicks – The Undertones   11. The Wall Street Shuffle – 10cc
12. You Might Just See Me Cry – Our Kid

So, back up the M5 onto the M6 north and then the M62 west passing Burtonwood services and Knotty Ash on your way into Liverpool. When you come off the motorway turn right on Queens Drive, following the road until you get to West Derby and then turn left on Millbank, passing the Mormon chapel on the left and down to Tuebrook roundabout, turning right onto Lisburn Lane and Sandringham Road is the ninth turning on the left. Flat 2, 8 Sandringham Road is on the right-hand side. This is the journey I took on my return to Liverpool in late spring, 1978, just a few weeks before I turned 20 years old.

Waiting for me in his first floor flat was Steve Power. I had met Steve at the Mormon chapel earlier in the year during my first aborted foray to Liverpool. Sympathising with my predicament that led to me having to return home to Bristol, Steve kindly offered to share with me his humble abode. And humble it was too. The accommodation was essentially one room, maybe 12 by 15 feet, that contained Steve's single bed, a couch which became *my* makeshift bed, a small TV, a record player, and a small table with a couple of chairs. Off this room was a tiny kitchen with a stove and a fridge. Bathroom and toilet was shared with the occupants of the flat next door and was up a short flight of stairs and, joy of joys, hot water was available for the bath after depositing 10p in a meter. If we were frugal enough with the hot water both Steve and I could have a lukewarm bath for one 10p coin. This was a luxury compared to my previous flat on the other side of Newsham Park where I'd had no running hot water and had to boil a pan on the stove for a wash or a shave. I ended up living with Steve in that flat on Sandringham Road for nigh on 18 months and I've been perennially grateful for his generous hospitality ever since. Without it I'm not sure I could've made it back to Liverpool.

Steve also played guitar, acoustic mostly, and very well. A party piece (not *my* kind of party you understand but, you know…) of his was 'Cavatina', the theme to Michael Cimino's *Deer Hunter*. To this day I can't hear that piece of music without thinking of Steve. We'd sit there with blankets over our legs to keep out the cold and compare and exchange guitar chords and riffs. He introduced me to the music of Steely Dan and I played him Television and Talking Heads. I remember the first Kate Bush album, *The Kick Inside*, being a particular favourite of ours as was Blondie's *Plastic Letters* and Deaf School's *2nd Honeymoon*. At night Steve would lie in his bed and I'd be cocooned in my sleeping bag on the couch and we'd listen to *Low* by David Bowie or Brian Eno's recently released *Music For Airports* until we'd both drift off to the Land Of Nod.

Besides wanting to immerse myself more in the burgeoning Eric's scene the principle reason I wanted to make it back to Liverpool was to have a play with Ded Byrds, the band that Dave Wibberley had recently joined as rhythm guitarist and was praising up a storm. They were rehearsing on the top floor of an empty office block on Fleet Street, a couple of streets over from Bold Street, a building that the Everyman Theatre used as temporary storage for their costumes, props, and stage sets. I daresay it's prime real estate these days but back in the late spring of 1978 there was severe economic depression in Liverpool, as well as the rest of Britain, and many warehouses and office blocks stood empty and unused in the city centre.

Through benevolent friends at the Everyman Ded Byrds enjoyed the use of the space rent free, and because there were no other businesses in the same building or even in the local vicinity they could make as much noise as they wanted during the day. The top floor was a big open plan space, so there was plenty of room to set up and make a right racket.

Through Wibbs bigging me up I was invited down to join them one Monday morning. As well as Wibbs the band comprised David Knopov, a well-known character around town, who was, aptly, the singer. Ambrose Reynolds, whose father, Stanley, was a very well-respected *Guardian* journalist, played bass. Jon Moss, who fancied himself as a photographer and worked in the city centre Virgin Records store, and not to be confused with his namesake who later kept rhythm and more for Boy George, battered the drums. And Jon's girlfriend's little sister, Denyze D'Arcy, played saxophone. They already had maybe three or four tunes kind of worked out so as I was setting up my amp and guitar they ran through the songs for my benefit. Pretty ramshackle they were it has to be said, although they definitely had a spark and an originality. Once I had tuned up I started playing along, adding lead guitar lines and making suggestions as to the arrangements, dynamics and instrumental parts.

I was certainly a pushy, opinionated bugger in those days, very driven, nakedly and unashamedly ambitious at a time when 'careerist' was a very dirty word amongst my peers and in the music press. What was wrong with wanting to make music my life's work, my career? It's all I had wanted to do since I was 14 and had first picked up a guitar. I wanted desperately to be a musician. A rock star. I always knew I would be so why pretend otherwise? I'm sure I was an uptight, egocentric pain in the ass but I could play and I knew how to arrange a song and how to organise a band to make them sound good.

So Ded Byrds asked me to join and, like a marauding Genghis Khan with hobnail boots, I stormed in there and took over. Within a couple of hours we honed the three or four songs they already had into gleaming diamond-sharp slabs of noise. Ded Byrds needed me and I needed Ded Byrds. It was fate, written in the stars. They knew it, as did I. Before I joined it was all a bit aimless and haphazard. I wasn't there to be liked and didn't care if they did or they didn't. I just wanted us to be as good as I knew we could be. And we *were* good.

I don't think my attitude has really changed too much since then. I am still the one that pushes the others in rehearsals and in the studio, making 'em play it 'just one more time' before the next tea and fag break. I do believe I have lightened up a bit though in the intervening years and I am not now, and possibly never was, the dictatorial ogre to work with that I know some people believe me to be. The number of musicians that have passed through the ranks of The Mission through the years is often cited as evidence in support of this bogus accusation. I also know that with my later use of amphetamines these tendencies of mine to be manic and totally absorbed by the process of making music became heightened and accentuated, and it's during this period that I probably acquired this unenviable reputation. But those traits were there innately in me from the very beginning. Sans drugs, booze, or the power of success, relative or otherwise.

I like to think it's passion and drive and having the confidence to take the lead. I don't believe pure democracy can work in a band environment, there always has to be one, or even two, pushing and pulling the others along; someone who has the vision, sees the big picture. 'Our Glorious Leader' is the moniker that Craig Adams, Mick Brown, and Simon Hinkler christened me with in the early days of The Mission. I'm not sure they weren't taking the piss but even if they were I liked my new nickname and endeavoured to live up to it. Others may call it arrogance and bull-headedness. I don't care as long as the job gets done, and done well.

I do like and welcome collaboration though. There's nothing quite like feeding off other musicians and being excited by the music that we're making together. And just as I am comfortable working on my own I do prefer, however, the interaction of sitting face to face with another musician and trading ideas. And, contrary to the opinion of some, I do listen to other people's ideas and suggestions and will always try them rather than dismiss them outright.

Simon Hinkler once said about me in an interview, and I'm paraphrasing, "Wayne always listens to what you have to say but then goes ahead and does what he wants anyway." In the end I believe you have to be able to stand behind what you do and to do that you have to feel you've done the very best you can at any given time. None of that, "Oh, that'll do" for me. All that aside though, and while I think I've learned to be more relaxed and forgiving in my musical relationships, certainly since I've given up the 'fasties', when I look back I think I would now really despise having to work with the younger pre-drugs me. What a sanctimonious, obnoxious little toad I could be. But you won't catch me apologising for that. No way.

After that first day with Ded Byrds I went home and started putting some new songs together that I thought would suit our new band and over the course of the next few weeks we rehearsed every day and gradually pulled a set together ready to take to the stage.

And our first stage was at the Everyman Bistro on Hope Street. In the absence of a diary or any info online then I'm guessing that must've been June 1978. The room was packed with other curious local musicians as well as thespian types popping down from the theatre upstairs after they had finished work for the night, but mostly with friends of Knopov and Ambrose as they were both already well-known faces around town. We went down fantastically well. I guess you could describe Ded Byrds as being satirical art-school punk if you're into classification and feeling pretentious enough. With songs such as 'Lily's Off To Paris', 'Plastic Love', 'AWOL' and a rousing version of The Beatles' 'Why Don't We Do It In The Road' it was all very chic, trendy and arty, a world I had never really ever inhabited or been exposed to before. Not for the first or the last time did I feel out my depth, insecurity betraying my arrogance but only to myself. I wondered how I was getting away with it. It's a thought that has persisted throughout my life.

We started playing more shows around town – Kirklands on Hardman Street, the Masonic on Berry Street and, further afield, the Bluebell in Huyton, amongst others – until we were offered our, and my, very first show at Eric's supporting John

Foxx's Ultravox on September 23, 1978. Being a Saturday there was also an earlier matinee show for under 18s as well as the later show for those of legal boozing age. It was Eric's policy, and a very good one, to always add a matinee show on Saturdays so that younger kids could get to see the bands that they were hearing on the radio and reading about in the music papers. These younger audiences tended to be more natural and demonstrative in their reaction to the bands. If they liked you then they *really* liked you and would show their appreciation with a hailstorm of coughed up phlegm. If they didn't like you then they would show their disdain with a hailstorm of coughed up phlegm. Either way, most bands came off stage covered in gob. Fortunately by summer 1978 this trend of spitting at the bands was starting to peter out, particularly with the older audiences, but the younger kids still thought it was the *appropriate* way to exhibit their fervour.

The dressing room at Eric's was off to stage left, a tiny room about the size of a bus stop. We were to share that dressing room with some notable musicians of the day, Ultravox being the first. I remember them being very friendly and accommodating. Their guitarist, Robin Simon, and I had what must've been a very tedious conversation to any eavesdropper about guitars and amps and FX pedals. Probably quite tedious for Robin Simon too, now I think about it.

Our second show at Eric's was again on a Saturday, November 4, headlined by the Bard Of Salford, John Cooper Clarke with Ded Byrds second on the bill. First on that afternoon and evening was a new Manchester band called Joy Division.

Liverpool and Manchester have a long history of rivalry, probably best exemplified by the sometimes vicious animosity between the warring hordes of football supporters of both cities' more historically successful clubs, Liverpool and United (sorry, Everton & City, but it's a fact). Musically, the intercity rivalry has been ever present too but on a far less toxic level. In the Sixties Liverpool produced The Beatles, while the best Manchester could offer in retort was Herman's Hermits and Freddie & The Dreamers. To borrow the football analogy, 1-0 Liverpool. The early Seventies wasn't a particularly brilliant time for music in either city, if truth be known, but it did see Manchester produce 10cc while Liverpool, beneath the shadow of The Beatles cast ever longer and darker, could muster no one of any real note. 1-1. Then, in 1976, the Sex Pistols played twice in Manchester during the summer and inspired a whole new generation of young musicians to form bands of their own with Buzzcocks becoming the first to reach national prominence.

Contrary to popular legend – perpetrated no doubt in Manchester – the Pistols did make it to Liverpool late in '76 but were supposedly so awful that the budding scenesters that attended that night were not swayed in the least. As a consequence Liverpool was culturally a step behind. The best Merseyside had to rouse in '76 was Our Kid. 2-1 to Manchester. However, in late 1976 Roger Eagle, Ken Testi and Pete Fulwell opened Eric's, quite possibly the best music club *ever* in the north of England.

The Liverpool punk epiphany occurred in May of '77 when The Clash's White Riot Tour, the tour I'd seen in Bristol on my birthday at the Colston Hall, swung by. 2-2. Manchester came back with the Factory in 1978 and Joy Division's *Unknown Pleasures* in 1979. 3-2 to the Mancs. 1980-82 saw Liverpool finally shedding the weight of suffocating Beatles achievement and come of (new) age with a flurry of quite brilliant new pop bands, most of them flowering out of the very creatively fertile

Eric's scene – The Teardrop Explodes, Echo & The Bunnymen, Orchestral Manoeuvres In The Dark (OMD) to name just three, some of whom began to infiltrate the upper echelons of the British music charts. 3-3.

All this is by the by as it's well into the future as far as *my* story goes but, as much as it pains me to admit it as I do still have a huge fondness for Liverpool, unless I'm missing something I'd say it currently stands at 5-3 to Manchester courtesy of The Smiths and Oasis. Stone Roses don't count as they only had a couple of good songs.* But sod it, thinking about this a bit more I'm awarding Liverpool three more goals for The Beatles and their huge global cultural and social influence as well as the great songs and the fact that they are the biggest and best band the world has ever witnessed. So 6-5 to Liverpool.

But during the punk revolution and the immediate following years, 1978-80, Liverpool and Manchester were reasonably close in terms of their music scenes. Obviously there was still *some* rivalry but generally it was good-natured amidst an atmosphere of co-operation between the cities and the two main music venues – Eric's in Liverpool and the Factory in Manchester.

The Factory was a club night fronted by Alan Erasmus, Alan Wise, and Tony Wilson at the squat Russell Club, slap bang in the middle of the god-forsaken Sixties planning atrocity that was Hulme. Most days of the week the Russell Club featured reggae but at weekends it was taken over by the Factory mob putting

---

*   Of course it's only my personal opinion and I'm sure I'm in a minority but The Stone Roses got lucky when they captured the zeitgeist of the 'baggy' movement. For me, they were like The Monkees; looked great, made a couple of great singles and a half decent album, but, really, there was very little there of any real substance. A lot more pose than poise. Says he.

on local and national punk and, the newly unimaginatively christened post-punk musical movement, *new wave* bands.

In this spirit of bilateral concertation Manchester bands would be booked into showcase gigs at Eric's on local bands night supporting Liverpool bands, and Liverpool bands would be invited over to the Factory to support Manchester bands. In this way I got to see Ludas, Manicured Noise, The Fall, Durutti Column, a Mick Hucknall-fronted Frantic Elevators and, of course, on this particular occasion, Joy Division. And as part of this intercity cultural exchange we, Ded Byrds, played the Factory a couple of times, one of which was a couple of weeks later, with us being first on before Joy Division and John Cooper Clarke.

As I mentioned before, the dressing room at Eric's was small, with the one at the Factory even tinier still, and with us all having to share it was impossible to ignore each other, try as we might. Nods and grunts were the order of the day rather than any real bonhomie between the two bands as introductions were made. Like some naughty schoolboys looking for trouble on an away day trip, Joy Division laughed a lot amongst themselves although, and I can't be sure that this memory isn't tainted with time and legend, I remember Ian Curtis sat in the corner with his pint being very quiet and slightly separate from the rest of that Manc rabble.

Anyway, I also remember watching Joy Division's set and being mightily impressed by their gravitas and intensity on stage. Only moments before in the dressing room it was Just William and his Outlaws. Remember, this was almost a year before the release of *Unknown Pleasures* but it was already evident that Joy Division were a cut above.

That being said though it would've been impossible to predict that Joy Division were going to be as globally recognised as they are today. I see young kids in shopping malls at home in São Paulo wearing the cover of *Unknown Pleasures* on their t-shirts like it's some young, hip fashion statement, much like I also see the Ramones logo. I'm not even sure that a lot of these kids know what they are wearing. Just that it looks cool. And it does.

Without stating the obvious, I'm pretty sure that wouldn't have happened if Ian Curtis hadn't committed suicide. Ian, and Joy Division by association, have become canonised, a symbol for the 'outsider' by virtue of his early death and the lyrics he'd written for their brilliant second album *Closer* that seemed so sadly prophetic once the tragedy of his passing had unfolded. But maybe if it had been that other Ian, McCulloch, or Julian Cope or Robert Smith or any of the other bright young emerging talents of the time that had taken their own lives, then the same lionisation may well have occurred for them. Maybe our generation, as do all generations, needed its *own* martyr.

It is too hypothetical to speculate just what would've happened to Joy Division had Ian lived. Just look at New Order and what they went onto achieve without Ian. Who knew? Who knows?

Which reminds me, I saw New Order's first ever gig. I have since spoken with Hooky about this and he has no recollection of this happening and it isn't chronicled anywhere in the New Order mythology but I am absolutely certain and utterly convinced it happened.

I'm jumping ahead here but in the summer of 1980 I was fronting my own band for a few weeks called ...And The Dance, more of which later. Ian Curtis had taken his own life on May 18 and, like everyone else I knew in Liverpool, I was shocked, stunned, and deeply saddened at the news. Eric's had been forcibly closed down earlier in the year but it had reopened by this time under the guise of Brady's and it was maybe late June or early July and we were scheduled to play the local band night on this particular Thursday. Anyway, I remember someone from the office at Brady's calling me the day before and asking if I'd mind if they postponed our gig, promising in return for compliance a later prime support slot which was, in the end, never forthcoming. Oh, the vicious and cruel fickle mistress that is the music business. I digress. Anyway, the reason for the postponement was because the three remaining members of Joy Division – Bernard Sumner, Hooky and Steve Morris – wanted to play an unannounced warm-up show. I don't think they even had the name New Order at the time. Gillian certainly wasn't in the band at this point; it was just the three of them.

Like the hustler I was I managed to wangle myself onto the guest list and I was surprised to see the place less than half full, maybe 100-150 people at the very most. News spread slower in those pre-internet days. I clearly remember being impressed, and this is such a vivid memory, because Barney played a melodica on stage and I hadn't seen that instrument being used in that way before. So inspired was I that I went out and bought myself one the very next day from Hessy's. I still have it in my studio but it rarely gets taken out of its box anymore.

Anyway, that was New Order's first gig that history, and Hooky, has conspired to forget. I was there and I remember it and before you lay any accusation at my feet of having a mixty-maxty* memory this was at a time before I'd started using illicit drugs of any kind.

So, back to Ded Byrds and Eric's. As well as playing a couple of times on local band night Thursdays and even one Friday in early 1979 supported by Teardrop Explodes and OMD, we also ended up supporting The Undertones in early March. They'd

---

* Jumbled, muddled, addled.

just had a big hit with 'Teenage Kicks' and I seem to remember Knopov getting into some kind of altercation with them. They, The Undertones, wouldn't let us share the dressing room. Knopov took umbrage at their haughtiness. So much for them not having airs and graces and being just five street kids from Derry. Bah, spoilt brats.

Knopov could be a gobby bugger though and wind people up, but he was a good and colourful front man, it has to be said, despite having a voice that sounded a bit like Elvis Costello with a mouthful of marbles. I believe he performs a very creditable Frank Sinatra cover show these days, must catch it sometime being a huge Frank fan myself. Walking through town with him he seemed to know *everyone*, still does, and we'd be stopping every two minutes for him to have a natter with someone he knew.

It was on one such occasion that I was first introduced to Bob Wooler who was, famously, the DJ at the Cavern in the days that The Beatles played there and, as legend would have it, introduced Brian Epstein to the soon-to-be-world-famous lovable mop-tops after one of their lunch-time shows. It was also Wooler that John Lennon, again famously, beat up at Paul McCartney's 21st birthday party because ol' Bob had made some quip calling into question Lennon's sexuality after he had holidayed in Spain with Epstein. Wooler, of course, dined out on his proximity to the early Beatles for years, and who can blame him?

Another character I met through Knopov with links to The Beatles was Alan Williams who had managed them before Epstein and taken them out to Hamburg for the first time. And there were others too – Roger McGough, Paul McCartney's younger brother Mike McGear, Bill Harry, Adrian Henri, and more – I'd regularly see walking around town. Knopov knew them all. Being such a huge Beatles fan since I was knee high it was amazing to me to be walking where The Beatles had once walked, to drink where they had once drank, to talk with people that had talked with them, that had known – still knew – them.

Through Ambrose I met Nathan McGough whose mum was Thelma Monaghan, née Pickles, who was John Lennon's first girlfriend, and who also went out with McCartney. Nathan was a very pretty boy, curiously looking not unlike a young Macca. As a result, Nathan was nicknamed Nacca. I remember once staying over at Nathan's, or rather his adopted dad Roger's house, and, waking in the morning, Nathan telling me that I had just missed Paul and Linda leaving who had also stayed under the same roof that very night. I don't know how true that was but if it was then that was the closest I ever got to meeting a Beatle. Nathan, of course, went on to manage, if that's the correct job description, the unmanageable Happy Mondays.

When I first joined the band, Ambrose, the Ded Byrds' bass player, lived on Menlove Avenue, just a few hundred yards or so down on the same side of the road from number 251, named Mendips, where Lennon was raised from the age of five by his aunt Mimi. Catching the bus to Ambrose's for songwriting sessions I would exit a stop early just so I could walk past where John spent most of his childhood and teenage years. The propagated myth has it that John grew up in a very working-class environment but Menlove Avenue was, and is, a very middle-class area of Liverpool. In those days in the late Seventies Mendips was a privately-owned home with a sign on the front gate declaring that 'trespassers will be prosecuted' but now, of course, it is owned by the National Trust and open to the public as part of a Beatles tour. Strawberry Fields is just around the corner. A short walk from Ambrose's in the opposite direction and I would find myself in Penny Lane. McCartney's childhood home is a short bus ride down Mather Avenue from Penny Lane, the next street over from where Knopov's family home was. Everywhere I went in Liverpool there was a little piece of Beatle's folklore and I lapped it all up like a parched puppy.

Aside from gigging as much as we could during this time, including memorably supporting Cheap Trick and the ridiculous five (two's enough, right?) necked guitars of Rick Nielsen at the Liverpool University's Mountford Hall, Ded Byrds recorded demos in Amazon Studios, an eight-track facility situated on an industrial estate in Kirby on the outskirts of Liverpool. This was my very first time in a recording studio and, sadly, I don't personally have a copy of those recordings. If memory serves we recorded such potential classics as 'I Wanna Be A Monk', 'Teenage Apathy' and maybe 'Summer In Russia'.

This recording session is memorable for two things. Firstly, the producer for our session was a young Liverpool lad by the name of Gil Norton who has since gone on to be a top record producer, working with such bands as Foo Fighters and Pixies. The second memorable incident was when Ambrose's dad, the carousing journalist Stanley Reynolds, turned up at the studio one evening clearly under the influence of a drink or ten and, for no reason any of us could fathom, took a swing at Fraser, the engineer. In an attempt to diffuse the situation, Ambrose, quiet, gentle Ambrose, with one punch that John Conteh would've been proud of, decked his dad. That put a stop to that, then. Stanley was shunted into a taxi and sent home apparently waking the next morning with a black eye and no recollection as to how he got it. I'm not sure Ambrose ever told his dad the truth.

It was also around this time that Ambrose and I got together with Ian Broudie on guitar and Budgie, who went on to be one of my favourite drummers while playing with The Slits and the Banshees, for a couple of days at the Open Eye Studio in the city centre on the corner of Whitechapel and Roe Street. The idea was to put a new band together but in the great Liverpool tradition of brilliant bands that never get out of the rehearsal room we didn't have a singer or even a band name and we only lasted two days before Ambrose and I returned to our day jobs with Ded Byrds.

CHAPTER 8

Burning Up In A Blaze Of Glory

At some point in late summer 1978 we, Ded Byrds, lost our rehearsal space in Fleet Street and had to find a new home. Enter the very handsome and charismatic Hambi Haralambous. Hambi was a rock star. At least in his own mind. If I had been a betting man in 1978 I'd have put my giro on Hambi becoming a bona fide pop star. He should've been. He had the looks, the voice, the personality, the swagger, and he could pen a decent tune too, that was for sure. He was the front man for perhaps my favourite new Liverpool band of the time, Tontrix. As well as being quite possibly the most self-confident person I had met up to this point in my life, he was also a member of the Ananda Marga organisation.

The Nandas, as they were affectionately known around town, were based in a big four-storey house at number 8, Ullet Road, the road that dissects the two parks, Princes and Sefton. According to their website: "Ananda Marga is a global spiritual and

social service organisation founded in 1955 by Shrii Shrii Anandamurti. The mission of Ananda Marga is self-realisation (individual emancipation) and service to humanity (collective welfare): the fulfilment of the physical, mental and spiritual needs of all people." What this meant to me at the time in very basic terms was that it was some kind of commune that existed at their Ullet Road, Liverpool centre. I won't say hippy as that would be stereotyping and unfair so let's call it spiritual, shall we?

The top two floors of the house was where their devotees, practising families and individuals lived – Hambi being one of them with his wife, Josie, and their two young children. Strict vegetarians and devoted to the disciplines of transcendental meditation and yoga, theirs was a lifestyle that invited derision from non-initiates, the ignorant and the more worldly, at a time when their practices were maybe still perceived as being esoteric and slightly suspicious. Today, in a more enlightened era in many ways – and in other ways more like a reversion to the dark ages but we won't go there – and with 60 years of life experience behind me, I personally view this philosophy, theology and attendant disciplines as being very humanitarian. Although I don't practice yoga or meditation or subscribe to any specific spiritual movement myself, I do wish the world would, could, adopt more principles and practices such as these in dealing with each other, the animal kingdom and our environment.

On the ground floor of the Nandas' house were three large, beautifully wood-panelled rooms with big bay windows overlooking an unkempt garden.* These three rooms were used as a morning nursery for their children and for meditation workshops and classes held in the evenings and sometimes at weekends. In the cellar were another three or four rooms of varying sizes and in varying states of repair, the largest of which Hambi used as a rehearsal room for his band, Tontrix. We rented the room across the corridor that had a bay window that looked up into the back garden. It was a smaller room with bare walls and ceiling that we adorned with egg cartons, heavy blankets and thick cardboard and polystyrene in a valiant attempt at soundproofing to keep the noise levels down for the inhabitants upstairs. Nonetheless we couldn't start rehearsing until midday when the crèche on the floor above would close for the afternoon. Which was okay with us as, being musicians, a midday start to our working day tallied with our preferred lifestyle. We'd generally work all afternoon until five or six, finessing new songs and preparing the set for any upcoming shows. Much work was done in that small room, plenty of arguments too, of course, but also a lot of creative activity. In September-October of 1978 one thing for which we rehearsed very hard was our first ever TV appearance.

So It Goes was a late night Granada TV culture, events and music show hosted by the legend that was Tony Wilson. When *So It Goes* was cancelled by his Granada bosses due to Iggy Pop's on-air profanity, Tony, who was a main anchor for the daily evening *Granada Reports* news programme, managed to persuade the board-room suits to let him, for one evening every week, feature a local band performing a live song over the closing

---

* This is an aside but I have always preferred gardens that are allowed to grow a little wild rather than the manicured lawns and flower beds that many prefer. There's something magical and mysterious about fighting your way through a thicket of brambles and undergrowth.

credits. So, for a short period in 1978 on *Granada Reports* you could catch bands such as us, Ded Byrds, enjoying our first TV exposure.

The song we chose to perform as our introduction into millions of homes at teatime in the north-west of England was our anthem of abstinence, the self-penned 'I Wanna Be A Monk'. Another band that made their first TV appearance in this way was Joy Division performing 'Shadowplay'. Fortunately for the world at large some bright spark at Granada TV had the initiative and foresight to archive the Joy Division tape, as evidenced by its presence today on YouTube but, maybe with the same instinctive foresight, recorded over Ded Byrds' paean to abstention. Sadly for me but probably better for you, our performance has long since disappeared from the Granada vaults.

Aside from Manchester, Ded Byrds started to play more and more gigs out of town; at the F Club in Leeds, supporting 999 at Preston Uni, and Straight 8 at the Marquee in London, amongst others. Later in March 1979, the same month that we played with The Undertones, at Eric's we supported The Pretenders who were flying high in the UK Top 40 at the time with their recently released 'Stop Your Sobbing' single. Again, it was a Saturday so that meant, again, two shows.

We were sat in the dressing room waiting to soundcheck when The Pretenders arrived and in walked Chrissie Hynde, took one look at us and announced, "Oh, I see the groupies are already here." Cheeky bint. They were great though, a fantastic band at that time, and in James Honeyman-Scott they had a guitarist whose playing I adored. Another friendly bunch, unlike the mardy Undertones, and I again recall cornering Mr Honeyman-Scott in the dressing room and having a very one-sided conversation about guitars. He obviously had better things to do with his time than to talk with some young Woody Allen lookalike from the support band but he was gracious enough to answer my prying queries about his guitar and amp set-up and how he obtained that jingle-jangle sound that I so loved. Pretty and cool as you like and everything a guitar hero should be, just listen to the guitar playing on 'Kid', The Pretenders' follow up single to 'Stop Your Sobbing', if you need evidence of Honeyman-Scott's ability. The guitar break is sumptuous and the harmonics at the end of it leading back into the bridge in tandem with Chrissie's falsetto vocal is spine tingling. 'Kid' is a great, great pop song and still my favourite Pretenders single. Sadly James Honeyman-Scott was to die in June of 1982 aged just 25 of, according to Wikipedia, heart failure caused by cocaine intolerance. Fucking drugs.

With The Pretenders that day came Seymour Stein. Being the record label boss and a friend of Chrissie's he'd come along to see their show. He caught our show too and loved it as we, apparently, reminded him of his then-current-favourite band, The B52's. Seymour approached Knopov and Brenda, who was our manager at the time as well as being Knopov's girlfriend, and expressed a fervent desire to sign us to his label, Sire Records. At this time Sire was a very cool independent label distributed by WEA. Alongside The Pretenders on their roster were The Ramones, our 'mates' The Undertones and one of my absolute faves, Talking Heads. Seymour would, of course, famously later go onto discover and launch the career of Madonna and introduce such bands as Soft Cell, The Cure, The Smiths, Depeche Mode and Echo & The Bunnymen to North America. I guess ol' Seymour would have to concede that Ded Byrds was one of those rare occasions when he got it wrong. And it had all started off so promisingly for us with Sire as well.

A deal was easily and quickly agreed but one proviso that Seymour insisted on was that we change our name as he thought Ded Byrds was too close to the Dead Boys who were also on Sire, and that Ded Byrds would be a difficult name with which to attract airplay on mainstream radio. None of us were particularly attached to the name and we were easily persuaded. I came up with the new moniker, The Walkie Talkies. Silly and poppy, the rest of the band agreed and that was that. From that moment on we were known as The Walkie Talkies.

One other change suggested to us by management before we signed the contract was to sack Dave Wibberley. Yes, I know, it was harsh and cruel and even maybe a little reminiscent of The Beatles sacking of Pete Best just before they signed *their* record deal, although history was to decree that The Beatles would go onto be the biggest band ever while Ded Byrds split up after one failed single. So Wibbs didn't miss out on much, if truth be told. I personally felt strongly that getting rid of Wibbs was the right move because in the time the band had been together I felt we'd all improved as musicians both individually and collectively and had become a pretty tight beat combo... except for Wibbs and his sloppy rhythm guitar playing, which was often out of time and tune.

Okay, I know the punk emphasis was more about energy and attitude over technical expertise but my feeling was that with just one guitarist, namely me, we'd be better and tighter with more space in the music without Wibbs and his constantly strummed heavily distorted barre chords. And he danced funny as he played, the lolloping lummox. Anyway, my style of playing guitar had developed into a hybrid of rhythm and lead at the same time so we had our bases covered.

Apart from the ever loyal Ambrose, lovely boy that he was, the rest of the band agreed and so Wibbs was out. When Ambrose, who took upon himself the unenviable task of having to break the news to Wibbs, told him Wibbs broke down and cried. When I heard about this I felt like a right heel, particularly when you consider it had been Wibbs who had brought me into the band in the first place. But it was the right decision at that time and I've never shied away from having to make difficult decisions when it's come to my work.

A strange scenario occurred at the next couple of local Liverpool shows we played. Wibbs turned up with his small coterie of friends and fans and sat right in front of the stage with tears streaming down his face while his posse all gave me the beady eye and chanted his name between songs. Wibbs has, probably justifiably so, nary a good word to say about, or to, yours truly ever since.

And the same could've been said of Knopov if it wasn't for the fact that he and I have become reacquainted while I've been researching this book. There was always a little tension between the two of us, probably the result of a power struggle within the band, but generally we agreed to disagree and to just get on with it. More and more of my songs were being performed by the band and Knopov, being the singer and unable to play an instrument at the time, was not only finding it harder to get his ideas heard by the rest of the group but was reluctantly obliged to sing the lyrics that I was writing. Even on stage on occasion he took to slagging off my lyrics by introducing 'Summer In Russia' with the comment, "These words are so shit they're not even worth the toilet paper they were written on." Nice.

Now, many years later and being a singer myself, I can understand his frustration at having to sing someone else's words without having an outlet for his own metrical efforts. A couple of times our disagreements would flare up into fisticuffs, more slapping than punching though being the soft-boy types that we were, with one particular occasion being, I remember, when the two of us had to be dragged apart by a passing Ian Broudie outside of the Armadillo Tea Rooms on Mathew Street. I can't remember now what the fight was about but it was probably something as trivial as Knopov expressing his dislike for the colour of the beret I was wearing at the time. Yeah, I know. A beret.

With juvenile bickering put aside and Wibbs ejected from the band, Ded Byrds travelled to London and the Sire Records office on Floral Street and signed our recording contract. When the deal was inked and the advance banked we were in the fortunate position of being able to pay ourselves a weekly wage of £25, if memory serves, which wasn't a huge amount but more than enough to live on and keep me in berets. And we had enough to buy ourselves a few new bits of kit. I traded in my Music Man combo for a new Roland JC60 amp, the JCs being my amp of choice pretty much ever since, and bought myself a white Yamaha SG2000 as my spare guitar. For the uninitiated the Roland JC amps have an inbuilt chorus that is very sweet and despite trying every chorus pedal and computer simulation plug-in since I've not found anything that can come close to matching the quality of the JC chorus. In years to come with The Mission between Simon Hinkler and myself we owned nine or ten of the JC120s and we still both use this venerable oldie on stage to this day. Just don't ever use the JC distortion; it's rubbish, sounds like a wasp in a bottle.

With Seymour Stein flitting between continents it was left to his UK label lackey, Paul McNally, to run Sire's London office and it was he that suggested we use an up-and-coming engineer-producer by the name of Colin Thurston to record our debut single. Colin had fairly recently been engineering Bowie's *Heroes* and Iggy Pop's *Lust For Life* albums which was kudos enough in anyone's book let alone mine. The famous Virgin-owned Townhouse Studios on Goldhawk Road, Shepherds Bush, was booked for a week in the summer of 1979. It was to be my first time in a 'proper' recording studio. We stayed for the duration in the apartments above the studio and I shared a room with Jon, our drummer. We were working in the studio closest to the reception, Studio One I guess, while XTC were recording their *Drums & Wires* album with producer Steve Lillywhite in Studio Two further down the corridor.

Colin Thurston, who would go on to enjoy huge success producing Duran Duran, brought a black-and-white Fender Stratocaster guitar into the studio that he claimed had been given to him by the Thin White Duke himself during the recording of *Heroes*. Obviously I had to use it during the course of *our* recording, it would've been rude not to. We spent a couple of days setting up and getting levels and recording the basic backing tracks in the traditional way, playing together in the studio – drums, bass, and rhythm guitar – and then overdubbing more guitars, sax, and vocals throughout the course of the week.

After consultation with Colin and Paul McNally we decided to record three songs during this period, two that I had written: our live fave 'Summer In Russia', and a new song called 'Rich And Nasty'. The third choice was a Knopov-Ambrose composition, 'Pop Star'. All three songs being lyrically satirical, I wrote 'Summer In Russia' after reading a story in a newspaper about how Russians were planning to develop certain parts of Siberia as holiday resorts in the hope of attracting foreign tourists. 'Rich And Nasty' was about lusting after fame and fortune and how when it finally arrives most people then become arseholes. Like I'd know. Not the typical quasi-mystical Hussey fare of later years.

As it happens 'Rich And Nasty' was chosen as the A-side of our 7-inch while 'Summer In Russia' got the nod ahead of 'Pop Star' as the B-side. It was really quite thrilling to finally hold the single in my hands and look at the label on the record and see (Hussey) as the writer underneath both titles.

Released in September 1979, 'Rich And Nasty' wasn't a hit, barely got a mention in the music press, garnered just a couple of radio plays, and sank without trace. Described in one *Record Mirror* review, I remember, as ska-punk it did sell a few copies in Liverpool and that was about it. It became, however, a much sought-after relic once The Mission became successful and fans began to realise that, yes, the same Wayne Hussey they knew and loved that wore purple crush velvet loons and big black hats and lipstick was pictured on the back cover of The Walkie Talkies' sleeve leaning against the window of the Townhouse Studios, along with the rest of his band mates, looking forever like a new wave John Lennon with little round national health specs, skinny tie, and light cream jeans... aargh, no beret but more sartorial inelegance nonetheless.

I mentioned earlier that XTC were also recording in the Townhouse during our time there and the studio had a communal recreation room with a TV, pool table and a fridge stocked with beer, all studio pre-requisites. This is where we would adjourn if our presence wasn't required in the studio and this is also where XTC would hang out too. West Country boys from Swindon, just down the road from my home town of Bristol, a friendlier bunch you couldn't wish to meet with singer/guitarist Andy Partridge the most gregarious of them all. He was like the older geek kid at school, a sixth form prefect maybe, wanting to constantly show off his new toys – his guitars, his keyboards, his pedals – inviting me into their studio, the big live stone room where Phil Collins later recorded *that* drum sound, to let me try his guitars and amps.

I remember one evening being sat at the back of their control room with Lillywhite and engineer Hugh Padgham at the desk while Dave Gregory, XTC's quite brilliant guitarist, was recording a guitar overdub. He was playing with a cloth duster over his fretting hand, the idea being to dampen the strings. Normally a guitarist would dampen the strings with the palm of his strumming/picking hand but that also kills any resonance or overtone. The sound they were after was one where the plucked strings would ring out but be muffled, rather than muted, and with less sustain. The actual track is 'Day In Day Out' and if you listen to the intro you can plainly hear the guitar and effect. It's a trick I've tried myself a few times since in the studio but without ever achieving the same sonic satisfaction. Must be using the wrong duster.

Drums & Wires is, for me, one of the truly great guitar albums of all time with really good songs fantastically performed and produced. While all the playing on the album is exemplary, I particularly adore Colin Moulding's bass playing, it's the guitar playing that is incredibly creative and inventive throughout, not once resorting to cliché. I spent many hours playing my guitar along to this album on its release but, frustratingly, I was never really able to work out many of the guitar parts. The only downside to the album for me, and this will no doubt enflame the more zealous fans of XTC, is Andy Partridge's vocals which can get a bit wearisome and sometimes border on the histrionic, much like my experience of him as a person.

My path would cross with Andy Partridge again 11 years later with tumultuous results but more of that another time. On its release in the autumn of 1979 I went to see XTC play at Eric's and, being an acquaintance of the band, blagged a guest list spot and watched the show from the side of the stage. They were brilliant. It's a great shame they stopped playing live a year or two later because of Partridge's chronic stage fright. For most musicians playing live is our life-blood, our pulse, as essential to us as air, but we all suffer with stage fright to varying degrees and all have our own idiosyncratic and sometimes peculiar ways of dealing with it. It must've been particularly intense and debilitating for Andy to even consider giving up playing live. I couldn't.

While XTC went on to greater commercial success with subsequent releases, for me they never quite matched the creative zenith of *Drums & Wires* ever again.

Assisting Paul McNally at Sire Records was Mick Houghton. Mick began as a journalist writing for various rags in the Seventies, including *Zigzag*, *Sounds* and *Time Out*. In 1979 when I first met him he was working in promotion at Warner Bros, Sire's parent company. Mick has enjoyed a long and illustrious career in the music business, working mostly as PR and has represented many fine artists including Echo & The Bunnymen, Julian Cope, The KLF and The Jesus & Mary Chain as well as The Sisters Of Mercy during my tenure with the band. Mick began writing again for a couple of the UK music monthlies in the early Noughties before later writing two very enjoyable and well-respected books, one on the life of Sandy Denny and the other on the founder of Elektra Records (the E in WEA), Jac Holzman. In the online info I read about Mick The Walkie Talkies were omitted from his every biography. My guess is that he would probably, if he even remembers us, think of us as an episode best forgotten. And to be fair, it's probably a very valid point.

I remember once having a conversation with Mick and Paul about The Teardrop Explodes whom Paul was thinking of signing to Sire. At the time the Teardrops were fledgling and raw and I was asked my opinion of them. Feeling threatened by Paul's interest in what I regarded as local rivals, to my eternal shame I proffered the judgment that they weren't worth pursuing as Julian Cope couldn't sing, the band couldn't play, and they had no songs. Oh, what an insidious self-serving brat I was. And how wrong I was about the Teardrops and Julian in particular. Within less than a year they would release what would become one of my all-time favourite singles in 'Treason' and go on to substantial commercial success with Julian becoming one of the genuine maverick pop stars of the era and beyond. And I know it's taken nigh on 40 years but I wish now to publicly apologise to Julian and the other Teardrops and offer myself up to penitence.

To help promote the stumbling 'Rich And Nasty' single, The Walkie Talkies were booked onto an upcoming UK tour as support to The Ramones but Da Brudders pulled out at the last moment, leaving us bereft and squabbling amongst ourselves. The only respectable thing left for us to do was to split up which we duly did in November of 1979.

Oh, and I dumped the berets.

CHAPTER 9

And The Dance Goes On And On And On

After the demise of The Walkie Talkies in autumn 1979, aged 21 and impatient for impending 'success' to arrive, I was in a state of flux, unsure what my next move should be. Having garnered a nascent reputation around Liverpool as a decent guitarist I received a few offers to join local bands and even played on a couple of recording sessions but nothing really sparked my imagination or enthusiasm sufficiently to make me want to nail my flag to anyone else's mast. It was a frustrating limbo for what was, in retrospect, probably just a matter of a couple of weeks but at the time felt like an eon.

And then, fortuitously for me, Hambi's band, Tontrix, split up. During the time that The Walkie Talkies had been rehearsing in the basement at 8 Ullet Road I had become friendly with Hambi, sharing a mutual love for Television and Blondie, old Phil Spector productions and 'classic pop', although I never fully understood his passion for Bruce Springsteen. Still don't, to be frank. Anyway, as Hambi was at a loose end and so was I it seemed a natural conjoin to start playing and writing songs together. Hambi owned a four-track TEAC reel-to-reel tape recorder and we put a small demo studio together. The large bay-windowed room at the front of the house that we'd used for rehearsing became the main playing room while a small adjacent room became the control room. We knocked a hole in the wall between the two rooms and fitted a double-glazed window and, voila, we had our own demo studio.

Our equipment was spartan at best. We had a very basic small MM (nicknamed Mickey Mouse) 16-channel mixing desk, a few cheap Shure 545 microphones, and one Yamaha E1010 FX unit, all monitored through a pair of huge domestic hi-fi speakers that Hambi had nicked from the Ananda Margas upstairs. Hambi, christening the studio Pink, the rhetoric being it's the colour of universal love of oneself and of others, would develop the facility through the years and eventually move its location from Ullet Road to Lark Lane whereby it has now changed hands and is these days owned by Andy McCluskey from OMD and called The Motor Museum. And it still churns out the hits. From small acorns...

As Hambi and I were both too busy writing and playing we needed a lackey to press the buttons and watch the recording levels. I thought of my flatmate, Steve Power. He could play guitar, and I knew he had a good ear and was interested in the recording process. I suggested him to Hambi and, with a little cajoling, Steve was invited over to Pink to become the house engineer.

Steve was an avid student, a fast learner, and, with me as his very willing guinea pig, he would spend long hours in the studio experimenting with EQs, microphone positions, mixing and remixing; just basically learning how to get the very best out of the rather primitive equipment he had at his disposal. Steve ended up working at Pink for quite some time after I had left Hambi and he oversaw many improvements and upgrades at the studio before eventually leaving himself and moving to London to further his own career. A career that saw him go onto production work with such luminaries as Robbie Williams (there is a 'Hambi' link here which will be explained later in this chapter), Diana Ross, Tom Jones, Kylie Minogue, Blur, Andrea Bocelli, and many others. And it all started for Steve in the little four-track Pink Studio at 8 Ullet Road, Liverpool 8.

Now we had Steve ensconced behind the desk Hambi and I were recording every song and fragment of music that we came up with. Being slightly impoverished we just used the same three or four tapes that we owned, recording over what we had previously recorded when we'd come up with a new song. I'm sure much good music was lost forever in this way but we had no choice, we couldn't afford new tape every time we wanted to record.

Not yet having a permanent band we'd rope in friends to play on our demos. Glynn, an eccentric neighbour of mine and Steve's in Tuebrook who had a huge Kate Bush fixation (and, let's be honest here, who didn't?) came in and played drums and percussion on a few things but didn't really hit it off with Hambi. Glynn was a bit too outer space while Hambi was defiantly earthbound. Chris Hughes, later known as Merrick when he was one of the two drummers in Adam's Ants and who went onto produce massive sellers for Tears For Fears, also came into drum on a track or two. A young 15-year-old Guy Chambers occasionally came into the studio after school to play piano and keyboards. Guy went onto play with The World Party and The Waterboys and, of course, later played piano on The Mission's *Carved In Sand* album while also scoring parts for an 80-piece orchestra employed, at a cost of over £10,000, to accompany a piano piece I had written that became 'Sweet Smile Of A Mystery', an absurd exercise in excess that saw the light of day as merely a track on The Mission's compilation, *Grains Of Sand*. But all of this pales in comparison to his later work with Robbie Williams. Guy penned the tunes and became Robbie's musical director and co-producer (along with Steve) for the ex-Take That star on some of his hugest hits.

We'd sometimes get Mike Score to come in and play bass. Mike, he of the famous haircut in A Flock Of Seagulls that for some epitomised the early Eighties, was previously the bass player in Tontrix but had left to start his own band. Mike owned a hairdressing salon on Whitechapel in town, next door to where NEMS, the Epstein's family business, used to be. With my being on the dole and a fellow aspiring musician, Mike would offer me free haircuts and every time, as he'd be snipping away at my forelock, he'd ask me to join his new, fledgling band. Mike had switched to playing guitar and keyboards and singing. A fellow employee at his hair salon, Frank, was playing bass and Ali, Mike's brother, was bashing the drums.

They were roundly derided by all the cool, trendy cats in Liverpool, as always jealousy masquerading as contempt, probably because they were a very well-equipped band with their very own rehearsal space in the room above their shop. I don't think it helped their cause any by being poncey hairdressers either. They needed a lead guitarist and Mike believed I was the man for the job. But I resisted all entreaties despite the promise of free haircuts for life, feeling that they were maybe a little too frivolous for my burgeoning pseudo-intellectual sensibilities. Mike had the last laugh though, eventually finding his guitarist and, being the first Liverpool band of our generation to do so, going onto great international success with hits such as 'I Ran (So Far Away)' and 'Wishing (If I Had A Photograph Of You)'. Unfortunately, A Flock Of Seagulls are probably best remembered for the outlandish haircuts rather than the quality of their music but Mike, it has to be said, certainly did have a way with a tune.

After Mike had enjoyed some success in the US he came back to Liverpool for a few weeks in late 1982 and, while I was again helping Hambi out in the studio on some demos he was recording, Mike was invited down to add some 'celebrity guitar' on one of the tracks. He plugged in his Gibson Flying V (ugly looking guitars, imho) and proceeded to play a guitar solo that I can only describe as sounding like a feral cat's mating yowl. At the end of the take Hambi, voicing what the rest of us were thinking, said, "Well, that wasn't very good, was it?"

To which Mike replied, in all earnestness, "You can't talk to me like that, I'm an international rock star!"

You could cut the quiet with a breath… Until I burst out laughing and then everyone else joined in. Thank bugger for that. I ended up replacing the guitar part myself after Mike had left the studio. My solo sounded more like the howling dog we were after.

My path would cross again with Mike's in the late Nineties when I was living in Orange County, Southern California. I call this period 'my wilderness years' as, having split up The Mission in late 1996 and moved to the US, I was floundering in both spirit and creativity and to help make ends meet I was remixing tracks for the LA-based label, Cleopatra Records. One of the projects I was asked to be involved with was A Flock Of Seagulls. I ended up doing a remix of their song 'The More You Live' and in the process I spoke – for the first time in 15 years – on the phone with Mike who was then living in Florida. We had some catching up to do. As always it amazes me how the smallest decisions you make can sometimes have the biggest effect on your life. And conversely, what you feel to be the biggest decisions can have little or no affect at all.

While the studio at Pink was in the basement the toilet was on the ground floor, up a narrow winding set of stairs to a long L-shaped corridor. At the far end of the corridor the loo was on the left just before the door to the beautiful wood-panelled room that during the mornings was used as a children's nursery. The light in this part of the hallway never worked, the spent bulb never having been replaced, with the only light coming from around the bend of the L by the front door. It was okay, there was enough light to find your way.

Late one night working with Hambi and Steve, I needed a pee so off I toddled towards the toilet. Afterwards, as I exited the bathroom back into the hallway, I heard a child crying to my left, the sound coming from the end of the corridor. I turned to look at the child and, although it was really quite dark, I could see it was a young girl in a white dress.

"Are you okay, love?" I asked, my initial reaction being one of concern.

Without really thinking I presumed she must be lost or maybe locked out of the nursery room. As I stepped towards her the crying stopped and she disappeared. Just vanished. Looking around I walked to the end of the corridor and tried the door to the wood-panelled room. It remained locked. She was nowhere to be found. Bafflement was my next reaction, and with a dawning realisation, quickly followed by fear. I hurried back down the corridor and the stairs to the studio without nary a backward glance. I related what had just happened to me to Hambi and Steve. Hambi replied, "Yeah. A couple of people have seen her before, that little girl. She's a ghost."

Trembling with shivers racing down my spine, I couldn't work anymore that evening so I left immediately and caught the bus home. I didn't believe in the afterlife, still don't to be honest. This is it, once we're gone we're gone for good is my belief. "It's unto· dust one day we shall return whether we lie in the ground or we burn."

I'd like to believe there's something more but the rational part of me is agnostic despite my religious upbringing. I have no explanation for what I saw and heard that evening though; none whatsoever and I gave up trying to rationalise it years ago. And, no, I wasn't tripping or stoned, this was before I started using any kind of hallucinogens. Anyway, the next day I went out and bought a new bulb for the empty light socket in that part of the corridor. I didn't feel threatened at all by the ghost but I really wasn't keen to make her reacquaintance.

In the first few years I lived in Liverpool I very rarely had any money to speak of and any I did have usually went on new guitar strings, or an album or suchlike. Unable to afford coach or train fare, I used to hitchhike back to Bristol a couple of times a year, for Christmas especially and then maybe once in the summer. I'd catch the bus to the Rocket in Broad Green, the on-ramp to the M62, and I'd stand there with my thumb out never having to wait more than half an hour before getting a ride. Sometimes just to the M6, sometimes to Birmingham, once or twice actually all the way to Bristol. I never encountered any problems hitchhiking, no pervy come-ons or threats, just occasionally having to put up with chatty Manchester United-supporting lorry drivers. Well, this one year Christmas was fast approaching and so I rang my parents as I did regularly once every couple of weeks, always reversing the charges of course, and informed Mum that I would be home the following weekend.

After catching a couple of rides I made it back early evening. I was dropped off at Yate shopping centre and walked the last mile or so to my parents' home. Dark and bitter cold, but with Christmas lights adorning all the windows of the houses I passed, a growing sense of excitement and inner warmth gripped me. I loved Christmas. It's the one day of the year I made every effort to spend with my family. I was looking forward to seeing my parents and my siblings, eating some proper hot food and relaxing in a heated living room watching crappy Christmas TV. It made a very welcome change from the frugal existence I normally lived in Liverpool.

I arrived at our front door, the curtains were drawn, but through the heavy drapes I could see the silhouette of the Christmas tree with its twinkling lights in its normal place in the corner of the front room. Aah, all was as it should be. I rang the doorbell and waited a few seconds for Mum or one of my brothers or sisters to answer the door. When the door opened there stood a strange woman I had never seen before.

"Hello. Who are you? Do I have the wrong house?"

"What number are you looking for, son?" asked the woman.

"Number 48. Yeah, this is 48. Where's my family?"

The woman looked me up and down, then answered, "We live here, have done for a couple of months now. Are you looking for the Husseys?"

"Yeah, I'm their son come home for Christmas. I've just hitchhiked down from Liverpool. Have they moved?"

"Yeah. They didn't tell you?"

"No, and I spoke with my mum a couple of days ago and she didn't mention a thing. They haven't changed their telephone number so how would I know they'd moved? Do you have their new address by any chance?"

"Yeah, hang on, I've got it written down here." She disappeared briefly and came back with a slip of paper with an address written on it. "Here you go. It's not too far, just the other side of the estate. Shouldn't take you long to walk there."

The kindly woman gave me directions and after thanking her and wishing her glad tidings I set off on my way. Fortunately it wasn't that far, maybe another 20 minute walk. So, my feelings of Christmas cheer having dissipated a little at this unfortunate oversight on Mum's part, I made my way to the new family home. On arrival I knocked on the door and Mum answered it.

"You didn't tell me you'd bloody well moved! I've just come from the old house and there's some strange people living there."

"Oh. I didn't tell you?" laughed Mum, "Mmm, sorry about that. Well, you're here now so no harm's done. Merry Christmas, Wayne. Come on, give yer ol' mum a cuddle."

The Ananda Margas ran a health food shop and vegetarian lunch restaurant called Food For All on Hardman Street, next door to Kirkland's. Nowadays there are loads of these places in every city and very welcome they are too, but back in 1980 they were few and far between and viewed with suspicion or mockery by the general public. Hambi was still very involved with the Anandas at this point, so we'd often pop down to the restaurant for lunch while he'd conduct a little business.

One of the girls working behind the counter, a ravishing beauty named Louise, had caught my eye and gradually over the course of the ensuing weeks I summoned up the courage to speak with her. Put me on stage in front of thousands of people and I'm okay but I was, and still am, incredibly shy and gauche when it comes to 'normal' social interaction. Drugs and drink have certainly helped through the years and that's maybe a conversation for another time but at this point I did neither so I had to overcome my natural timidity by sheer force of will. I liked Louise and I began to suspect that she liked me back. Still too insecure to ask directly for her phone number I got my mate Hambi to do it for me one day when I had made my excuses and left the restaurant early. I caught the bus back to Ullet Road and the studio and waited with sweaty palms and a stampeding heart for Hambi to arrive a little while later. In through the door he walked with a grin broader than the Mersey and a piece of paper in his hand with Louise's phone number written on it.

"She really likes you, give her a call," relayed the swarthy Cupid stood in front of me.

That evening when I arrived home I went to the phone box at the end of the street, and mustering up all the courage I could, I called her.

"Can I speak with Louise, please?"

A man answered. "Can I ask who's speaking?"

"Uh, my name is Wayne."

"Wait a moment, I'll get her for you."

After seconds that seemed to stretch into eternities, she came to the phone. "Hello, this is Louise."

"Hi, this is Wayne. I was wondering if you'd like to go to the movies with me sometime?"

There ensued a lengthy pause, as if Louise was deliberating what her answer would be. Hambi, you bastard, you told me she liked me. If she did then she would have said yes by now. Shit, shit, shit. I can never go back to Food For All for a piece of flapjack or some cauliflower cheese. Oh God, what have I done? Blushing in the quiet I held my breath waiting for her answer.

"Yes," she replied, then paused. "But don't ever say 'movies' again, I hate that word, it's so American. I almost said no because you said 'movies'. Yes, I will go to the cinema with you. What would you like to go and see?"

Spluttering and stammering I suggested, "What about *Alien?*"

And so the following weekend Louise and I went to the cinema together, not the movies, in Liverpool city centre to watch Sigourney jettison the Alien. I may have held her hand in the dark of the cinema, I may have not, I can't remember, but I do know we became boyfriend and girlfriend after that evening and within a matter of weeks I had moved out of the flat I shared with Steve in Tuebrook and into a first floor bedsit at 97 Arundel Avenue, near Sefton Park, with Louise.

Despite the guest musicians playing on our demos Hambi and I soon realised we needed a permanent band to play our new songs. We found ourselves a cracking little rhythm section, the two Pauls, Curran playing bass and drummer Barlow, who would later go onto play with The Christians, It's Immaterial, and even later still, The Pogues for a brief stint.

While I was just 21 and the two Pauls even younger, Hambi was veritably ancient at 28. I got on very well with the two Pauls and we'd laugh and giggle while Hambi would throw withering looks our way in much the same way an adult would misbehaving children.

Probably because of the age difference Hambi did have an annoying tendency to be patronising, didactic even, which obviously caused a little friction, particularly with three stroppy know-it-alls with me as the eldest barely out of my teens. It was a combustible dynamic and likely to flare at any moment, all four of us being very opinionated and not shy to voice those opinions. It never quite reached the point of fisticuffs but it came close on occasion. Hambi was the kind of man who would always tell you what you are doing wrong and how to redress that wrong. Even when you are absolutely right.

Ian McCulloch, of Echo & The Bunnymen, was the best man at Hambi's wedding to his second wife, Lesley, and whenever he is in Brazil, either with the band or solo, I always try to meet up with Ian. I am often his first port of call for some, ahem, refreshment on his arrival into São Paulo. I can't always oblige but I do know a man who knows a man. Let's leave it there, shall we? Anyway, I always ask after Hambi and Ian says Hambi even now is the only person that still tells him what he's doing wrong and how. That I can believe. But there is no malice or ill intent with Hambi. He has always seemed happily oblivious to any insensitivity he may be exhibiting.

The main bone of contention with the two Pauls, and I was on Hambi's side on this one, was about the way they looked and dressed – plain ol' blue jeans and t-shirts – not good enough, ever, in my book. I was sporting the presently trendy 'David Byrne collegiate pseudo-intellectual' look while Hambi was more into Elvis-type lamé jackets with sharply creased black pants and Brothel Creepers. It has to be said that Hambi did look, and act, the part. I was recently reminded by drummer Paul of an occasion when we were playing at the Bluebell in Huyton, which was a hard pub in a rough area. Hambi, dressed to the nines in a gold lamé suit, was vamping it up in his usual inimitable fashion and addressed the audience, "Yeah, I know you guys have your problems out here in Huyton. This one's for you, it's called 'Stranded'." Took a lot of bottle, that, and lucky not to *be* bottled.

Hambi, in a prescient act that foretold of Eldritch's request for me to change my name when I joined The Sisters Of Mercy just a few short years later, tried to persuade the two Pauls to change their surnames to something more glamorous than Barlow and Curran. Hambi suggested Pacino for drummer Paul and De Niro for t'other Paul. Amongst great guffaws they less than politely declined the suggestion. I actually thought it was quite a good idea myself.

We rehearsed and recorded every day at Pink and put together a good bunch of songs and, despite our sartorial differences, musically we gelled very quickly, sounding not unlike our influences: Springsteen, Blondie and Costello's Attractions. Within a few short weeks, under the moniker of Hambi & The Dance, we were gigging around the pubs and clubs of Liverpool, building a good reputation and audience. But good things never last, do they? You never realise they're good until they're over, do you?

A few months in, and with record companies starting to sniff around us, the question of ownership of our songs was raised. A heated and fractious meeting in Food For All spelled the beginning of the end for Hambi & The Dance, Mk I. Hambi wanted to take all the credit for the songs while myself and the two Pauls felt the credit should be shared equally, or at least a division that was commensurate with the amount of input we'd had on the songs. We were definitely contributing chord sequences and parts that were integral to the songs above and beyond just playing our instruments. And I felt, personally, that I had a genuine claim to a share of the publishing on pretty much all the songs, many of which were written by Hambi and I before the two Pauls had even joined the band.

Song publishing credits can be an area of great resentment within bands and I'm not sure there is an absolutely fair way to divvy up the proceeds. Without the band the songwriter may not even have a vehicle to record the songs, resulting in the songs not being 'hits' if the writer is on his or her own. On the other hand, good songs are gold-dust, and good songwriters are rare to unearth. Hence writing songs can be very lucrative if you are successful. If one member of the band takes all the publishing credit then the other members may see the writer living a Life of Riley driving around in a flash car while they are still paupers having to catch the bus. That kind of situation will only foster rancour and grievances.

The traditional way of splitting songwriting credits is 50% for the writer(s) of the music and 50% for the writer(s) of the lyrics. I've been in bands where one guy writes a vocal melody with a lyric but with no music, maybe just a drum beat, and I've fleshed out all the music around the voice and received no credit; and at other times received 50% of the song for merely contributing a simple guitar part. I think it's crucial to establish an agreement over publishing at a very early stage when you're working with somebody for the first time.

When we started The Mission, having learnt from my past experiences working with bands and seeing and feeling the resentments engendered when someone isn't receiving the credit they feel they deserve, or when someone receives credit without having any input, I proposed a policy of splitting the songwriting credits thus: 80% for the music and 20% for the lyrics. With there being four of us in the group we'd split the music credit equally four ways, giving each member of the band 20% of every song. Then, being the principle songwriter, I would take the extra 20% for the lyrics making my share of the songs 40%.

Now, I know that some would probably argue that 20% was still too much for my lyrics. I was never seriously gonna threaten the Dylans, Bob and Thomas, in the poetry stakes, but the way I figured it I would still make twice as much as the rest of the band for the songs that I'd be writing. And deservedly so. And with this arrangement in place from the beginning it gave me license as the songwriter to sometimes go to the band with fully fledged songs knowing exactly what the bass line should be, what the drums should do, having all the guitar lines worked out, and getting the band to play the song exactly as I heard it. Or, conversely, I could go into rehearsal with just a few very sketchy strummed chords and we'd all work on the idea together. This, to me, was a good way to work and a very fair way to split the publishing, certainly for a newly formed band. At least, that is, as long as we were *still* working together as a band.

When the original members, first Simon, then Craig followed by Mick, started leaving one by one I kept the band going and we were releasing live albums, and compilations, and re-recordings, and playing the songs live, and the original members of the band were still receiving their 20% of the publishing, sometimes on songs that they didn't even play on in the first place. I started to resent this, certainly at times of financial hardship, as I was working my balls off while they were sat at home with their feet up making money on songs I'd written. But it was the agreement we made in the beginning and it had to be honoured. With each successive line-up change of The Mission I altered the way the publishing credits were structured, again learning from experience, and now we adhere to a policy of the full writing credit going to whoever writes the song. It does seem fairer particularly at this stage in our lives.

So with squabbles and open hostility becoming more frequent within Hambi & The Dance, and a deep-rooted malcontent festering because of the publishing dissension, we played a few more gigs, the last one at the Everyman Theatre in summer 1980, and then the two Pauls and I bid Hambi adieu and it was mercifully all over.

Hambi rallied and continued on as Hambi & The Dance with a new band of sillitonian* musicians, and managed to get himself a huge record deal with Virgin Records. On the eve of signature he apparently sacked his new band and signed the deal himself. With the substantial advances he received he upgraded Pink Studios to a commercial 16-track facility and recorded his one and only album there with Steve Power in tow. Steve was even a member of the band for a while but he quickly saw the error of his ways and reverted to being an engineer and producer. Hambi got the big promotional push from Virgin but it didn't happen for him. I believe his one and only UK TV appearance was on *The Basil Brush Show*. It's hardly the stuff of legend, is it?

Listening to his album now there are three or four songs on it that I consider I had a large part in writing, with arrangements very close to the arrangements we worked out together with the two Pauls. But c'est la vie, he went his way and I went mine. I'd have put money on Hambi being successful though. He had the whole package and I don't quite know why it didn't happen for him. Maybe I'm being inequitable here but karma is a word that's scratching at my mind.

---

* Meaning silly or gullible person, esp. one considered as belonging to a notional sect of such people.

So what did I do next? Myself and the two Pauls formed a new band with me taking over vocal duties and, in typical Paul & Linda or John & Yoko style, I persuaded Louise, my girlfriend, to join us on keyboards and backing vocals. Oh my. To be fair Louise went about her task with great diligence and genuine enthusiasm if not musical ability. And in an act of pure spite and malevolence directed at Hambi we called the band ...And The Dance. We managed a few gigs around town without causing any great stir. I hadn't yet really found my voice and was still feeling more comfortable as a sideman rather than a frontman at this juncture.

Undeterred, I scraped together enough cash to pay for a day at the Open Eye four-track studio. We recorded and mixed five songs in eight hours with one track, 'And The Dance Goes On', making it onto a local compilation album, *A Trip To The Dentist*. In years to come, much like the Walkie Talkies single, this album became a much sought-after curio amongst avid Mission collectors purely for the fact that it included a track listed as being by yours truly. The cover photo was of all the bands and artists that appeared on the album gathered together as one big group in a field. Much time was squandered by Mission fans analysing the photograph with a magnifying glass trying to work out which one was I amongst the dishevelled rabble, but to no avail. I didn't turn up for the photo shoot and didn't admit that fact to anyone for years.

Aside from her lunch-time job at Food For All, Louise was a full-time student at the Liverpool College Of Art, the same school that John Lennon and Stuart Sutcliffe had attended and where John had met his first wife, Cynthia. I loved walking around those hallways and stairwells with Louise imagining how it had been 20 years earlier when I might've bumped into Lennon himself or heard him playing his guitar and singing his songs in the Common Room. I was nothing if not the fantasist, eh? But Louise's time at the Liverpool college was coming to an end and she was going off for further studies at the Middlesex School Of Art that autumn. Louise and I continued to see each other sporadically for about a year after she left for London with us, as with the band, eventually drifting apart but more because of distance and absence rather than the apathy that afflicted ...And The Dance. I do remember travelling down to stay in the halls of residence with Louise a couple of times, the nearest underground station being Cockfosters, the end of the line. And, yes, it was.

During my brief flirtation with obscurity as ...And The Dance a Scottish fanzine called *The Next Big Thing* sent their Liverpool correspondent, Kris Guidio, to interview me. In contrast to his sallow junkie pallor, Kris was clad all in black leather, skull earrings, jet-black hair and jet-black shades, as snout-fair* as the devil himself, tall, Italian, literate, sinister and beautiful, a black angel with a soul as dark as sin and a smile that could smite even the coldest heart. Eloquent, learned, and irreverent, godforsaken and glorious, infernal but unsullied, affected and the most genuinely beguiling man I had ever met. I instantly fell in love with Kris. Not in a physical or romantic way but in the way that all devoted acolytes come to worship their master. We became fast friends.

Kris was married at the time to Nina Antonia who, some years later, would go on to write well-respected tomes about her beloved Johnny Thunders, The New York Dolls, and, as her book was entitled, the homme fatale, Peter Perrett. I think it's fair to say that Nina had a junkie fixation, a fascination for skinny white boys who injected heroin into their veins. Kris was

---

* Handsome; having a fair countenance; fair-faced, comely.

her ideal partner. As well as writing for fanzines Kris was also a truly gifted poet, Byronic in tone and temperament, and, dare I claim, a huge early influence on my lyric writing. An illustrator of prodigious talent working mostly with black ink and influenced by Aubrey Beardsley, Kris produced a series of startling comic strips featuring his biggest love, the American band, The Cramps. Kris was art and culture and rebellion and experience and the education that I'd always craved but up to this point in my life had never known I needed. I didn't know my heart and soul ached for the shadows as I'd always lived in the light.

With Louise having flown the coop and left for London it was a struggle for me to financially maintain the bedsit that we had shared. Kris and Nina, who had recently become parents for the first time to the girl infant Severina*, had a spare bedroom and offered it me. There was no hesitation, I moved right in and my instruction in the dark arts began.

23rd August 1985 by Kris Guidio (reproduced by kind permission)

I should have kept my mouth shut
It was never what I wanted
Not to hurt you
Of course it's true I wanted blood on
My teeth
But then you became the ghost in my
Heart and the purpose behind my
Silence
I spent hours in the mirror

---

* Named after the character Severin in the Velvet Underground song 'Venus In Furs' and the Leopold von Sacher-Masoch novel of the same name.

Training for the perfect
I love you
Your shoulders will always taste
Sweeter than needles
And once again I'm sure
I won't hear your voice tonight
I did not live for honour
The mysteries of slavery became clear
I left my heroin in an old coat
Cigarettes and occasion flawed me
Your privacy was respected while I
Waited for morning
I thought about empty rooms and
All the ceremonies that might fill them
These are the prayers that poisoned
In the vicious small time hours
I did not live for honour

CHAPTER 10

Searching For Heaven

PLAYLIST:

1. The End – The Doors   2. Venus In Furs – The Velvet Underground

3. I Wanna Be Your Dog – Iggy & The Stooges   4. Suzanne – Leonard Cohen

5. Frankie Teardrop – Suicide   6. Human Fly – The Cramps

7. Sex Beat – Gun Club

8. Searching For Heaven – Pauline Murray & The Invisible Girls

9. Animal Crazy – Pauline Murray & The Invisible Girls

10. Atmosphere – Joy Division

11. Another Girl, Another Planet – The Only Ones

12. Fools – The Only Ones w/ Pauline Murray

It was late 1980 and having taken Kris and Nina up on their invitation to lodge with them at 13 Lambton Road, just off the top of Aigburth Road, I was, with Kris' guidance and mentorship, immersing myself in new (to me at least) music such as The Doors, The Velvet Underground, Iggy & The Stooges, Leonard Cohen, Suicide, The Cramps, Gun Club; the literature of Burroughs, Kerouac, De Sade, Sacher-Masoch; the poetry of Plath, Lorca, Byron and the French bards, Baudelaire, Rimbaud, and *Cheeks On Fire* by Raymond Radiguet; films such as *The Nightporter*, *Death In Venice*, *Zombie Flesh Eaters*, *The Warriors*; and the TV show *The Addams Family* with the proto-goth Morticia played by the delectable Carolyn Jones.

Being a registered junkie Kris had legal access to the heroin substitute, methadone, and various other opiated pharmaceuticals and he'd hand me various pills and capsules saying, "Here, try this. You'll like this." And mostly I did. I didn't know or care what I was consuming, I was searching for the altered and higher state. This was the education that I craved. Sometimes the brightest light comes from the darkest place.

Although I enjoyed being the front man again for the first time since my school days, I was by this time getting a bit tired of flogging the dead horse that was …And The Dance. Apart from a little tentative interest from Carol Wilson* at the Dindisc record label we were going nowhere fast. I started buying *Melody Maker* every week to scour the 'Musicians Wanted' personal ads at the back of each issue in the hope that someone would post an ad along the lines of: 'Guitarist wanted for established name artist. Fame and fortune and endless orgies await the successful applicant. Must look a little like a cross between Woody Allen and John Lennon, wear little round national health glasses, long grey overcoats, and monkey boots, and be influenced by Television and Talking Heads'. Of course I never came across *that* particular ad but, one week, I did come across one that read simply, 'Guitarist wanted for recording & touring. Please send tape, photo, and telephone no. to…' and a PO box address was given.

I waited until my next giro arrived and caught the bus into Liverpool Lime Street Station where there was a coin-operated photo booth. You know the kind, four passport-sized photos for 50p. Got my photo taken, cut one out and saved the other three

---

* Carol Wilson had signed my publishing to Virgin Music when I was with The Walkie Talkies and, surprisingly, she would reappear later in my life story when I was with The Mission.

for later. Put the one in an envelope along with a cassette of some demos I'd recorded that showed off to the best possible advantage my scintillating (ha!) guitar playing abilities, and a little note with the Guidios' telephone number and what I suppose you'd now call a resumé but at the time was just a very, very short list of my musical achievements thus far. I walked to the post office and sent it off to the PO box in London listed in the ad.

For days every time it rang I'd rush downstairs to answer the phone but the call was never for me. Forlornly I'd traipse back to my room. And then one day a few weeks later when I'd almost forgotten about sending the tape and photo, I arrived home to be handed a piece of paper by Nina with the name Robert written on it and a telephone number with a town code I didn't recognise and a request to call him back.

"Can I please use the phone, Nina? I'll put 10p in the jar."

"Sure, go ahead."

I dialled the number and a male voice answered.

"Hello, is that Robert?"

"Yes."

"Uh, my name is Wayne and I'm calling you back. Apparently you called me earlier."

"Ah, yes. Wayne the guitarist. Well, you sent us a tape a few weeks ago and so we've now had a listen to it and we like your guitar playing."

"Wow, that's great, thank you. May I ask who 'we' is?"

"Yeah, of course. My name is Robert Blamire and I work with Pauline Murray. Have you heard of her?"

"Yeah. Of course, you both used to be in Penetration, right, and Pauline released a solo album with The Invisible Girls recently."

Which she had. A great album, actually, recorded with Martin Hannett who had, over the course of the previous couple of years, come to prominence as the producer of albums by Joy Division, among others, and who was fast becoming legendary as a maverick sonic wizard. Martin had a group of musicians he regularly used for recording sessions called 'The Invisible Girls', based around Vini Reilly from Durutti Column, John Maher from Buzzcocks, and keyboard whizz Steve Hopkins. He used this nucleus of musicians on Pauline's album as well as albums by John Cooper Clarke.

Back to the phone call. Robert: "So, would you be interested in coming up to Durham for a couple of days and having a play and seeing how we get on?"

"Yeah, of course, if you'll pay for my train fare."

With negotiations and times and a rendezvous settled before my 10p ran out we said our goodbyes. A week or so later, my prized Telecaster guitar in one hand and a not-so-prized Tesco carrier bag containing toothpaste, toothbrush and a change of underwear in the other, I set off from Liverpool Lime Street on the train to Durham. On arrival I was met at the station by the tallest man I had ever seen (though I've since met taller).

"Hi, Wayne, I'm Robert, my car is parked outside. Do you want a hand with anything?"

"Oh, good to meet you, Robert," I said, standing on tip-toe to shake his hand. "Yeah, you could carry my carrier bag, please, if you don't mind."

And off we sauntered to his car. "Wow, you have a car. I don't know anyone else apart from grown-ups who owns a car. You must be very successful."

"Nah, my mum and dad bought it for me for my 18th birthday."

"Ah, right, I got a silver neck chain from my folks on my 18th."

Oh, how the other half lives, eh? But I still have, and cherish, to this day that silver chain while I bet Robert has changed his car many times since. Just saying.

So, with my guitar and carrier bag safely stowed away in the boot of his sporty number off we drove to Robert's house. Robert was still living with his very generous and welcoming parents at this time and I was staying for the duration in a spare room at their spacious family home. Coming from a cramped council house background in Bristol and having had to share a tiny bedroom and bunk beds with my two brothers, this was, indeed, the height of luxury to me – a proper bed and my own room. "Can I live here?" I thought to ask Robert's mum but thought better of it as I'd only just arrived. Maybe I could endear myself to them over the next few days and they'd invite me to stay, like a Little Orphan Annie. Alas, it didn't happen, and it was back to the Guidios for me and a screaming Severina at all hours.

Once I'd carefully placed my Tesco carrier bag and guitar in my room we were off to meet Pauline. At this time, she was married to Peter and lived in a first floor flat in Durham town centre with a separate living room, kitchen, bedroom, and their very own bathroom with hot and cold water. We sat around and drank tea; talked about music and bitched about pop stars and they played me lots of cool music I'd never heard before.

Peter, I seem to remember, owned and ran an independent record store in Durham. Their flat was very bohemian and cultured compared to the hovels I had been used to. Books, records, esoteric art on the walls, a bean bag, even videos and a video recorder, carpet on the floor instead of bare floorboards, and it was warm, they had heating, I remember that. Introductions having been made it was then time for Robert and I to leave and return to the Blamire homestead where mummy Blamire had a lovely hot dinner waiting on the table for us when we walked through the door. I really could've gotten used to this.

Once we'd finished our meal Robert took me into another spare room, which he had set up as a home studio with an eight-track tape recorder and a big mixing desk. Nowadays, home studios can and do exist on a laptop and pretty much anyone has access to what was once million pound studio environments and equipment for a couple of hundred pounds. Back then I didn't know anyone else, apart from Hambi, who had a studio in their home like this. I was green, both with envy and naiveté. Robert set about playing me a few new songs that he and Pauline had been working on and I proceeded to play along and work out some guitar parts that we then recorded.

Next morning, not *so* early, Pauline came around, had a listen to what we'd recorded the previous evening and gave it the thumbs up. We then started 'jamming' and came up with a couple of ideas for new songs that we bashed down onto tape. It was a very productive day and we all seemed to be getting on great with very similar tastes and an empathetic sensibility to making music. That evening, after Pauline had gone home to Peter and their flat 'La Boheme', Robert and I went out to his local and we downed a couple of pints in an evening of male bonding. Good lad, Robert, I really liked him, still do.

Next morning, after being reimbursed my train fare, I bid my fond adieus, with Robert and Pauline promising to call me once they'd had a chance to digest my time in their presence and have a chat – and no doubt audition other guitarists, which they *didn't* mention – to let me know if I'd got the job or not. I was pretty cocky in those days and knew I was a more than decent guitar player. I felt fairly confident that they'd call and offer me the job as I had never up to that point, or since, failed an audition.

And lo and behold a few days later Robert called and said the job was mine if I wanted it. Of course I did, this was a step up for me and about time too, I thought.

That winter I travelled back and forth between Liverpool and Durham a few more times to work on the new songs with them, simultaneously also learning the songs from the album as we had a European tour planned for the spring of 1981. It would be my first ever tour if you don't count the pubs and working men's clubs of Liverpool!

Around 9am on the morning of Tuesday, December 9, of 1980, I woke up in my room at the Guidios and, unable to afford a TV of my own, turned on the radio. 'Imagine' by John Lennon was playing. Nice, I thought, beats the usual breakfast-time fare. And then, when the song ended, the DJ announced that John Lennon had been shot dead in New York just a few hours previously. Shocked and saddened beyond belief as was the rest of the world at the violence of his death, I cried. John was and remains my favourite Beatle, we all have one, don't we? Being in Liverpool on that day and witnessing the communal grief the city felt at losing one of her favourite sons was an experience that made a huge and lasting impression on me. Liverpool is an emotional city, a city of passion that wears its heart on its sleeve, with a people loyal to their own. Ignoring the national outpouring of love for the slaughtered Lennon the Guidios were unmoved by his slaying, with Kris wrapped up in the needle and Nina in motherhood. I think it's safe to say that they weren't Beatles fans.

I continued to work with Pauline and Robert and once we had the new songs pretty much written and ready to go in early 1981 we convened to Stockport and the 10cc-owned Strawberry Studios to record a single. Producing again for Pauline but for the first, and sadly the last, time for me was Martin Hannett. Having not had much experience of 'proper' producers up to that point it was certainly an education.

John Maher was on drums, Robert was playing bass, with Steve Hopkins on keyboards, and little ol' me on guitar. You know that feeling where you wonder how you're getting away with it? Despite my bravado that was I. This was different league to what I had been used to before. Big studio, big producer, proper gear and name musicians. We started with recording basic backing tracks for three songs – 'Searching For Heaven', 'Animal Crazy' and 'The Visitor' – before moving onto overdubs.

I seem to remember we were there for the best part of a week and one eventful, and some may some fateful, day a visitor was welcomed into the studio. Within minutes white powder was being chopped out with a razor blade on top of one of the tape boxes. I'd only ever seen white powders being chopped out once before and that was by The Only Ones backstage at the Factory in Manchester a year or two previously when I'd inadvertently stumbled into their dressing room uninvited. There were soon a few lines at the ready and a pound note rolled up and proffered. Not everybody partook, that much I can remember, but Martin Hannett did for sure.

And then the pound note was passed to me. I'd never put anything up my nose before apart from my little finger and a pea when I was a toddler, and wasn't really sure what to do or how to do it. Martin, bless his cotton socks, rather than taking the piss out of my naiveté showed me how you put the note up your nose and snort, first one nostril and then the other in quick succession, and then tilt your head back so that the powder runs to the back of your throat. I did the right nostril fine but had trouble with the left and ended up blowing the rest of the line onto the studio floor, whereby Martin got on his hands and knees and started dabbing at the spilt powder.* Waste not, want not, eh?

That was my first ever line of cocaine. And boy, did I like it. Within ten minutes I was asking for more lines to be chopped out. I was easily seduced and readily corruptible. I surrendered unhesitatingly to taking the first steps on the road to ruin; that dark, alluring, mythical place where caricature and rock'n'roll cliché exist.

Anyway, cocaine aside I really enjoyed the recording. It was interesting to see the working interaction between Martin, Steve (who was *kind of* Martin's musical director), and Chris Nagle, the engineer (who I would work with again later with The Sisters Of Mercy). Martin loved AMS and Eventide harmonisers and delays and tended to use them on pretty much everything that was recorded. Somehow, despite a multitude of overdubs and layers of sound, and this was his genius, Martin was able to achieve a beautiful, crystalline spaciousness to the sound. His working processes were certainly not conventional. For example, on one track, 'Animal Crazy' I think it was, Martin had Steve pressing an aerosol can, Pauline's hairspray I believe, in time to John's snare beat. He then took the best 'presses' and sampled them into an AMS and flew them into the track alongside John's snare to make a great synthetic electronic snare sound. This was long before sampling became standard practice.

---

* In all the years I have put powders up my nose I was never able to master using my left nostril, just the right, and because of that practice, today I suffer from regular bleeds only in the right-hand side of my nose. That'll teach me.

I also remember an evening when I was overdubbing a guitar part on 'Searching For Heaven'. I was playing in the studio next to my amp to fashion a very present guitar sound and monitoring the track through headphones. To create a mood for me Martin turned down the lights in the studio and control room very low. The tape rolled down to me and I played along the guitar part that I had worked out previously. At the end of the take I heard the tape rewind in my headphones and start again and so I played along, again, through the song. This happened four or five times and without any word from the control room I was starting to wonder if I was doing something wrong or if Martin wanted me to try something different. A few more runs at it and still no communication was forthcoming. After the eighth or ninth take I put the guitar down and walked into the control room. It was very dark in there apart from the lights of the desk and the FX units and at first I thought there was no one there, but then after the tape stopped to rewind yet again I heard soft snoring and looked down under the mixing desk and there was Martin. Fast asleep. I had put Martin Hannett to sleep with my guitar playing. Brilliant. That was good for my self-esteem. Martin had put the machine on automatic record and rewind and so, in theory, I could've been there all night while Martin slept, playing along without any idea of whether what I was playing was any good or not.

After we wakened Martin and completed recording my guitar parts I went back home to Liverpool to leave Pauline to record her vocals and for Martin to mix the tracks. A week or so later I received a cassette in the post with the finished mixes and I was surprised to hear an additional guitar on 'Searching For Heaven' that I didn't play. Putting aside my bruised ego I acknowledged that it was actually a pretty decent part and wished I'd thought of it myself. I phoned Robert to ask who had played it. It transpired that while mixing Martin felt the song needed another guitar part in a certain section of the song and had roped in his mate from Joy Division and New Order, Bernard Sumner.

The single, 'Searching For Heaven', for which I shared the writing credit with Pauline and Robert, was released in April of 1981 on their own label, Illusive. It enjoyed a few plays on Radio One and generally favourable reviews in the music weeklies and went into the national charts at number 83, my first ever chart entry. Listening to it today I think it's fairly easy to hear the beginnings of what was to become my signature guitar sound and style. Lots of arpeggiated hanging open chords effected with delays, chorus and phaser.

Sadly Martin Hannett passed away of heart failure in 1991 at the criminally young age of 42, another victim of excessive living, but his legacy remains in the wonderful records that he produced of which, I am proud to say, 'Searching For Heaven' is one.

Pauline re-released her *Invisible Girls* album in 2013 and the three tracks we recorded with Martin were added to the album. When I played a solo show in Newcastle that same year Pauline and Robert came to see me and they gave me a copy of the re-release which then became the preferred listening in our van for the rest of the tour. It's a great album and stands up very well sonically to the test of time. I do love Pauline's voice, there's something wistful and fragile about it even though, with Penetration, she came out of the punk movement where shouting was largely the order of the day.

And maybe my love of the album is engendered by the fact that these were the songs that I had to learn to play for my first ever tour and whenever I hear them I am transported back to that time.

Rehearsals commenced in mid-March in Liverpool and the touring band, besides myself, was Robert on bass, John Maher on drums, and Peter Barrett on keyboards, and obviously Pauline. Our first show was in Oslo on the 27th. We drove in a mini bus to Newcastle and caught the overnight ferry to Norway. This was my first time abroad apart from a family camping holiday in Spain when I was 12 or 13.

Anyway, on the ferry to Norway I bought some duty free John Player Black cigarettes for my landlord, Kris, intending to take them home for him as a present as I was not smoking myself at the time. I would be by the end of that ferry crossing. Of course, as bands and football supporters do, we convened to the ferry bar and we started drinking, and because there were several smokers among us, and not for the first *or* last time bowing to peer pressure, I opened Kris' John Player Blacks and started puffing away to feel more a part of the gang. Eventually that evening we adjourned to the ferry disco and somehow I ended up being taken to bed in one of the cabins by a Scandinavian beauty. So this was what touring was all about, eh? Booze, ciggies and sex with strangers. Good start, Hussey. All that was missing was the drugs but they would come later. Copiously.

As with any tour the shows themselves are a bit of a blur unless something out of the ordinary happens. I have little or no memory of most of the shows on my first Euro tour but looking at the itinerary now it's amazing to me that some of the venues I played on that tour with Pauline in 1981 I ended up playing again, and again, with both The Sisters Of Mercy and The Mission; venues such as the Underground in Stockholm, the Trojan Horse in Den Haag, Amsterdam's Paradiso, and the Markthalle in Hamburg which I played again for the umpteenth time as recently as November 2016 on The Mission's 30th anniversary tour.

After the first show in Oslo we drove over to Stockholm and played a couple of shows there. We were then scheduled to drive down to Holland but over the course of the first few days on that tour Pauline and Robert, unbeknownst to the rest of us, had got together as a couple.* What with Pauline's marriage to Peter coming to an end and the stress induced by her new-found situation, it was felt by Pauline's manager, John Arnison (an easily likeable chap who also managed Marillion at the time), that an extra day in Stockholm was needed for Pauline, especially, to come to terms with it all. It was decided that the crew would drive on with the van and the gear while the band would fly the following day. So, from Stockholm to Amsterdam I flew for the very first time in my life. I've since taken many, many flights but like sex and gigs, you always remember your first, don't you?

According to the tour itinerary our last show of this part of the tour was in Paris on April 14. I have no recollection at all of visiting Paris on this tour which is strange as Paris, along with Rome, came to be one of my favourite cities. I know for certain I was in Paris with my girlfriend, Louise, later that same year, in July in fact, the week of the royal wedding of Prince Charles and Lady Diana. We just had to get out of England when all that razzmatazz was going on. A royalist I am not. *That* was when my love affair with Paris commenced.

Anyway, after we finished the mainland Euro leg of the tour we returned to the UK and in April played a handful of shows that culminated in a sell-out at London's Lyceum. The Only

---

* They're still happily together to this day and now have a couple of grown-up kids.

Ones' Peter Perrett, along with his wife, Zena, came backstage after the show. Pauline had sang a duet with Peter on the song 'Fools' from The Only Ones *Baby's Got A Gun* album, an album coincidentally produced by Colin Thurston who had produced the sole Walkie Talkies single. I must confess to being a little awestruck when Pauline introduced me to Peter Perrett.

Like everyone else in the world I had loved their single 'Another Girl, Another Planet' from their mostly brilliant eponymous first album. The Only Ones had broken through as part of the UK punk movement but they were far more than that to me. Despite being English they had more of a New York sensibility than London to my ears, spiritual bedfellows to my favourites, Television. The band could really play and weren't afraid to show it, unlike a lot of the older UK punk bands who had dumbed it down in an attempt to foster critical and commercial acceptance from the punks. I had seen them play at Eric's and been so impressed that I followed 'em over to Manchester the following day to see 'em again at the Factory. That's the night I walked in on them snorting lines off a table backstage. Despite having a complete stranger in their midst they made no effort to hide the fact, and why should they? It was their dressing room, their sanctum, and I was there uninvited. In years to come I'd possess the very same attitude, not caring a jot who saw me with a pound note up my nose.

The following day, the day after Pauline's Lyceum show, we went to Peter and Zena's home, a large house stuffed with antiques in Forest Hill, south London. Pauline and Robert were there to pick up a couple of films on video cassettes. We were shown into the front room where two whole walls were covered with banks of VCR recorders. I'm not quite sure what business Peter and Zena were in and didn't like to ask. The only conclusion I could draw was that maybe it wasn't entirely legal.

There was nowhere to sit. Every surface was piled high with books and newspapers, and there were full ashtrays and empty tea cups strewn around all over the place. It was safe to say that the housekeeper hadn't cleaned up that week. Or maybe even that year. My impression of Peter was of a man obviously learned but removed, not quite in this world, or even *of* this world. A chain smoker with smokers' rasp, smokers' cough, thin as a toothpick, ravaged but gloriously so. I remember comments after we'd left that neither Peter nor Zena looked long for this world. But guess what? They're both still here with us some more than 35 years later.*

The tour finished in early May and with Pauline's marriage having ended and her and Robert wanting to set up home together, they felt it best to make a clean break and leave Durham. They moved to Liverpool. I'd like to believe that in their desire to continue working together with me I was instrumental in their decision but I suspect it was more pragmatic than that. But anyway, to Liverpool they did come and set up home in a first floor flat on Princes Avenue, very close to the gates of Princes Park. Of course they didn't have the same amount of living space as Robert enjoyed at home with his parents but they still managed to put together a small recording set-up in their living room. And for a while I would go around there and we would play and try to write new songs, but it all kind of fizzled out in apathy, I felt, on their part and frustration on mine.

---

* In a case of weird symmetry, Richard Vernon was Peter Perrett's bass player during the years 1992 to 1996 or thereabouts. Richard went on to join me in The Mission in 2002 until we disbanded, again, in 2008.

I was, and remain, very driven and creative inactivity for any length of time drives me crazy. I was itching to get to work again and sitting around smoking dope was not in my plans.

After a year or so Pauline and Robert moved back north to Newcastle where they still live today. They run a rehearsal studio for local bands and have continued to release records and sporadically tour, more recently as the reformed Penetration. In fact, Pauline with her band The Storm supported The Mission on one of our early tours and Pauline as a solo artist played with us on shows in 2016 and 2017 with Robert as her driver and guitar tech. It is always lovely to see them both, and whenever they come to see me when I play in Newcastle I'm always reminded of my very first line, tour and flight.

Nota bene: As mentioned above, it was while working with Pauline that I met John Maher, the Buzzcocks' drummer. John was a great, down-to-earth northerner who was more interested in drag car racing than being a pop star. In fact just a couple of years later he gave up playing drums to concentrate on his passion for cars, starting a business building custom engines and transmissions that became very successful. But the main thing for which I have John to thank is that he wore prescription dark lenses in his spectacles. Until then I never knew that it was possible to buy them and as soon as I returned home from Pauline's tour, I bought my first ever pair of prescription shades with some of the proceeds. I never looked back. They revolutionised my life.

CHAPTER 11

Wanted: Dead Or Alive

PLAYLIST:

1. Shangri-La – Nightmares In Wax   2. Touch – Lori & The Chameleons
3. Rumble – Link Wray   4. Zuvembie – The Mogodons   5. I Want More – Can
6. Alone Again Or – Love   7. I Keep A Close Watch – John Cale
8. Sex Dwarf – Soft Cell   9. Reward – Teardrop Explodes
10. Blue Monday – New Order   11. Dear Prudence – Siouxsie & The Banshees
12. Love Cats – The Cure   13. This Is Not A Love Song – Public Image Ltd
14. Whammy Kiss – B52's   15. If I Had You – The Korgis.

I was on tour with The Mission in Europe, Bratislava, Slovakia, to be exact, on Monday, October 24, 2016, eerily enough exactly a year ago today as I'm writing this. I was sat quietly in the dressing room with the rest of the band, Craig, Simon, and the relatively new drummer boy, Mike Kelly. George, our manager, was flitting around doing his usual pre-show fussing – set-lists, towels and drinks for stage, and, as his alter-ego 'Georg Of Bath', pronounced gay-org, my hair. Wine o'clock had just come and gone and I was taking the first sips of a bottle of Shiraz that is part of my pre-show routine. Of course we were all on our iPads or phones social media'ing or attempting level three sudokos. I received a message notification on my phone.

It was an email from Ramone, the original Eskimo, who lives in Liverpool. "Hey, mate, I know you're on tour in Europe somewhere. Just wondering if you'd heard the news? Your ol' mate, Pete Burns, died yesterday. Shocking."

I couldn't believe it, Pete Burns was dead. I'm not ashamed to admit I shed a tear or two. Not for the Pete Burns that became celebrated as I didn't know that Pete, but the younger Pete that I once knew and admired so much, even loved. That night when we played 'Tower Of Strength' on stage I dedicated it to Pete. It was the very least I owed him.

After my working relationship with Pauline Murray and Robert Blamire slowly and apathetically dissolved in a cloud of marijuana smoke during the summer of 1981, I was approached to join Pete Burns and Dead Or Alive by their then-manager, Francesco Mellina. Having recently changed their name from the far more descriptive Nightmares In Wax to the prosaic Dead Or Alive, they were in the process of a line-up overhaul and needed a new guitarist. Unbeknownst to me at the time, this is something that Pete habitually did every now and then, wielding his scythe to cut down the chaff that grew around him.

When I'd first moved to Liverpool I'd encountered Pete at Eric's and while I can't claim to have been friends with him we were on nodding terms with the occasional "How are you?" I preferred to keep my distance as at any given moment Pete was very capable of an unmerciful jibe and I wasn't yet a strong enough personality to come back with a witty riposte. Pete and his wife Lynn both worked in Probe Records on the corner of Button Street and Rainford Gardens, literally a 100 yards, if that, around the corner from Eric's. Probe was a social hub on a Saturday afternoon when the punk waifs and strays of the city would congregate waiting for Eric's to open later.

Like every other 'alternative' kid I would go into Probe to buy my more, shall we say, esoteric records, records that you couldn't find at any of the other more conventional record shops around town. I'd be scared to death it would be Pete who would serve me as he'd quite often make some loud, withering remark about the taste in music of his customers, sometimes throwing the records at them in disapproval, or even point blank refusing to serve them if he really disliked the record. The fact that the boss, Geoff Davis, also treated clientele in the same derisive manner obviously encouraged Pete and the rest of the staff to do the same. It was a terrifying gauntlet to run in the cause of obtaining the very coolest of music.

It would be an understatement by a country mile to say that Peter Jozzeppi Burns was a colourful character. Born in the delightfully named Port Sunlight, and unmistakably Leo, as well as his extravagant clothes and fearsome tongue Pete would also very often wear black contact lenses, thereby rendering the whole of his eyes impenetrably black. Unable to tell whether he was looking at you or not, having a conversation with him could be an unnerving, disconcerting experience. Much like, I guess, people having conversations with me while I'm wearing my shades.

As we all now know, in later life Pete would go onto have many cosmetic procedures carried out on his face but when I knew him this was all way off in the future. I know I'm probably rousing the ire of many Dead Or Alive fans when I say that, for me, Pete was never pretty. Always looking good, most times even beautiful, but Pete wasn't what I'd call naturally handsome. He had to work really hard to look as good as he did and in his own mind he was a breathing, living work of art. I know that the impulse for him to change the way he looked was there right from the first moment I knew him but I never dreamed it would manifest itself in such an horrific manner with such tragic eventual consequences.

I'd seen Pete perform the one and only show with his first band, The Mystery Girls (with Pete Wylie on guitar and Julian Cope on bass), supporting the abhorrent oiks Sham 69 if memory serves, and later with Nightmares In Wax, and while he was an arresting figure on stage I must confess that I wasn't overly enamoured with either his singing or the songs. He did look great though, intimidating too, and it's the only time I can recollect the audience moving *away* from the stage rather than getting closer to it when the band came on.

Hoping for a guitarist position in a more established band I was playing hard to get and it took an impromptu home visit from Pete, sans contact lenses, and Francesco to entice me to at least have a play with Dead Or Alive. Also Kris, my mentor and landlord, was a fan of Pete's and from him I'd hear a daily mantra of "My dear boy, you won't get your candies if you don't join", which, of course, ultimately had the desired effect.

I played with the band one day at The Ministry rehearsal rooms in the city centre and that was enough to persuade me to finally say yes. The band at that time consisted of Joey Musker on drums, new boy Mike Percy on bass, Marty Healey on organ, and, of course, Pete and that voice of his. While the world at large would later come to identify Dead Or Alive more with the 'You Spin Me Round (Like A Record)' type pop, when I joined it was full-on gothic rock before the term had even been coined. Heavy tom-toms from Joey was something different compared to most drummers of the day who splashed about on hi-hats and cymbals. We had tall pretty boy Marty playing Manzarek-style drone organ. With his long silky black hair reaching way down his back, always clad in black and with black pointy boots and the face of an innocent choir-boy, it was clearly evident that Marty, being far prettier than Pete, wouldn't be long for this band. Couldn't be doing that, having a member of the band prettier than the singer – except in The Sisters Of Mercy and The Mission, of course (and I don't mean Craig... work it out).

Marty's girlfriend was Lori of Lori & The Chameleons who enjoyed a minor hit during this period with the glorious still fresh as a daisy single, 'Touch'. Lori followed it with 'The Lonely Spy', another pop gem and then promptly retired from the music business, disappearing into the briny leaving barely a ripple. That's the way to do it. The pair of them, Marty & Lori, were the bonniest couple in Liverpool at this time. If it had been America they'd have been the homecoming king and queen.

On bass in Dead Or Alive was Mike Percy, newly acquired from where I remember not. A little too happy to be slappy on his bass, in my humble, his playing style a precursor, maybe, of things to come.

And then there was Pete who, I have to say, took me by surprise with his prodigious talent. Despite my initial reservations I came to *love* that voice. It was huge. Pete didn't need a microphone in rehearsals. He was able to sing above the full band hammering away and still be heard without the aid of a PA. When we did have microphones, my God, it was an awesome noise that the five of us made together.

I can't vouch for his later working methods but while I was in the band Pete never wrote lyrics down. They were always in his head. We'd be jamming new songs and he'd just reel off all these brilliant words and remember every line the very next time we played the song. Pete was an extraordinary talent but, sadly, that gets overlooked amid all the celebrity nonsense that his life later became.

We rehearsed a lot, pretty much every day, but in the two years, more or less, that I was in the band we played only a handful of shows, the highlights probably being second on the bill to The Damned at The Futurama Festival in the Deeside Leisure Centre, and supporting Killing Joke at Manchester Rotters. Not for us slumming it in the pubs and bars of Liverpool.

With such a dearth of dates in our calendars we were left with plenty of spare time in which to entertain ourselves. It was during this period that my drug use escalated. Of course it did. With cocaine far too expensive for anyone in my circle of acquaintance, speed became a firm favourite for me as it was with all the band apart from Joey. Joey liked a pint with his Scally mates. Salt of the earth, that lad, still is.

With my giro I'd buy a gramme of speed, a loaf of bread and a few oranges, and that would see me through the week if I wasn't too excessive. As well as providing me with a steady supply of opiate-based narcotics, Kris, Severina's dad and my usher into this new netherworld, introduced me to the wonder of LSD. Mostly tabs of blotting paper laced with a touch of lysergic acid that could be bought for £2 each, a hit that would last the best part of a night. If taken at 8pm, say, I'd be coming down as the sun'd be coming up.

It became well known among my friends and peers that I'd become a bit of an acid head and so for a couple of birthdays everybody would buy me a tab or two as a present. I'd drop acid and go clubbing. I'd think nothing of dropping four or five tabs in a night if I was in the right company. And accompanied by a line or two of happy whizz the trip could be intensified and prolonged. The holy grail of LSD was the microdot. They didn't come along very often but when they did it was well worth forking out the extra quid or so for the privilege.

I can't explain to you what an acid trip is like. If I have to explain then you'll never understand. But what I can say, and I know it's a cliché, I do feel it opened my mind. I loved the surrender of my senses, my thoughts, my body, to wherever the trip would take me. I'm not gonna sit here and write that drugs are bad or drugs are good. Some drugs are obviously more dangerous than others, heroin probably the most perilous of course. Most people, in my experience, could take 'em and then leave 'em until next weekend. Some, though, became enslaved to the high or the low of their drug of choice although the same can be said of alcohol and nicotine or even bloody chocolate if it comes to that. They don't work for everyone, that much is clear, and for some they are a danger to their physical and mental wellbeing, but drugs worked for me at a time that I was open to new experiences and new ways of thinking. I enjoyed some great trips, with some great people, and it was a practice I continued into the early Nineties, giving up LSD for, first, ecstasy, and then later, fatherhood when it came along for the second time. Acid is really the only drug I miss nowadays. That and ecstasy.

I remember one Saturday night going to see Kris' beloved Cramps supporting the loathsome Police. Kris, being friends with Lux and Ivy, had managed to blag us onto their guest list. I thought The Cramps were blinding, and The Police's predominately teeny-bop audience was appalled and spellbound in equal measure. There were small pockets of Cramps fans scattered throughout the Liverpool Empire auditorium but not enough, sadly, to unsettle Sting and his cronies when they came on stage. The Police were longueur in the extreme and I made my excuses to Kris and Nina and left early to go and spend the rest of the evening in the underground sanctum of Eric's.

Later, I made my way home at 2am closing time and let myself into the darkened house, the Guidios already soundly in the Land of Nod, and crawled into bed. In the late morning I awoke and after my ablutions I made my way downstairs to the lounge. Imagine my surprise on opening the living room door to find Lux Interior and Poison Ivy from The Cramps perched on our couch sipping tea and nibbling on toasted crumpets.

Kris introduced me as "the best guitarist in Liverpool" which I obviously shucked at and we proceeded to have a conversation about how tedious The Police were, both on and offstage. Far from the menacing types that I was led to believe they'd be from their on stage personas, Lux and Ivy were gracious, polite, quiet and seemed to me to be, like me, quite shy.

Kris, Nina and myself formed a band, the ingeniously named Mogodons, an extracurricular distraction for me from my day job with Dead Or Alive. With Nina on vocals and Kris writing the lyrics and in charge of art direction, and enlisting the help of the two Pauls from …And The Dance as rhythm section, we went into nearby Hambi's Pink and recorded two songs for a single. It was great fun. It was dark, it was eerie, seedy and narcoleptic, Link Wray *Rumble* type guitar… and then Kris sold the tapes to another studio when he needed money for a fix and they were recorded over. The priorities of a junkie, eh?

Sadly there is not even a cassette of these recordings and, in my admittedly addled memory, I remember this as being one of the very best records I was ever a part of. Damn that smack. The Mogodons did go back into the studio a year or so later to re-record the classic-in-waiting 'Zuvembie' using another guitarist as I was unfortunately committed elsewhere at the time. Before Kris could scalp the tapes again the single was mastered and released. Without my *genius* on guitar it didn't set the world

on fire but it did reach number seven in the *Zigzag* alternative
Top Ten. That's something, isn't it?

It was during this period that I started DJ'ing at the Warehouse
on Fleet Street. Since the demise of Eric's in March 1980 and a
lacklustre attempt to resurrect its bonhomie atmosphere in the
same location as the re-named Brady's, there hadn't really been
a regular club venue in Liverpool for bands that could pull
between 200 and 600 people. There was no real centralised hub
anymore where we could all congregate to bitch about whoever
wasn't present that night and, more importantly, where we
mostly didn't have to pay to get in. The Eric's scene was
dispersing. The Warehouse attempted to fill that gap and kind of
did for a short while but by that time the main players in the
Eric's scene were all in bands and enjoying degrees of success
which kept them out on tour and away from the city for long
periods of time. And when they were home the last thing they
would want to do is spend their evenings in a nightclub where
they would be subjected to bitchy barbed comments from the
jealous locals with whom they once drank and fraternised, rather
than the fervour and fawning from fans they had gotten used to
on tour. How do I know this? Because it happened to me a few
years later when I lived in Leeds and The Mission first became
successful, sometimes even to the extent of being physically
threatened. It really wasn't worth the bother.

As DJ at the Warehouse I got to play my favourite records
between bands and while I can't claim my selections were as
eclectic as they once were at Eric's it was still a pretty groovy
way to impose my music taste on a captive audience. I'd play
Can, Love, John Cale interspersed with Soft Cell, the Banshees,
and 'Reward' by the Teardrops. I would take requests but refused
to play anything by Simple Minds or Level bloody 42. Some of

the gigs I saw there while I was DJ'ing were a blistering early Birthday Party show, Virgin Prunes, Thompson Twins and Nico pumping away on her harmonium, serenading us in that deep Germanic baritone of hers. I was invited into the dressing room after the show to meet her but I couldn't get a coherent word out of her, just a very limp shake of the hand, the same hand that had once reputedly held Jim Morrison's not so limp dick. That was enough for me.

It was one night while working at the Warehouse not long after I had joined Dead Or Alive when I was approached by Holly Johnson asking if I would be interested in joining a new band he was forming.

"Eh, Wayne, I'm startin' a band, like. I need a guitarist, are youse up fer it, la?" he asked in his whinny whiney camp scouse.

"Well, I've just joined Pete and Dead Or Alive. I think I'm gonna stop there for a bit," I replied in my 'ark at 'ee thick Bristolian burr.

"Aw, cum on, we'll be bigga and betta than Dead Or Alive."

"I don't know, Holly, mate. What are you called?"

"Frankie Goes To 'ollywood."

"What a crap name, you'll never get anywhere with a name like that."

"Oh, sod ya then, you'll be sorry when we're on *Top Of The Pops* and you're still DJ'ing in this shitehole."

"Yeah, Holly, sure."

Oh, the fickle hand of fate...

Around this time I produced some demos in the Open Eye studio for a band of kids, mid-teens maybe, called The Dancing Girls. The drummer was named Ped, the guitarist Nasher and the singer, Ged O'Toole. Not long after, the band were playing a gig in town and Holly went along to see them. He got so carried away that in his enthusiasm he jumped up on stage and started singing with them. Within a week Ged had been jettisoned and the band had changed their name to Sons Of Egypt, changing it yet again a short while later when John, the bass player, and Julie, the keyboard player, left. Ged's younger brother, Mark, came in to play bass, and Paul Rutherford, lovely man, joined as dancer/viber. Yeah, that's right, Frankie Goes To Hollywood.

I don't know whether Holly harboured a grudge because I turned him down. I'm probably flattering myself to think he even remembered asking me as he seemingly asked every other guitarist in town to join at one point or another, but when The Mission started taking off Holly took to slagging me off in the music press. By then the Frankie star was waning and mine was on the rise and I was an easy target. As Morrissey once sang, we hate it when our friends become successful – and Liverpool was one hell of a bitchy scene. Of course The Mission's success didn't remotely compare to the Frankie's but when you're on your way down every band on their way up is perceived as a threat and usurper. I know, I experienced it myself a few years later with The Stone Roses and Happy Mondays.

Speaking of which, Nathan McGough had started hosting nights at Pickwick's called Plato's Ballroom with a modicum of success, catering more for the whimsy of bands like The Pale Fountains, The Wild Swans, Aztec Camera and Orange Juice. Come to think of it Dead Or Alive played Pickwick's too during my tenure with the band but I don't believe it was a Plato's Ballroom night as I'm sure we didn't fit in with Nathan's 'sensitive' aesthetic. It's all dribbling back to me now; I also played there switching between guitar and bass with a short-lived electronic band from the Wirral called The Games whose album I had played on.

The best larger venue in town was the Royal Court which started putting bands on in 1980. With a capacity of 1,500 maybe, and no seating in the stalls, this was by far the preferable larger venue to both play and see bands. I saw some fantastic shows there in the early Eighties – Iggy Pop, Siouxsie & The Banshees, the Bunnymen all springing to mind – and later played some humdingers there myself with Pauline Murray, and The Sisters Of Mercy, and my favourite ever show with The Mission.

New clubs were always starting up as old ones closed down. Cagney's, to start with, was a Sunday night club with an emphasis on dressing up and being into music such as Roxy Music, Japan, Gary Numan and Bowie, of course. Its popularity grew and it soon became the place to go on a Friday and Saturday as well as a Sunday night. Its patrons evolved into what became known as the New Romantics. Steve Proctor was the DJ at Cagney's and when the State Ballroom on Dale Street opened in 1982 Steve would also DJ the Thursday night there, taking most of his clientele with him. The State, a shiny, art nouveau venue, boasted Liverpool's first laser disco light show, the complete antithesis to what we had known and loved at Eric's. How times changed. The best club since Eric's though, to my mind, opened in June of 1983. Planet X.

Long before goth become a media swear word I was a goth. Or at least that is how my history has been written. In terms of perceived goth, my pedigree is rather good. Early Dead Or Alive, mid-period Sisters Of Mercy, and lifelong Mission, and I don't suppose you can really discount my stint as an Invisible Girl with Pauline Murray either. But at the time I had no concept of what goth was. None of us did. Anybody that claims differently is a poseur and would never have made it as a member of our coven.

There was certainly a gathering of like-minded souls gravitating towards a similar darker aesthetic in music, art, film and literature, but the movement wasn't yet named. Clubs catering to this new burgeoning scene started springing up in most big cities in the UK, with the Batcave in London, which started in the summer of 1982, being primary. Specimen members Ollie Wisdom and my old Mormon scout troop mate, Jon Klein*, ran the Batcave, situated in Meard Street in Soho, with such luminaries as Siouxsie, Robert Smith, Marc Almond, Peter Murphy and Nick Cave patronising the establishment.

I would go a few times myself when I was in London recording with Dead Or Alive. The music played was glam meets punk and all its hybrids veering off into new and uncharted musical territories. We didn't call ourselves Goths, it was the media that did that. Whatever it was called, the brush stroke was so broad in the beginning. Almost everything was permissible, allowable. From Joy Division to Soft Cell to the Bunnymen to Depeche Mode to the Cure to Fad Gadget to Killing Joke to Bauhaus. And on and on. And while the Top 40 generally continued to be the same old conservative fare we would cheer

---

* When Jon and I were boy scouts together in our early teens in Bristol, we both started to play the guitar around the same time. As kids we challenged each other to see who could make it onto *Top Of The Pops* first. When I left for Liverpool a few years later Jon and I drifted apart, but I did hear tale that he was on *TOTP*'s miming with The Korgis on their hit, 'If I Had You', some six or seven years before I made my first appearance on that venerable, institutional TV show. I emailed Jon for clarification and he sent me a YouTube link: https:// www.youtube.com/watch?v=PnIInWCFsC4 Jon is the guitarist at the back playing a Stratocaster. Don't snigger. Compare Jon's transformation to mine. Both sweet, innocent Mormon boys to prime movers in the decadent goth scene within just a few short years.

the occasional alternative band infiltrating the charts – New Order's classic 'Blue Monday', 'This Is Not A Love Song' by PiL, The Cure's 'Love Cats' and the Banshees sublime cover of The Beatles 'Dear Prudence' to name just four.

We'd congregate in these darkened clubs and drink cider and cheap white wine. We'd indulge, in contrast to our black garb, in cheap white powders, and second generation LSD. We'd have sex by candlelight while listening to The Doors, the Velvets and Iggy's Stooges. We'd read Baudelaire and Rimbaud out aloud while tripping. We loved Dirk Bogarde and Charlotte Rampling in *The Night Porter*, and purred and pored over Honor Blackman clad in black leather in *The Avengers*.

It wasn't a contrived movement. No true movement ever can be contrived. Its evolution was natural, propelled by a need, a desire and a reaction to what had gone before. Much like the original punk ethos was about the encouragement of individuality and uniqueness so was this new scene in 1983. It is history that has decreed it was a movement and conferred upon it the name Gothic. We just saw ourselves as kindred spirits, living down in the cellars, but with our heads in the stars, who didn't want to walk the straight line. And like any fledgling, vibrant, evanid* youth movement, as soon as it was recognised and given a name it became corrupted, diluted and infiltrated by charlatans and sciolists, and hence, fashionable. Then, as it goes mainstream, we see the beginning of its demise.

By the time goth was christened, the prime movers, the forward thinkers within the scene, were already moving onto pastures anew and goth had become just another uniformity, much like Punks, like Teds, like Rockers had become. What goth is today bears very little resemblance to what it was when

* Anything fleeting, transitory, short-lived, liable to soon dissolve or collapse.

it all kicked off. Goth has survived and managed to sustain itself over the years by becoming more musically linear with its acolytes and adherents seemingly abiding by an ever-increasing set of rules and strictures, and a dress code that has become ever more uniform. Like any musical movement though, the best music always transcends the time and place – the fashion – and survives and flourishes. In 1983, the future seemed bright and the possibilities seemed limitless; we weren't bound by convention, expectation or a fussy morality. Maybe there's a point where each generation needs to feel this way, their very own zeitgeist moment. Punk in 1976 was one but I was just a little too young and provincial for it to seriously affect me. I think for me, for us, it was now, 1983.

Originally just a Friday night at McMillan's in Concert Square, just off Bold Street, and owned by the same people that owned the Warehouse, Planet X was the brainchild of Liverpool legend, Doreen Allen, and her partner, Kenny Dawick. Doreen had one time also visited the Batcave and when the opportunity arose for her to start her own club in Liverpool she, in tandem with Kenny, knew just what they wanted it to be like.

I'd known Doreen since the first night I'd gone to Eric's back in early 1978, when she'd issued me with my membership card. Whenever I found myself in the city centre during the daytime I'd pop into the Eric's office for a natter and gossip, as we were always most welcome there. Once Eric's finally closed after a police raid in early 1980, Doreen ran the office of the Eric's and Inevitable record labels and was also working the door at the Warehouse when I was DJ'ing there. But it was with the birth of Planet X that Doreen ultimately made her own unique mark on the Liverpool scene. Doreen and Kenny were fabulous club hosts and patently cared about their nights and their patrons.

Much attention was lavished on the decor, the Everyman Theatre props department dressing the club with bloodied mannequins hanging from the walls, white gauze and cobwebs made from butchers' cloth draped from the ceilings, a collection of broken doll body parts in a large net suspended over the dance floor and, of course, coffins in which members could stand with their arms crossed across their chests like a freshly embalmed corpse. All fairly de rigueur these days for a goth club but at the time it was new and exciting and faintly blasphemous, plucky, and derring-do. This was Planet X, so named by Frankie Goes To Hollywood's Paul Rutherford from a lyric in a B52's song, 'Whammy Kiss'.

With Doreen and Kenny both good friends of mine I was beholden to support them in their new venture and would turn up whenever I was at home in Liverpool. For the first few months I'd do a stint as guest DJ to give Kenny a break so he could slouch off and, ahem, entertain admirers in a darkened corner somewhere. He was a *bad* boy, was Kenny, but who am I to cast stones?

As personified by Doreen herself, Planet X was such a friendly place and I can't remember there ever being any trouble when I was there. And great fun. A lot of 'love' was in Planet X, years before ecstasy came along. Regarded mostly as a goth club, the city's first, it was much more than that. It was Mecca for those whose music taste, indie, alternative, whatever you wanna call it, ran outside the mainstream Top 40; and a comfortable, safe haven for those who liked to dress up, or down, outside of the norm.

The Stone Roses played an early gig there, as did Primal Scream, Ride and many others. Even The Mission played a very sweaty secret show there one night when we were at the zenith of our popularity and selling out Wembley Arena and Birmingham NEC. That was bonkers.

The thriving scene was soon to explode into the national mainstream so no doubt there would have been other clubs sprouting up to cater for this specific fashion, but I'm pretty sure the scene that would soon be inaugurated as goth wouldn't have flourished in Liverpool the way it did without Doreen and Kenny's Planet X. The club changed location a few times before Doreen and Kenny secured their own premises later in the decade, finally going out of business in 1993 when Doreen hung up her Liverpool Queen Goth crown.

Although I was still on the dole, when I wasn't DJ'ing I'd spend most evenings of the week out on the town. I knew most of the club owners and, being a minor local celeb, I could finagle myself into venues for free and, once inside, could always find someone more affluent than I willing to stand me a pint and maybe a line or two. Not having a regular girlfriend after Louise, I shook off any residual Mormon guilt and got myself shagged on a regular basis, most nights heading for home with different partners for a bit of rumpy-pumpy. It wasn't just me, it was the scene – Cagney's, the State, the Warehouse, Planet X – everybody was shagging everybody. Relationships were a no-no, hedonism a go-go. I have no idea how many partners I have enjoyed sexual shenanigans with over the years but, despite my late start, if you put 'em all in the Shepherds Bush Empire, I'm guessing that if it's not quite a sell-out then I've certainly broken percentage. I think that's one gig I wouldn't turn up for though.

CHAPTER 12

I Know How It Feels To Be Alone In A Crowd

PLAYLIST:
1. Living On The Ceiling – Blancmange   2. Whirlpool – Dead Or Alive
3. It's Been Hours Now – Dead Or Alive
4. Nowhere To Nowhere – Dead Or Alive   5. The Stranger – Dead Or Alive
6. Some Of That – Dead Or Alive   7. I Feel Love – Donna Summer
8. You Make Me Feel (Mighty Real) – Sylvester
9. You Think You're A Man – Divine   10. Misty Circles – Dead Or Alive
11. See That Glow – This Island Earth   12. Never Stop – Echo & The Bunnymen
13. No G.D.M. – Gina X

One day I arrived home and Kris and Nina sat me down and told me they were moving to London. Damn. I had to find new digs, man. As upset as I was I was kind of relieved in a way because bringing home strange new people every night to their home when Severina, their daughter, was still just a toddler wasn't a particularly cool thing to do. I'd miss them, Kris and Nina, though, very much. Kris had done his Svengali work on me and now my metamorphosis from naive country hick to deviant city slick was almost complete. Kris was a brilliant teacher and perhaps the most influential person, ever, on the person I have become. To this day there is a dark corner of my heart that will forever be in thrall to Kris and despite huge periods of my life where he just disappeared like an infernal Lord Lucan he has often been in my thoughts, and I am eternally grateful for the pedagogy in the esoteric and arcane arts he endowed – some may say damned – me with.

Anyway, getting turfed out of the Guidio household provoked me into looking for a place of my own where I could come and go as I please at any hour of the day or night. Bemoaning my fate at band rehearsal one day Francesco Mellina, the band's manager, overheard then informed me that there was a flat going in the house he lived in at 11 Lancaster Avenue, the other end of Ullet Road, very close to Sefton Park. Serendipity. My new flat was on the first floor at the back of the house, Francesco's being at the front. We shared a toilet and a bathroom as well as a landing. A strange but welcome coincidence was that Steve Power was living on the top floor with Bonce, his girlfriend whom he had met and fallen for while he and I had lived together in Tuebrook. They're still together today although now they count John Motson and Ronnie Wood as their neighbours as opposed to Francesco and I. Yep, Steve's done very well for himself I am so very pleased to be able to say.

My flat was two rooms, unfurnished, one the kitchen and the other, bigger room the living/sleeping area. Again, there was no heating to speak of except for a three-bar electric fire although I did have a cooker with two of the four rings working. I think it must've been left by the previous tenant. No fridge though but that was okay as it was always so bloody cold I didn't need one. I bought a cheap mattress which I threw into the corner of the room. No couch or chairs. I had my guitars and my record player and that was all I really needed and wanted. With no wardrobes or chests of drawers, I kept my clothes in cardboard boxes or on wire hangers on the back of the door. Winter mornings I would get dressed in bed after warming up my clothes under the blankets. In many ways this was my absolute favourite time of living in Liverpool. Living on my own but with friends nearby, finding myself and my way in the world, with barely anything to my name, very little money, no responsibilities, living on speed, acid and oranges, playing music every day with Dead Or Alive, and bonking my way through the Liverpool phone directory. Life was good.

Francesco was good company and would very often accompany me on my sorties into town but he abstained from the excessive drugs and drinking to which I became prone. He became a very good minder and made sure he got me home in one piece whether I was alone or with company. Francesco, known among friends as the Italian Stallion, certainly wasn't averse to bringing female consorts of his own home with him either. A right pair of rampaging lotharios we were.

Most of my records were kept at the Warehouse for my DJ'ing, hundreds of pounds worth. Too many by far to carry on the soddin' bus every time I DJ'd so I just left them at the club and took home the ones I fancied listening to that week. One day, while wandering through town on my way up to The Ministry for rehearsal I met Planet X Doreen.

"'Ere, Wayne, did you hear the Warehouse burnt down last night?"

"What? All my bleedin' records are in there!"

"It's gutted, luv, I'd pop around and see if there's anything you can salvage."

Posthaste I made my way to Fleet Street. The Warehouse was, indeed, gutted. Anything not ash was singed with smoke and left sopping wet from the hoses of the fire brigade. I managed to find a few of my records not completely destroyed, the covers all soggy with scorch marks at the corners. Animal Magnet's 'Welcome To The Monkey House' was one, I remember, and 'Living On The Ceiling' by Blancmange another that I managed to salvage. Not my favourites.

I saw the owner of the Warehouse and he told me not to worry, everything was insured and I'd be taken care of. Didn't like the sound of that, to be honest. The later rumour to surface around town was that the fire was arson, an inside job contracted by the owners to collect the insurance money. Only a rumour, mind, I'm not saying it was true. The insurance was paid out but did I get anything for my records? Did I heck and going after Liverpool club owners for money you think they may owe you is not the best of ideas if you wanna keep the use of your legs. That was the end of my budding career as a DJ. How could I be a DJ with no bloody records?

Not long after I joined Dead Or Alive we were booked into Cargo Studios in Rochdale to record my first single with the band. Produced by ourselves, we recorded and mixed three new songs over the course of two or three days engineered by studio owner, John Brierly. With my natural inclination to take control it was the first time I was allowed to get my grubby mitts on a proper mixing desk while recording and mixing. I was full of ideas and suggestions, no doubt making a pain in the ass of myself yet again. But the results were worth it and still sound great to these battered old ears of mine even today. Just take a listen to one of the B-sides, 'Whirlpool', which is my favourite track on the EP and should've, in my opinion, been the A-side. Layered with six and 12-string acoustic and electric guitars, it probably more so than anything else I'd recorded up to that point exhibits the guitar sounds and style that I would employ later in my work with The Mission.

The single was released early autumn, on Black Eyes Records, the first release on Dead Or Alive's own label and distributed by Rough Trade. It featuring four songs: the A-side 'It's Been Hours Now', with three extra tracks, 'Whirlpool', 'Nowhere To Nowhere', another new song, and a dub version of the A-side with all hands on the desk for the mix as we didn't have computerised mixing in those days, certainly not in Cargo. The single sold well, making the Top 10 in the UK Independent Chart. Around the time of release we made our one and only TV appearance with this line-up, augmented by Steve Coy on congas, on Granada TV's *Exchange Flags*. It's still on YouTube if you fancy a peek. Please ignore the brown suede pants I was wearing, I still hadn't quite sorted out my 'look' as of yet. Some would argue I never did.

Again recorded at Cargo, we quickly followed up the 'It's Been Hours Now' EP with another single in late 1981. This time it was just a 7-inch, 'The Stranger' as the A-side and the tribal 'Some Of That' as the B. Feeling more assured in the studio this time, I was more 'hands on' on the production side of things, almost ousting poor John Brierly from his engineer's chair at times. 'The Stranger' starts with a small Dr Rhythm beat box before a strummed 12-string Ovation guitar comes in, the song building in intensity until the full band arrive and join the fun. Listening to it now I can see how this arrangement was the template for perhaps The Mission's most popular ever song, 'Tower Of Strength'. It *is* very similar, I confess, but nought wrong with a bit of recycling in my book. Again the single was released on Black Eyes Records and again hit the Independent Chart Top 10. To coincide we were invited to the BBC Maida Vale studios to record a John Peel session, something we were never to do with The Mission. Obviously we didn't appeal to Peelie's indie sensibility.

We were close as a band and would regularly go out en masse to clubs and gigs but we started to get bored of the rock clubs and ended up going to gay clubs such as Jody's and, as a result, we were beginning to listen to, and be influenced by, dance music – Donna Summer, Patrick Cowley, Sylvester and, one of Pete's favourites, Divine, he of dubious notoriety after eating freshly excreted dog poop on camera in John Waters' *Pink Flamingos*. When we decided to have a night in we would congregate at Pete & Lynn's flat on Catherine Street, drink a little wine, share a few lines, and watch and laugh uproariously at Bette Davis and Joan Crawford in *Sweet Baby Jane* and Gloria Swanson in *Sunset Boulevard*, two of Pete's very favourite films.

We'd have dress-up nights when we would root through Pete and Lynn's cast offs and parade around the living room in various states of dress (and undress) to hoots of laughter. Pete and Lynn generously insisted we keep some of the clothes if we promised to wear them next time we went to a gay club. At Pete and Lynn's behest and with their encouragement, I started wearing dresses and experimented with blurring the conventional gender lines by wearing make-up and nail polish, and letting Lynn fashion my hair in more and more outlandish styles and colours. The fact that it was a blossoming trend among the youth of Britain at the time was merely coincidental. My mum and dad were apoplectic the next time I visited them in Bristol, finally and forever giving up hope that I would one day serve a mission for the Mormon church. There wasn't much chance of that now, was there? Mum looks back at this time and reckons, "That was your weird period."

Pete was a big man, in more ways than one. As well as a cutting wit and acid tongue, Pete could intimidate with his size. He was a couple of inches taller than me, getting on for six feet tall

(1.8m). I'm five foot eight inches (1.75m) if you're asking. Too bad if you're not, now you know anyway. And Pete was broad, big boned some might say. Far more of a man than I could ever be, he could look after himself. While not quite bellicose he'd happily return lip back to anyone giving him some on the streets of city centre Liverpool. He was a well-known figure around town and most people just stopped and gawped as he and Lynn flounced past. Any ignorant scally who hurled abuse Pete's way would soon regret it. He very rarely resorted to physical retribution, although he wasn't averse to giving someone a slap if they deserved it. He much preferred cutting them down to size with a rapier quip. In the time that I knew Pete there was only one person I knew who could take him on and give as good as they got. More of her a little later.

While Pete was famously generous and brilliant to have on your side he could also be incredibly jealous and possessive, hating it when any of us had girlfriends. Unless they were lesbians, we weren't allowed to bring friends of the female persuasion to our nights out and certainly not to our movie dress-up evenings at his flat.

If perchance I'd be in a club with Pete and I'd be talking to a girl Pete would walk past and either purposely spill his drink over her or make some stinging remark like, "Look at the state of 'er, she makes Hilda Ogden look like a beauty queen" or, "God, she's so fat she'd have to fart to give you a clue", all within easy earshot of the poor girl and all because she was talking to me. Not a very becoming side of Pete, it has to be said, funny though it sometimes was.

Pete was particularly scathing when I would go off and play with or produce other bands in the studio or guest on stage with them. His philosophy was that I should "save all my talents" for Dead Or Alive, while I just loved playing with anyone and everyone. It was a bone of contention between us right up until the end of my time in the band.

Once your time in favour with Pete had run its course then you became a pariah, persona non grata, ostracised from the circle of sycophants and minions that Pete liked to surround himself with. When Pete had decided, without conferring with the rest of us, that he wanted Marty out of the band and with his new lackey, Steve Coy, in tow they went to the band's storage unit one evening and took Marty's organ and sold it for next to nothing. When Marty found out it was missing Pete asked him, "How can you be in the band without an organ?"

"Well, I'll buy a new one then."

"Don't bother, what's the point, you're sacked anyway."

It was the same when Pete wanted to get rid of the drummer, Joey. It has to be said that Joey never really looked like he was a member of the band, more like the scally he actually was. He never really socialised with us although he and I did go out a few times together, but he was a damn fine drummer and it was the beginning of the end of my love affair with Dead Or Alive when Joey got kicked out in callous underhand circumstances similar to Marty. For all his bluster and seeming arrogance Pete could be a bit of a coward when it came to 'real' confrontation.

Around this time two young American girls, Courtney Love and her friend Robyn, turned up in Liverpool bearing gifts of acid and acid tongues. Being fans of The Teardrop Explodes they had followed Julian Cope and his band of merry men back from the USA to Liverpool. Courtney and Pete, it's safe to say, didn't like each other very much and would go at it hammer and tongues*

---

* I know the expression is 'hammers and tongs' but in this instance I thought it more appropriate to replace tongs with tongues.

on the streets of the city centre whenever their paths crossed. Eventually, when he saw Courtney and Robyn coming, Pete would run into the nearest shop doorway to hide and avoid the noisy altercation that would inevitably ensue if they spotted him. Courtney, even then, had a mouth to equal the most vicious and sardonic wit in Liverpool and I believe that Pete, despite his protests to the contrary, was a little in awe of this, his words, "stinking little gobshite slag".

I never had any issue myself with Courtney and Robyn. I even procured a couple of tabs of acid from them once or twice, but I was very wary of being on the end of one of their loud foul-mouthed rants of which they were both prone, particularly Courtney.

Mike Mooney was a mate of mine at the time and I'd bump into him again a few years later when he was playing second guitar in The Psychedelic Furs. As legend has it – and as claimed by Courtney herself – Mike took her virginity. Nevertheless, Mike has always denied this. Whatever the truth, and what has truth got to do with a good story anyway, I prefer the story that Pete loved to recount about Mike having to go to hospital one night because, in an amorous altered state, he'd coupled himself to a hoover and had to get medical help to be disentangled. I always wondered whether he took a taxi or a bus or whether an ambulance was called. How much truth is in that story too I don't know. I never had the nerve to ask Mike outright.

Another example of Pete's sometime cruel tendency is a story recalled to me recently by Hambi. One day Pete, Lynn and Francesco were travelling down to London by train from Liverpool Lime Street. Also on the same train was Hambi and his new paramour, Lesley (who are still together all these many years later). Anyway, being a long standing acquaintance of

Francesco's, Hambi and Lesley were invited to join the party and the five of them shared a compartment on the journey down to the capital. On arrival they all then spent the day together shopping at Vivian Westwood's World's End and Kensington Market as well as visiting Rough Trade where Pete and Francesco agreed a deal for the indie doyen to distribute their new Black Eyes Records label's releases.

Much celebrating ensued on the train back north later that evening and, seemingly, a budding friendship between Hambi and Pete blossomed, to the extent that on arrival in Liverpool Pete invited Hambi and Lesley around to his and Lynn's flat for dinner one evening later that same week. So, arriving at the appointed hour, Hambi and Lesley rang the doorbell to Pete and Lynn's top floor flat on Catherine Street. No answer, Hambi rang again. The window on the top floor opened and Pete's head appeared. "Oh, it's you, hang on a moment." Hambi and Lesley waited for a minute or two and then without warning a full bucket of water was poured over their heads from on high and the window closed. Of course no dinner was served that evening and from that day onwards Hambi, understandably so, never spoke another word with Pete or Lynn.

Pete had a real bugbear for Boy George who he felt was copying all of his ideas in clothes and hair. Pete detested Boy George, and issued endless tirades about how ugly, fat and untalented George was. His antipathy towards George would go on for a long, long time which is why I find it very surprising that Pete eventually relented and, apparently, he and George eventually became friends. Even so, it was a gracious and generous act on George's part to pay for Pete's funeral on his untimely passing in October 2016.

One of our favourite bands of the time was Mari Wilson & The Wilsations. She was probably noted more for her three-foot-high beehive than for her singing which was a shame as Mari was really rather good and they did put on a very good soul revue show. We travelled a couple of times to see their gigs and friendships were struck up. Of course, Pete and Mari – being two divas – were fated to meet. Theirs was a platonic relationship but with lots of oohing and cooing going on between the pair of them. Pete and Mari both unsubtly played matchmakers between myself and one of Mari's backing singers, Candide, engineering situations where the two of us were left alone. Eventually, after a few furtive glances and whispered sweet nothings, Candide invited me down to London to spend the weekend with her in her flat in Chalk Farm. Our tryst wasn't to last though. We were both geminis and too mercurial for each other. We soon realised it wasn't a match made in heaven and parted company, never to see each other again in the flesh, so to speak. Candide and I were both to go onto bigger and better things.

After being instrumental in the ousting of both Marty and Joey, by this time Steve Coy had joined the band permanently. Steve was a drummer by trade although nowhere near in Joey's league. Steve moved in with Pete and Lynn and double bunk beds were installed in their bedroom in the Catherine Street flat with Steve sleeping on the top bunk. Lynn would go off to work at Probe in the mornings, Pete by this time having given up his post behind the counter and thereby relieving customers of the terrifying prospect of a tongue-lashing, and, apparently, Steve would join Pete in the bottom bunk. The actual ins and outs of this arrangement were never made perfectly clear but we did conjecture as to the exact nature of their relationship. Steve was to stay with Pete and DOA for many years to come, eventually taking over Pete's management.

Ⓐ Humph, 1974. (Standing L to R) Brian 'Fee' Powell, Kevin 'Jam' Jarvis,
Wayne 'What Were You Thinking' Hussey. (Kneeling, as he should be) John 'Snob' Ashton.
Ⓑ Rough Justice, 1976. Powell, Simon Heathfield, Jarvis (on drums) and me.

Me, 1976. (Credit: Chris Reynolds)

C No heat, no hot water, but I do have a sleeping bag and a guitar. Liverpool, early 1978.

D With Steve Power in our one room Tuebrook flat, 1978.

Ⓔ Ded Byrds, November 1978. (L to R) Dave Wibberley, Ambrose Reynolds, me, Jon Moss, Knopov, Denyze D'Arcy.
Ⓕ The Walkie Talkies sign to Sire Records! (L to R) Seymour Stein, me, unknown, unknown, Knopov, Jon Moss, Denyze D'Arcy, unknown. Above: The front and back cover of the Walkie Talkies single.

G Home for Christmas with the Husseys, circa 1979.
H Me, Ullet Road, early 1980. (Credit: Peter Davies)

❶ Hambi & The Dance. (L to R) Paul 'De Niro' Curran, Paul 'Pacino' Barlow, Hambi, me. (Credit: Francesco Mellina)

❷ HATD in the newly built Pink Studio. (L to R) Paul Curran, Hambi, Paul Barlow and Steve Power. (Credit: Peter Davies)

Ⓚ

Ⓛ

Ⓚ Avoiding the royal wedding, Paris, July 1981.　　Ⓛ Kris Guidio: as snout-fair as the Devil himself.

My favourite time living in Liverpool was in this flat at 11 Lancaster Avenue, circa 1982.

Dead Or Alive in Pete's Catherine Street flat, early 1983. (L to R) Mike Percy, Pete Burns, me and Steve Coy.

The fact that Steve wasn't a great drummer was of no great importance anyway as we'd started using drum machines after Joey's exit. Steve's job, ostensibly, was to keep Pete happy and occasionally bash about on the congas. I had moved out of 11 Lancaster Avenue and moved into a top floor council flat on the corner of Catherine and Upper Parliament Street with my friend, John Hawkins, not a spit away from Pete & Lynn's. John fronted an electronic pop duo called This Island Earth and was signed to MCA for a brief period, enjoying a minor hit in 'See That Glow'. I did play guitar on some of his recordings but whether they saw the light of day I have no idea.

John had various synths and drum machines laying around the flat and I took to experimenting with some of his gear. Midi was in its infancy but I found out that if I midi'd a drum machine to the synth and plugged my guitar into the cv/gate input on the back of the SH101 I could play the guitar and it would sound like a sequencer synced to the drum machine. It was a revelation and proved to be the way forward for Dead Or Alive, moving us into a more dance orientated direction which we were all more interested in now that we'd gotten bored with the rock band format. We booked some time in Pink Studios and with Steve Power engineering we recorded three new songs: 'Misty Circles', 'Far Too Hard' and 'Selfish Side'. Brought to the attention of Annie Roseberry, who had signed U2 for Island, and the legendary A&R man, Muff Winwood, brother of Steve, the results earned us a recording contract with Epic Records, a subsidiary of CBS, which we duly signed in early 1983.

Another consequence of these demos was that Will Sergeant of Echo & The Bunnymen got to hear them and, one day when we met on the street in Liverpool, he asked me how I had got that triggered guitar sound. I explained how and lo and behold the next Bunnymen single, the brilliant 'Never Stop', featured sounds that were very similar. I mentioned this to Will many years later and of course he had no recollection of our conversation. Lovely guitar player, Will, one of the most creative and innovative Britain has produced in the last 40 years or so. Newly signed to Epic and with a sizeable advance we went out and bought a brand-new state-of-the-art Oberheim system; a drum machine, keyboard and sequencer, which all linked together to play in sync via midi. With none of us, myself, Mike, Steve, or Pete, having much experience with this level of equipment we enlisted the help of one of Mike's friends, Tim Lever, who had previously played guitar, keyboards and sax in another local Liverpool band, Modern Eon. Tim read the manuals and learned how to programme the system. Tim, Mike, and myself would spend our days working at the homes of either Mike or Tim, both of whom still lived with their parents out in Huyton, quite a trek for me on the bus from the city centre. We worked on the arrangement of 'Misty Circles' which had been chosen as our first single on CBS, programming my guitar lines into the sequencer. With the new direction the band were taking, this was another nail in the coffin for me. I should've seen it coming.

When the song was ready to record we travelled down to Martin Rushent's Genetic Studios in Berkshire. Rushent had earned his dosh in the late Seventies through success with The Buzzcocks and The Stranglers and had opened the facility in a barn at his home in Streatley in 1980, enjoying huge sales a year later after producing the massively popular album *Dare* by The Human League. Producing for us was Zeus B. Held, an eccentric German who had written and produced the club classic which we all loved, 'No G.D.M.' by Gina X. We were assigned the house engineer for these sessions, a young man by the name of Dave Allen. Dave and I would go onto work together again several times in the future, more of which later, but remember that name.

Genetic boasted chalets adjoining the studio which is where we, the band, stayed for the duration. It was a relaxed and happy few days and the track was sounding good. When we'd finished tracking we adjourned to Utopia Studios in the Primrose Hill area of London. Utopia was founded by Phil Wainman, a co-writer and producer of early Seventies hits for The Sweet, Mud, and The Bay City Rollers among many others. Again we were assigned the house engineer, another young lad this time by the name of Tim Palmer. Again, remember that name, our paths would cross again. The track was mixed and everyone, Zeus, us, and the record company were happy.

The single was released in May of 1983 and breached the UK singles chart at number 100. For one week. And that is despite a spirited performance on the Lisa Stansfield-hosted kids TV show, *Razzmatazz*. Reviews were indifferent apart from one particularly vile critique by Nick Heyward of Haircut 100 in the *Melody Maker*, the gist of which, I was reminded recently, was that Pete should die of AIDS. Now, Pete could dish it out, that's for sure, and had a biting tongue that could wither even the most impenetrable of egos, but Heyward's remarks were way beyond the pale and uncalled for. He'd get his.

Despite the disappointing chart performance of 'Misty Circles' we knuckled down to work preparing our debut album, again produced by Zeus and engineered by Tim and again recorded at Utopia. We were given the use of a luxury flat in Maida Vale for the duration, Pete and Steve sharing a room of course, with Tim and Mike in another, and lucky ol' me having a room all to myself. By this time I had become disillusioned with my ever decreasing role in the band; what with all my guitar melodies and arpeggios being programmed into the sequencer I was feeling increasingly redundant and ostracised. My only contribution on 'That's The Way I Like It', for example, was as part of the backing vocal chorus, "uh-uh uh-uh". Not the best use of my guitar skills, I'd contend.

Also assigned to us for these Utopia sessions was a tape-op/tea boy by the name of Jon Holness, son of Bob, presenter of the ever-popular kids TV quiz show, *Blockbusters*. He and I became fast friends, both sharing a penchant for darker guitar bands such as Killing Joke, the Banshees and The Cure. After finishing work in the studio in the evenings he and I would venture out into central London to the clubs of the yet to be christened goth scene, the Batcave being a favourite, to get royally fucked up and in the early hours stagger back to the flat where the other four members of the band were all tucked up in bed.

A division was developing between me and them, probably best exemplified by the day that Nick Heyward came into the studio. Unfortunately for him Tim was in reception and saw him go into the men's toilets carrying a newspaper. Tim ran back into the control room and excitedly reported the news. Immediately Pete said, "Right, let's get him. Come on, all of us." I declined, saying I was gonna stay put and continue reading my book. With looks of disdain and loathing aimed my way the four of them left the control room.

How I heard it afterwards was that each of them picked up a fire extinguisher and crept into the toilets where they quietly established that only one stall was being used. With one of them in each of the adjacent stalls stood on the toilet seats, one ready to go under the door and the last one going over the top, it was one, two, three and go – and they simultaneously let off their extinguishers onto the unsuspecting Nick Heyward who was sat quietly doing a crossword while taking a shit. I suspect it was a good thing Heyward was sat on the potty.

"That'll teach you, you cunt, to say such terrible things about me in the press," yelled Pete and they all came running back to the control room whooping and a'hollering and high five'ing.

I was no part of it, wanted no part of it, felt no part of it despite the sickening things Heyward had said about Pete, and I knew then, if I hadn't known already, that my time with Dead Or Alive was coming to an end.

During this time I was keeping a journal, more a notebook with thoughts and ideas rather than a daily diary, and in it I was expressing my doubts and disenchantment with the band. Indeed, I had actually written that I'd decided to leave the band but would finish the album first. About three weeks into the recording of the album I was again out one night with Jon and arrived back at the flat to find the four of them still up and ashen-faced. It transpired that the loathsome Tim Lever had been in my room while I was out, found my journal and read it. Then he showed the bit that related to the band to the other three. Despite this violation of my privacy, which was overlooked by all except Francesco, the manager who was visiting at the time and who argued on my behalf, bless him, it was decided that I should leave the band forthwith. I didn't care. I was glad and relieved to be out if I'm honest. I just would've liked to have finished the album having had a hand in writing a fair few of the tunes. Next morning I packed up my belongings and left, catching the train back to Liverpool.

Living so close to Pete, Lynn, and Steve it was inevitable that I would bump into them occasionally. Relations were strained but always civil. I did manage to get my equipment back, they didn't sell mine like they'd sold Marty's and in the end I was treated fairly by them. I think I have Francesco to thank for that more than anyone else.

A few years later, after The Mission had achieved a degree of success, I read an interview with Pete in one of the music rags. He said something like: "I was very hurt that Wayne left. We didn't want him to go but we didn't want him to stay if he no longer believed in the band. I loved Wayne, I really did, he's a lovely boy. He's such a talented musician, probably the most talented that's ever been in the band, but he has a serious problem with drugs. That didn't help."

It's obvious that Pete felt betrayed by me and my gradual withdrawal from the band camaraderie. But, in my defence, my detachment was borne out of my frustration engendered by feeling increasingly sidelined creatively. I'd come into Dead Or Alive while they were still a guitar-based rock band and in the two years I was there I'd been instrumental in helping to shape their new direction (sounds like Spinal Tap) but in the process I'd done myself out of a job. I was ready for a new musical challenge.

Dead Or Alive enjoyed a minor hit in early 1984 with their version of KC & The Sunshine Band's 'That's The Way I like It'. They also toured to coincide with the release of *Sophisticated Boom Boom*, the album I was recording with them when I departed. They were playing Leeds Warehouse. By this time I had joined The Sisters Of Mercy and was living in the city. I couldn't miss this, could I?

Still in touch with them, particularly their manager, ex-flatmate and my friend, Francesco Mellina, I went down to watch the show. The place was packed and they were good, very good. But what was strange was I could hear all the guitar parts and some of my backing vocals that I'd contributed to the records on the backing tapes they used live. It was like I was still with them on stage. Flattered more than insulted, I saw them after the show and we had a drink and laughed about 'my presence' on stage with them every night.

Of course, Pete and Co. later went onto deserved big international success with 'You Spin Me Round (Like A Record)' with which they very kindly paired one of the songs I'd co-written, 'Misty Circles', on the B-side. The proceeds came in very handily later when we were recording The Mission's early singles.

I also saw Dead Or Alive again in 1985 when we, The Sisters Of Mercy, were playing the Paradiso in Amsterdam. They were in town doing some TV show or other so came along to see us. Again, it was lovely to see them and any rancour there may once have been between us was clearly now a thing of the past.

The last time I saw Pete was in Habitat on Kings Road in London, around 1989-90. The latest issues of the music weeklies had just printed the results of their readers polls in which The Mission, and me personally, had swept the board. No doubt celebrating, I'd been up all night and looked like it. I was in a state of disarray both physically and mentally, attired in the same grubby clothes I'd been wearing for the last couple of days. Pete, Steve, and Lynn were all resplendent and gorgeous in their finest finery. Pete offered me his genuine congratulations. That was the last time I ever saw him.

Pete Burns was larger than life, beautiful not handsome, supremely talented, generous to a fault, funny as fuck as well as being caustic and sometimes just downright rude, cruel and wicked. He taught me so much about how to present myself, gave me the encouragement and confidence to finally become my own person. I wouldn't be the man I am today if it hadn't have been for the two years that I spent in his service. I felt like a small piece of me died with him that night in Bratislava when

I heard the news he had passed. The faint hope I had long harboured that we could possibly work together again one day was finally extinguished.

CHAPTER 13

In The Temple Of Love, Love, Love...

PLAYLIST:

1. Gimme Shelter – The Sisters of Mercy (TSOM) 2. Requiem – Killing Joke
3. Temple Of Love – TSOM 4. Spellbound – Siouxsie & The Banshees
5. Alice – TSOM 6. A Forest – The Cure 7. Body & Soul – TSOM
8. Ghost Rider – Suicide 9. Floorshow – TSOM
10. 1969 – Iggy & The Stooges 11. Ace Of Spades – Motorhead
12. Afterhours – TSOM

In the early autumn of 1983 I received a phone call from Andrew Eldritch. "Hello, I'm with a band called The Sisters Of Mercy and we're looking for a new guitarist and heard that you are quite good. Are you interested?"

Now, I had only recently become aware of the Leeds-based Sisters, my girlfriend at the time being into all things dark, but, shamefully, I wouldn't have known the difference between a Sisters or a Sex Gang Children or even an Alien Sex Fiend record. But that mattered not. Yes, I was interested. My time in Liverpool had run its course and it felt like the right moment for me to move to pastures anew.

Apparently, I had been recommended to Andrew by Annie Roseberry and Muff Winwood, the A&R people at CBS who had looked after Dead Or Alive during my latter time with the band and who were talking with Andrew about signing the Sisters. They had just returned from their first tour of the USA and Ben Gunn, one of the guitarists, had opted to leave to pursue university studies. Andrew and I arranged a time for me to travel to Leeds to meet with the band.

My friend, Kenny, who, along with his girlfriend, Doreen, ran the Planet X nightclub in Liverpool, owned a car and being a bit of a fan of the Sisters offered to drive me over to Leeds for the scheduled meeting. We set out from Liverpool one weekday morning and hit the M62. Within a couple of hours we were in Leeds and looking for number 7 Village Place, LS4, our rendezvous.

We arrived at our destination and wondered if we were at the correct house. All the curtains were drawn and the place looked deserted. I checked the address I had scribbled on a bit of paper. We were at the right location. Walking up the side of the house to the front door – a contradiction in terms I know but some houses do have their front doors on the side – we rang the bell. It was answered by a tall blonde woman who introduced herself as Claire and invited us into the living room. Adjusting our eyesight to the gloom of the room I spied a bearded figure clad in black curled up in an armchair in the far corner like some apprentice Erebus.

"Hi, I'm Andrew. Which one of you is Wayne?"

"Oh, that'll be me then," I replied, "and this is my mate, Kenny, who has kindly driven me over from Liverpool."

Introductions having been made and seats proffered on the couch we made ourselves comfortable. Claire asked if we'd like a cup of tea. "Yes, please, we are all English after all."

With the tea duly served Claire excused herself and left us boys to converse. To aid the breaking of ice some hefty lines of speed were quickly and ceremoniously chopped out on the coffee table. Once we'd partaken there ensued a rabid conversation about music, the gentlemanly sport of fencing, the Chinese language – a subject that Andrew had apparently studied at university – and football. With Andrew supporting Manchester United I should've known *then* that our relationship would forever be troubled.

After a while a tall man entered the room and introduced himself as Gary Marx. Gary, whose real name I was later to learn was Mark Pearman, was the other guitarist in the band and he lived in the house with Andrew and Claire. More lines, Mark abstaining, more tea and more conversation. Things were seemingly going swimmingly. With all the tea my bladder was rapidly filling and I needed to expel some liquid. After being told directions to the toilet I excused myself and left the room.

During my absence the doorbell rang and the bass player, Craig Adams, arrived. Thinking that Kenny was me, Craig asked him how long he'd been playing guitar, to which Kenny apparently replied, "Oh, just a few weeks. I'm more of a keyboard player really", which, of course, flummoxed our dear Mr Adams as he'd heard this bloke from Liverpool was some kind of guitar hot shot.

When I returned to the room the confusion was cleared up and I was introduced to Craig Adams for the very first time. A few more lines, many more ciggies, Craig smoked Silk Cut, same as me, Andrew Marlboro Reds, and a few more cups of tea and the meeting was deemed over. Armed with a newly acquired pile of Sisters records that I was expected to listen to before I made *my* decision we said our goodbyes with Andrew promising to call me in a day or two with *their* decision. Craig cadged a lift from Kenny and I into town and, for the first time but certainly not the last, tried to borrow some cash from me.

"Sorry mate, I'm on the dole," was my doleful reply.

"Yeah, so are we. Worth a shot as I don't know if I'll ever see you again."

Thereby endeth my first insight into the mind of Craig Adams.

Kenny and I drove back to Liverpool amped up on speed and excitement at the prospect of a new adventure that maybe, just maybe, was about to change my life.

I arrived back to the council flat in Liverpool I shared with my friend, John Hawkins, on Upper Parliament Street and sat down in front of the stereo in the living room and played the Sisters records I'd been given. 'Alice' and 'Floorshow' I kind of recognised from club nights at Planet X, 'Body Electric' and the *Reptile House* EP not so. And to be honest I wasn't initially overly impressed. I think it was the voice that put me off at first, sounding to me to be melodramatic and contrived, like some kind of Darth Vader character when in fact, in my mind, The 'Dritch himself in real life came across more like Rigsby from the TV series *Rising Damp*.* Next I played the 12-inch of the new single, 'Temple Of Love', which was being released shortly. While I enjoyed the A-side it was the B-side, their version of The Rolling Stones 'Gimme Shelter', that really sold me. I got it. I understood the artifice of it all, the vocals reminding me of Bowie on *Diamond Dogs*, my favourite of his albums. I loved it, playing it over and over for the next couple of hours, grabbing my guitar and strumming along.

---

* Andrew's speaking voice was unlike the deep baritone of his singing voice. Nae problem with that, there's a history of singers that sound very different when singing to how they sound when speaking. When Andrew spoke his accent was, to these ears, Home Counties and not unlike a slightly excitable, slightly helium'd Bowie. He'd also often sound amused and very impressed with himself. Again, no problem with that. Andrew is approximately the same height as I am, if anything slightly shorter, as is Craig. Mark is six feet, more or less.

Andrew called the next day. "The job is yours if you want it," he said.

"Yeah, brilliant. I do."

And then, startlingly, "About your name, we'd like you to change it. Any ideas?"

Uh?

"Well, both Mark and I have changed our names for the band, my real name is Andrew Taylor, and Ben Gunn was obviously a pseudonym. We're not very keen on the Hussey bit. Or the Wayne, to be honest."

After picking myself up off the floor I countered, "Well, actually, Mr Taylor, that'll be a no then as I am quite attached to my name. It's Wayne Hussey. My name comes with me or I don't come at all. Still want me to join?"

After a slight pause and a bit of a huff Andrew Taylor agreed that Wayne Hussey would be the new guitarist in the Sisters. I had passed the audition without playing a note though I suspect my skill with a blade and powder may well have had something to do with my appointment.

And so it was arranged that I would travel back to Leeds in a week or two with my guitars and equipment, stay for a while and start rehearsing with them after they had returned from another quick jaunt to the US. Again, Kenny kindly did the honours and, with Doreen along for the ride this time, drove me over to Yorkshire in his car laden down with my Aria 12-string electric guitar, my Fender Telecaster, my Fender El Rio 6-string acoustic, a Roland JC60 amp and assorted pedals that included a Memory Man Deluxe, Boss distortion, compressor and phaser. I also brought along a toothbrush and a change of underwear, just like I did when I went to Durham to meet Robert Blamire.

For the first few weeks I was rehearsing with the band I was sleeping (ha, that's a laugh) on the couch in the living room at 7 Village Place. Considering the amount of whizz that was being consumed sleep was in short supply and I could lie down only after Andrew, Claire and Mark had retired to their rooms. That living room was a social hub and people would turn up at all hours – Jez, Danny, Stevie Sex Pistol and others – to drink tea and to partake in the white line ceremonies. Interestingly, Mark (Gary Marx to you) would only rarely join the socialising in the living room and would mostly hide away in his room with his girlfriend Catherine. Or, as became more frequent as time went on, he would disappear to Wakefield where Catherine lived. I didn't think much of it at the time as I just thought he was not into amphetamine and staying up jabbering gibberish for hours which is fair enough really. Only later did I come to realise there was a problem there.

Our rehearsal room was a small, dank cellar. It was fortunate that a drum machine substituted for a real drummer, as we surely wouldn't have been able to rehearse there. As it was Andrew never deigned to grace us with his presence, preferring to sit in his favourite armchair in the living room directly above us watching daytime TV with the sound turned down. It was compulsory, however, to take a tea and ciggie break at 4:30pm so that Andrew could turn the volume up to watch *Countdown*. Andrew always did like his word games and very good at them he was too. Try to argue or play Scrabble with the bugger and you'll soon find out.

Andrew sat there all day listening to us rehearse, then told us we were "playing it wrong" when we adjourned for tea, but it was surely a blessing he didn't join us in the cellar as it certainly wouldn't have been able to accommodate all four of us at the same time. Or at least it would've required *very* uncomfortable contortions.

At the time we were running the drum tracks from a four-track cassette porta-studio as the Roland TR909 we were using had so little internal memory that we were unable to store a show's worth of rhythms on it. Each song had its own cassette tape and its own set of EQs that had been jotted down into a notebook. Up until I joined the band Craig was the one nominated to change the cassettes and adjust the EQs after every song. I think it was during this period, in the time between songs while Craig was changing cassettes, that Andrew, hanging onto his microphone stand for dear life, developed his dazzling caustic onstage wit and repartee.

The porta-studio was in one corner of the room while Mark, Craig and I had our small amps in the other three and then we stood nose to nose in the centre of the room with our guitars rehearsing the songs. At the time Craig was putting his bass guitar through a Marshall guitar amp head and 4 x 4 guitar cab. It certainly helped him achieve a unique bass sound as well as easing the space limitations, bearing in mind he has since gone on to use huge Ampeg stacks which require an army to lift and an HGV to transport. Mark used a small combo, HH if memory serves, just as I did with my JC60. We had a very small two-speakers-on-stands PA through which we monitored the porta-studio. It was a bit of a culture come-down to me as with Dead Or Alive I'd gotten used to spacious, air-conditioned, well-equipped rehearsal rooms with a café on the premises. The only café here was the kitchen upstairs where we could brew ourselves a cuppa, and then join Andrew in the lounge for a fag and a line and an investigation into how I was playing the songs wrong.

Andrew preferred the guitar parts to be played precisely while I came more from the school of visceral playing. Well, that's how I would describe it anyway. I liked to add my own colours to the palette. For example, I was playing a lot of songs now using the electric 12-string that became my favoured instrument during my tenure with the Sisters. I know I had come into the band to replace Ben Gunn but I had no intention of playing *like* him, I had more to offer than that. I was more about dynamics and exploring counter melodies than blasting out barre chords throughout, although the occasional big chord is never a bad thing. This was probably the first of the episodes where Andrew and I didn't quite see eye to eye. To my mind, Andrew, at least at the time, liked to approach the art of making music academically, intellectually, while I was more intuitive and prompted by how I felt 'in the moment'. Neither approach is wrong and there is merit in both. As was later proven, great results can be produced from the tension between the two attitudes.

Even though it was cold and damp, and in midst of the cruellest part of the Northern British winter, it was fun learning 'guitar' songs again after my recent experiences with Dead Or Alive's reliance on technology. And listening to the records belied the complexity of some of those guitar parts. These were, are, smart songs, I came to realise. Between them, Mark and Andrew helped me get to grips with the songs that currently made up the Sisters 'live' set. Craig played bass, operated the tape machine, made tea and smoked ciggies.

Pretty much every evening while I was in Leeds rehearsing we went out into town. Or at least Craig and I did. We became The Evil Children, eager brothers in arms in our nightly crusade to waste ourselves. Mark would mostly spend the evenings with Catherine. Andrew, being the *enigmatic* singer, would reclusively stay at home and compose cryptic postcards that he would ask friends from around the world to mail on his behalf to *NME*,

Sounds and *Melody Maker*. This ruse was to make it appear as if he had sent the postcards from LA or Berlin or NYC when, in reality, he was sat at home in Leeds LS4 with the curtains permanently drawn stroking his beloved cat, Spiggy. It was great mischief and early self-mythologising and the music rags easily fell for the stunt.

Claire, whom I discovered was Andrew's girlfriend, also liked to go out of an evening and as she was the only one of us who owned a car she became the designated driver. We used to go to the Faversham pub, which is still there near to the University, and drink with the students as the prices were cheaper than elsewhere. Having no money we became dab hands at playing on our local celebrity and managing to cadge pints and ciggies from the better-heeled students.

In fact, going out in Leeds soon made me realise that the Sisters were regarded as gods around town and this, of course, greatly appealed to my ever-burgeoning sense of self. 'Temple Of Love' had recently been released and was enjoying a stint at the top of the UK Indie chart and so, without me lifting a finger, the Sisters were getting bigger and more popular and I, for one, was reaping the benefits of this newfound by-proxy celebrity status. Suddenly, in Leeds I felt like one of the 'cool' people whereas in Liverpool it was something I'd always aspired to but never really felt I achieved. There was, and is, always someone who is cooler. And anyway, feeling cool is a misnomer, more of which another time.

Wherever we went we were feted and fawned over and didn't have to stand in line to get into the Warehouse on a Friday night. *The Warehouse on a Friday night!* Now that was something. Essentially an alternative night, we lorded it up down there. Always a group of people around us, being bought drinks, sharing white lines with strangers in toilet cubicles, having sex with strangers in toilet cubicles, even being asked for the occasional autograph in toilet cubicles. And most Friday nights I ended up in some strange bed with some strange person, finding my way back to Village Place usually sometime on Saturday afternoon. On the nights I didn't cop off I'd end up with Claire and our group of speeding carousers in a poky all-night café for a very early breakfast. How I managed to eat anything with that much amphetamine in my bloodstream I'll never know but I was young and foolhardy with the constitution of a giant sperm whale. And still as rake thin and translucent as a dry dead autumn leaf.

There was also Le Phonographique (The Phono), a tiny bar/club in a corner of the Merrion Centre. Monday nights were the popular nights there for our crowd. Claire was the DJ and she'd spin discs by the likes of Killing Joke, Suicide, and The Stooges and we'd drink cheap lager and cider. It was more of an elite crowd than the Friday night Warehouse lot, mainly because everyone there was on the dole and didn't need to get up for work the next day. There were a few exceptions. I do remember one particular Monday evening when this old soak was leaning against the bar and leering at all the bright young pretty things cavorting around the dance floor. I went to the bar to get myself a drink, the bar being the size of a medium-sized coffee table, and found myself rubbing shoulders with the lech. He offered to pay for my drink which I, of course, gleefully accepted and we fell into a conversation shouted above the volume of the music. It wasn't long before he propositioned me and asked if I would go back to his hotel with him. He'd pay me, he promised. "Right, fifty quid but no fist fucking, okay? And you have to buy drinks for me and my mates for the rest of the evening. Deal?" Concord was struck and I called my mates over to take advantage of my benefactor's good will and wallet. So, we drank and danced the rest of the night away until 2am came, closing time. At which time I did a runner.

I never found any genuine warmth in Andrew, either in a working or social environment. I can't speak for how he is today but back then he was never one who'd sling an arm around your shoulder and give you a hug. And I never felt I could do that to him either even though I am generally a big hugger. And that was fine. Our relationship was what it was and it worked, at least for the time being. The only moment of real warmth I can remember between us was when I went to see The Sisters Of Mercy at Wembley Arena a few good years later, when Tim Bricheno was in the band. Being a friend to us both Tim conspired for Andrew and I to be in a room together for the first time since we split. Polite conversation ensued until Andrew and I were left alone and he looked me in the eye (with both of us wearing dark glasses it's hard for the casual observer to tell but having worn dark glasses for years by this time we both *knew*) and said, "You're still the best guitarist I've ever had in this band!" And with his compliment warming the very cockles of my heart I threw my arms around him and gave him a big cuddle. I don't remember him recoiling.

So it was that for a few months I commuted between Liverpool and Leeds for rehearsals but ended up spending more and more time in Yorkshire until it became patently evident that I needed to move there. I'd met Gilly, an ex-girlfriend of Annie Hogan who at this time was working as a Mamba with Marc Almond. Marc, who also hailed from Leeds during his initial spell of success with Soft Cell, was by now spending nearly all his time in London but he still owned a house in Headingley that, I seem to recall, Annie and Gilly lived in for a while. Anyway, when they broke up Gilly bought a house nearby at the end of Ashville

Grove, number 27, right next to the railway tracks. It was less than a five minute walk from Village Place. Gilly offered me a room at a nominal rent and it was an offer too good to refuse.

I had the room on the left of the first-floor landing, opposite Gilly's room. Upstairs on the top floor was the bathroom on the right and an attic room on the left which looked down onto the street and which Stevie Sex Pistol moved into at around the same time as I moved into mine. I had, of course, met Stevie many times before, as he was one of 'our crowd' and was previously living nearby with Craig and Sisters roadie, Jez Webb. So Stevie moved out of Elizabeth Street and into Gilly's and Grape moved in with Jez and Craig. Around this time Mark moved out of Village Place to live with Catherine in Wakefield. Danny, who was later to form the band Salvation but was at the time the other Sisters roadie, moved into Gary's vacated room in Village Place. Confused? Yeah, me too. The upshot of all of this was that I had gotten myself prime real estate in the heart of Leeds bohemian district for a very fair rent and I moved from Liverpool over the moors to West Yorkshire.

One of the benefits of Stevie living in Ashville Grove with me, besides him being great company and a constant source of amusement, was that he was the local small-time speed dealer. As well as spending his time fly posting around Leeds for one of the 'organised' northern crews Stevie dealt in small amounts of billy* to his mates and the local bands. There was never anything really sinister to Stevie's dealing, never any ambition to deal big

---

* Billy; as in Billy Whizz, a fictional character featured in the British comic, *The Beano*. Billy is a boy who can't stand still and runs everywhere extraordinarily fast, his speed often causing chaos yet at the same time being an ability that can prove useful. Billy in this context is a euphemism for amphetamine, just as speed and whizz also are.

or to 'expand his market'. He never solicited business from strangers and he was never on the local playgrounds trying to sell to school-kids. He was selling to people like me who were relatively adult (debatable) and wanted it, knew its dangers but also knew its insatiable charms. Stevie was quite happy just selling to his mates on a Friday night. "You want something fast for the weekend?" he would enquire.

There was a steady procession of suspicious looking characters traipsing to our door and I met a fair few of the local druggies doing business in our living room. Stevie did have a code though. He would close for business at 2am, the same time the clubs closed, and only open again at noon. Quite often some reprobate or other would turn up at 3 or 4am banging on the door and shouting for Stevie and he would not so politely tell them to fuck off.

Delivery was always on a Friday afternoon for Stevie's whizz so I would try to make sure that I was at home when he took delivery of his latest batch. Quite often Craig would just 'coincidentally' be visiting me at that time too. Stevie always liked a taste for himself and whoever was around when the speed arrived. So we'd shovel up a few lines late on a Friday afternoon, buy our gramme each, usually £8, and then get ready to go to the Fav and then onto the Warehouse for a right roister-doister of an evening. Amphetamine was Stevie's main trade but he could also get us small amounts of smoke and, on the odd but always eventful occasion, acid. Speed use was so prevalent among my coevals, pretty much everyone I knew at least dabbled. And while no stranger to it previously, whizz became a daily habit for me. Even more so now that Stevie was around. Eating was always more expensive and, to someone on a budget determined by our government's benevolence, frugality was certainly a factor when considering the option of whether to eat or whizz.

After a while I began to notice that Andrew and Mark never spoke to each other. Literally. They lived in the same house but if one entered the room the other would leave. They carried on conversations but never spoke directly to each other, using Craig, Claire or myself as their go-betweens. It was bizarre. And when I was with one of them little snide comments about the other would pepper their talk; nothing too much or too malicious on either part, just enough to make me raise an eyebrow and realise that something wasn't quite as it should be. I don't know how long this had been going on previously before I joined the band but the silent rancour started to develop into more tangible animosity over time eventually leading to Mark moving out of Village Place to Wakefield.

I remember one occasion just a month or two after I'd joined the band, when Mark, Craig, and myself were on the top deck of a double-decker bus travelling from Leeds to Bingley to visit a music shop to look at some new amps and guitars. It looked very likely that we were going to be signing a record deal with WEA imminently and we'd be able to upgrade some of our equipment. Craig and I lit up a Silkie each – Mark never smoked – and then a conversation ensued.

Mark: "We wanted to talk to you, Wayne, about something?"

I look at Craig and through a cloud of smoke he nods agreement.

Mark continues: "We wanna split the band and form a new one without Eldritch. And we'd like you to join us. Are you up for that?"

Taking a big drag on my fag I inhaled, holding the smoke in my lungs for a beat or two longer than usual before exhaling.

"Well," I began, "I've only been in the band for a little while and we haven't even played a gig yet or done any recording. We're about to sign a deal with a major label. I dunno. I think I'd rather stay with Andrew for the time being and see how it goes."

And that was the end of that conversation, at least for the time being. We arrived in Bingley at the music store and proceeded to look at new amps and guitars and drum machines as though the conversation had never taken place. Things just reverted back to the way they were until a year or so later when the situation finally came to a head.

Fairly frequently, Andrew would disappear for a few days at a time, heading down to London to conduct business. We had no formal manager as such; Andrew took that role upon himself. And he was good at it although, I felt, unnecessarily uncommunicative and vague with us on his return about what was going on. But that was okay too. Craig's attitude and mine was pretty laissez-faire at the time and as long as we had money for ciggies, speed, and booze we were happy enough.

Along with managing the band Andrew also ran the label, Merciful Release, the label that the Sisters records had been released on up to that point. He also did all the artwork for the releases too so it was no real surprise that he never had any time to rehearse with us. I believe that Mark had been more involved in the business side of things previous to my joining the band but by the time I had Mark had pretty much withdrawn and just let Andrew get on with it himself. That being said though, I could sense that Andrew still took more notice of Mark's opinion than anyone else's on the odd occasion when he would relay an opinion through one of us to Andrew. It was a strange dynamic but I'd been in bands before with strange personal dynamics and it had worked so I didn't really question it or try to do anything about it. Maybe if I had then things may not have turned out the way they did. Or maybe they would have just come to a head earlier than eventually transpired. Either way it was none of my business really, I was the new boy in the band, and had yet to make a record or play a show.

One of the things we were doing as we were rehearsing was writing new songs. The same porta-studio we used for playing back the drum tracks we also used to record four-track cassette demos. Both Andrew and Mark already had a few new tunes that they were working on and during down time from rehearsing I would borrow the porta-studio and the drum machine and put together demos. The first tune I wrote and demoed for the Sisters ended up, with Andrew writing the lyrics, as the next single, 'Body And Soul'.

But there was a complication. My song publishing was still assigned to Chappell Music, the company I signed to as part of Dead Or Alive. I was angling for a release from that deal so I could sign a new one as part of the Sisters who were, at the time, negotiating with RCA Music Publishing. I had an option coming up for renewal that I didn't want Chappell to take. At Chappell I was dealing with Jeff Chegwin, brother of Keith and my friend from Liverpool, DJ Janice Long. Anyway, Jeff and I got on very well, enough for me to confide in him my present situation and enough for him to confide in me that he wouldn't take my option as he was leaving the company shortly anyway. But to make matters seem all above board it was deemed better that I wasn't seen to be writing any new songs. So, Andrew and I, in tandem for a change, came up with the plan that the publishing on 'Body And Soul' would be credited solely to Andrew and to recompense me he would credit me later, when the publishing situation had rectified itself, with one of his songs that I had no part in writing – which for the information completists among us ended up being 'Blood Money', a B-side to the later 'No Time To Cry' single.

In early spring of 1984 we recorded 'Body And Soul', along with 'Train' and the gloriously brooding 'Afterhours'* on which I played piano as well as guitar, with Andrew producing and Chris Nagle engineering at Strawberry Studios in Stockport, where I had previously worked with Martin Hannett while playing guitar with Pauline Murray & The Invisible Girls.

Even though we still kept the Merciful Release identity 'Body And Soul' was the first Sisters' release as part of the newly inked deal with Warner Brothers.** Released in early June of 1984 'Body And Soul' went storming into the UK singles charts at number 46 and over the course of the next five weeks gradually slithered down and out of the Top 100. Our first major label punt at the UK Top 40 ended rather ignominiously.

Making records is all well and good but the lifeblood of any real, true band is playing live. I made my onstage debut with the band at the Tin Can Club in Birmingham on Saturday, April 7. Ostensibly a warm-up show for our upcoming tour of the US, the Tin Can Club gig was free for Sisters fans. It was at this show that I first played with Andrew as during all the months we'd rehearsed prior he had never once blessed us with his presence at the microphone. It was a little strange hearing the songs with vocals after rehearsing for so long without. Despite

---

* I believe my playing of the piano on 'Afterhours' was the first time a keyboard was used on a Sisters record.

** Warner Brothers, Elektra, and Atlantic were the three main constituent record labels amalgamated to make up WEA. In the UK and Europe our records were released and distributed by Warners. In the Americas we were on Elektra.

the weirdness of the situation the show was a success and it was my first experience of the wonderful Sisters audience, many of whom I came to know very well over the next year or so.

A few days later, very early morning on Wednesday, April 11, we boarded the plane at Heathrow that would fly us across the Atlantic to New York City and the start of the Sisters' third but my first ever US tour.

CHAPTER 14

God Bless You, America

PLAYLIST:
1. Shoplifters Of The World Unite – The Smiths
2. Meat Is Murder – The Smiths
3. Gimme, Gimme, Gimme (A Man After Midnight) – Abba
4. Jukebox Babe – Alan Vega   5. Cheree – Suicide   6. Kashmir – Led Zeppelin
7. Dancing Barefoot – Patti Smith   8. No Fun – Iggy & The Stooges
9. Kick Out The Jams – MC5   10. War – Edwin Starr
11. I Heard It Through The Grapevine – Marvin Gaye
12. Panic In Detroit – David Bowie

The four of us were sat in a row at the back of the plane, the smoking section, on an early morning TWA flight from London Heathrow to New York that Wednesday; Craig Adams to my right, Andrew Eldritch to my left and Gary Marx, the only non-smoker among us, perched on the aisle seat beyond Andrew. It was only the second time I'd ever flown and I was on my way to America! The other three had been a couple of times before, of course, so knew what to expect. I'd heard nothing but epochal tales from the three of them about their previous visits, so anticipation and excitement was certainly high on my part if not theirs.

Craig and I drank ourselves to unconsciousness from the free bar offered on the plane, hospitality being a service that the airlines offered in those days as well as smoking seats. But not before we were asked if we could 'keep it down' as we were apparently disturbing some fusty passengers around us who complained to the hostess about our inebriated boisterousness. And no, I don't mean Andrew and Mark (Gary Marx), they had both long since fallen asleep.

Arrival at JFK in the mid-morning sunshine and through immigration and customs with no problem, to be met by John Hanti, our tour manager, sound engineer, and driver, and Ruth Polsky, our promoter.

John was a round faced, jovial, curly haired New Yorker who had played keyboards in the Alice Cooper band for a few years in the mid-Seventies, a self-made millionaire by the time he was 25 and a pauper again by the time he was 30. Now plying his trade as a live sound engineer, he had worked with the Sisters on their previous two visits.

Ruth is legendary. She was the booker at NY's Danceteria club, a multi-floor pleasure dome on 21st Street in Manhattan. Working at Hurrah's in 1980, it was Ruth who had booked the first Joy Division US tour that had to be cancelled a day or two before it was due to start because of Ian Curtis suicide. In the two years or so that she had been working at the Danceteria she had brought New Order, Echo & The Bunnymen, Teardrop Explodes, The Jesus & Mary Chain, Cocteau Twins, Depeche Mode and many others as well as TSOM into the country for their first ever US shows. When I first met her there was talk of her managing a new band from Manchester that had supported the Sisters just a few months previously and had just enjoyed a couple of minor UK hits. The Smiths. For some reason it didn't happen but Morrissey was to dedicate The Smiths single, 'Shoplifters Of The World Unite', to Ruth after she was tragically mowed down and killed by a runaway taxi on the steps of the Limelight in NY in September 1986. But that's more

230

than two years away from where we are in my story so we'll rewind, shall we?

We loaded our feeble amount of luggage and equipment into the back of John's minibus and, for my benefit as it was my first time in NY, he drove the scenic route over the Queensboro Bridge into Manhattan. Wow, bloody wow. NYC is one of the most iconic skylines in the world and instantly recognisable.

"Look, Wayne, there's the Empire State Building over there to the left, and the Chrysler Building just in front of it, and there off in the distance you can see the Twin Towers of the World Trade Centre, and shortly we'll be driving past Grand Central Station on your right," relayed my tour guide from his driver's seat.

I couldn't believe I was here in NYC! And to play shows with the band I was in, how brilliant was that? Having been to the US twice before the other three were somewhat blasé and playing it 'cool' compared to my giddy exuberant wonderment. I have since been to the USA many times, even living in Southern California for five years or so during the Nineties, but no memory of it compares with the exhilaration I felt the first time I saw the NYC skyline.

We arrived at the infamous Iroquois Hotel on West 44th Street, our home for the next few days. The Iroquois has since been renovated and is nowadays a high-end midtown boutique hotel but back in 1984 it was, like the rest of NYC, a dive largely patronised by lowly musicians, actors, artists, poets, drug addicts and dealers, pimps and whores, vying with the more famous Chelsea Hotel as the place to 'hang out' for the bohemians of the city. Like the hotel, many previously run-down areas of the city have since been developed and gentrified and as a consequence NYC is now a lot cleaner and safer than it was back then. It's obviously better for the tourist trade and for the city as a whole but, for me, it has lost much of the spirit and edge it had in 1984. Maybe the same could be said of yours truly; no longer seeking out and revelling in the seedy underbelly of the city as I once did and that attitude has coloured my viewpoint on my last few visits. It is still fabulously vibrant though, and a city I always look forward to visiting.

We checked into the hotel, me sharing a room with Mark while Craig had the dubious pleasure of cohabiting with Andrew. I think the rooming arrangement had been agreed beforehand without Craig and I being consulted in an attempt to keep the two of us, The Evil Children as we'd become disparagingly known, apart and out of mischief. No soddin' chance. We had time enough only to deposit our bags into the rooms and quickly freshen up before all meeting again in the hotel lobby. Our first show was that very same evening – in Boston. We were driving the four hours there and then after the show driving the four hours back to our base for the next few days at the Iroquois.

While Morrissey would be busy expounding his *Meat Is Murder* philosophy less than a year hence we stopped at a drive-through Burger King en route out of the city, tucking into two Whoppers each, a veritable feast on a pittance, two for $2 if memory serves. Because of the strength of the £ against the $ our per diems in the US, $25 per day, would go a lot further than they would in the UK. I couldn't believe how cheap burgers, ciggies and beer were. We were to live like kings for the next few days. Well, comparatively. Drugs were more expensive, as I was to find out.

To ease the tedium of being stuck in a minibus for four hours we started drinking the duty free spirits we'd purchased on the flight over from London. Craig and I were both on the blue label Smirnoff while Mark necked his bottle of Pernod. Andrew, sat between John the driver and Ruth the promoter like a teacher's pet, tutted at us from the front seat. Making the requisite piss stop about two hours into the journey, evidently I wasn't alone in my inebriation. All three of us were a bit Tipsy McStagger, lurching around the gas station forecourt like a pack of brainless Neanderthal zombies. It was great fun. Stumbling back into the minibus I was sat next to Mark. We both quickly passed out and my head drooped onto his chest. During the drive Mark vomited in his sleep all over my head.

Waking up in Boston with bits of undigested whopper and fries in my bird's nest hair I wasn't allowed into the venue where we were playing, ironically named The Spit Club, because of the vomitus.

"But I'm in the band!"

"Don't care, buddy, you're not coming in here with puke in your hair."

"What am I supposed to do then?"

"Go to your hotel, buddy, and clean up. Then I'll let you in."

"But my soddin' hotel is in New bloody York."

"Ain't my problem, buddy."

"I ain't your fucking buddy, buddy."

I stomped off in a tantrum *and* a sulk.

Mark had sick all down the front of his shirt so he just grabbed a new Sisters t-shirt from the swag-bag, changed in the street, and they let him in. The twat. Craig had already vanished into the club, no doubt in search of someone to score some speed from while Andrew just looked at me with something resembling pity, maybe disgust, and, shaking his head, disappeared into the dark of the Spit.

Ruth came to my aid. "Look, here's 50 bucks. There's a hat shop just over there. Go and buy yourself a hat to cover up the mess in your hair and then that jobsworth'll let you into his stupid club."

What choice did I have? I walked into the shop and bought myself a spiffy wide-brimmed black hat, the kind that matadors and Leonard Cohen might wear, to hide the offending mess on my head. Donning said hat I was allowed into the venue and on stage to play the show. And that was how the cult of the goth hat was born, I tell no lie, necessity being the mother of creation. Or rather, to cover up the sick.

My first ever show in the USA and I had sick in my hair. I can't remember much about the actual performance, to be frank, but I do remember the look of abject horror on the faces of the mostly black-clad legion when we started playing a cover of Abba's 'Gimme, Gimme, Gimme (A Man After Midnight)'. Irony is not a concept that is grasped particularly well by the common American, in my experience. Neither is sarcasm.

After the show our dressing room soon filled up with half of the audience come to lig. I found Americans, generally, to be very forward and assertive. My impression was confirmed when an insistent young lady, with barely two words exchanged between us, dragged me into the toilets and, without ceremony, knelt down, undid my jeans, extracted my knob and put it in her mouth. My first American blow-job. Pretty much the same as a British blow-job, it has to be said, except I didn't have to go through any of the usual ritual courting before fellatio was administered. I kept my hat on, I'll have you know.

It was on this particular evening that I first heard the phrase that Andrew would use like a mantra whenever he spied one of us slinking away to indulge in some carnal shenanigans.

"A gentleman always carries a condom in his wallet," he would pontificate.

"I don't even own a bleedin' wallet!" I thought. "What would I need a wallet for, I've never got any money. He's gotta wallet just to keep a condom handy? What a ponce."

This was long before any of us enjoyed the convenience of credit and debit cards, of course. I guess this was one sure piece of evidence of the higher breeding that spawned Von Eldritch. I wonder what else he kept in his wallet? It certainly wasn't cash as I never ever knew him to buy a bloody round. Among the many attributes for which he is renowned generosity isn't one of them...

Next morning, with Andrew taking a meeting with Ruth and John in the room he shared with Craig, and slugabed Mark wanting to sleep-in, Craig and I arranged to meet for a wander before we had to leave for Philadelphia for that evening's show at the East Side Club.

The Iroquois is a short walk down 7th Avenue to Times Square which was where Craig and I headed. We walked around the area. It was full of strip joints with pimps trying to tempt you into their establishments and separate you from your hard earned. It was squalid and sleazy and right up my strasse. I was fascinated by the comings and goings, the drunks and junkies passed out on the streets, the hookers with scabbed arms – "Hey, honey, you looking for a good time?" – and winking at us as we walked past. It was like being an extra in a film, Scorsese's *Taxi Driver* maybe, and, oblivious to any danger, I loved it. It felt like a million miles away from Leeds, Liverpool or Bristol. I was half expecting, hoping, to meet Tom Verlaine in Burger King or David Byrne in Denny's or even Iggy Pop propping up the bar downstairs in the Iroquois over the next few days but no such luck.

Craig and I headed back to the hotel. Andrew, still in his meeting with Ruth, had locked his room door from inside. Craig couldn't get in so he joined Mark and I in our room, Mark now being wide awake. The rooms were actually small suites; one room with two queen-size beds in, not like the titchy single beds we got in Europe which were no fun if you had company. The other room was a lounge area with a beaten-up couch and some frayed chairs, a TV, a fridge, sink and a microwave for the self-caterers among us. Obviously, what with Burger King and Denny's being just a stone's throw away self-catering wasn't on the cards. In fact, catering became our secret code for drugs as in, "Can we get any *special* catering today?"

There was AC in the rooms which only worked intermittently but that wasn't too bad as it was still only April, although it was hell when we returned to NY in August of that same year. If you walked on the carpet without shoes and socks your feet would stick to it, the carpet gnarled with years of various substances being ground into it. The cockroaches were everywhere. Although you very rarely saw them when the lights were on you could hear them scuttling about. When we'd been out for the evening and came back and opened the door and turned on the light for a split second you could see thousands of the buggers scurrying away to hide. You couldn't leave any opened cans of drink unattended or any leftover foods on the side as they'd be in like Flynn.

One time the three of us were in the room and Mark had passed out on the living room floor. Not being of the same robust constitution as Craig and I, Mark rarely drank and if he did it was generally in moderation, Pernod episode aside. On *this* occasion he'd fallen asleep with his mouth open so, being the two Evil Children we were, we started to lay little food trails from the edges of the room to Mark's mouth, delicately placing morsels on his cheeks and his lips. And then we sat back and quietly watched as cockroaches slyly and surreptitiously made their way along the trail to the gaping grand canyon of Mark's gob. If Craig or I moved the 'roaches would skitter back to their hiding places and we'd have to replenish the trail and start again. Eventually we got the 'roaches onto Mark's face and one even went into his mouth but quickly back out again when it'd copped a load of his boozy breath, too rancid even for a cockroach. Obviously disturbed by feeling something on his face and in his mouth Mark woke up and, startled, sat up and started flicking off the 'roaches as they scampered off to their dark corners once again. Craig and I were rolling around in boozed-up hysterics. "You bastards," Mark declared not without some justification. Nice friends to have, we were, uh? It was best to sleep with your mouth closed and with the lights on in the Iroquois.

Of course one of the first questions we'd always ask the promoter on our arrival *anywhere* was "Can you get us some whizz?" Trying to get speed in NYC was difficult, cocaine not a problem. But coke was too prohibitively expensive and didn't last as long as amphetamine. A waste of money in our book. But we weren't averse to hoovering up a few lines if they were presented to us on a metaphorical silver platter. But we never bought the shit, not until a few years later anyway by which time we'd made a bit of the ol' filthy lucre. We could get hold of crystal meth though and, in our ignorance, we'd snort it. Crystal meth came as small rocks that looked like broken glass and which we pummelled as best we could into powder and chopped into lines. It burnt like the infernos of hell when we'd ingest it into our nasal passages. It was only a few good years later that I came to find out that you were supposed to smoke crystal meth, not snort it. It's a wonder that none of us ever suffered a perforated septum. The good, hard-working amphetamine that we could get at home in Yorkshire was impossible to find in the land of the brave, so crystal meth it was then.

On one of these late nights back in NYC and the Iroquois after an out-of-town show Craig, having maybe ingested a touch too much billy, was lying in his bed wide awake with Andrew, in the other bed, in much the same state. With the TV flickering away in the corner of the room sleep wasn't coming easy for either of my compatriots. Andrew sat up in his bed and lit a Marlboro Red and proceeded to smoke it. Craig, in a case of monkey see monkey do, thought to himself, "Mmm, that's a good idea, I'll have a ciggie." Not having a lighter or any matches, he asked, "Andy, have you got a light, please?"

After an extra-long drag on his fag Andrew replied, "No, actually. You should've thought about this yourself earlier. I have worked it out and I have three matches left which is enough for three more cigarettes before the morning. If you want to use the next match after I have lit my next cigarette, which I calculate to be in about an hour, then you're very welcome. But you'll have to wait."

Craig, in a huff and eager for a puff, got up from his bed, left the room and came knocking on my door. Of course, being more of a forward planner than Craig I had more than three matches and was quite happy to give him a handful to see him through to the morning without having to resort to accepting Andrew's questionable benevolence.

As in Boston the night before there was another bout of the fast-becoming-regular après-show hi-jinks before setting off back from Philly to NYC. It was a gruelling schedule that would probably just about finish me off if we had to do it today but in 1984 and all being young and fuelled by adrenaline, excitement, and white powders, it was a doddle. Our motto was, as coined by Stevie Sex Pistol and not very politically correctly, "Sleep is for poufs."

The next day, Friday the 13ᵗʰ, we were to play the Danceteria in NYC. I would come to spend many a balmy party night here over the next couple of years but tonight was my first ever show in New York. On arrival, by virtue of the fact that we were carrying guitars and the star-turn for the evening, we skipped the lines at the door. Once inside Craig and Mark took great delight in showing me around while Andrew swanned off to the rooftop bar. Each floor was dedicated to a different musical theme, the basement being disco, the ground floor, le premier étage, or first floor as it is in the US, was the room where the shows were performed. This was where'd we be playing. The next floor was maybe hip-hop, with the next being possibly British alternative and so on.

I have no recollection of our show itself except that the room was swelteringly full but I do remember we convened post show to the rooftop and this was where the decadence really began. Ruth handed over a pile of drinks tickets which we'd exchange at the bar for the tipple of our choice and soon we were rubbing shoulders with New York's glitterati *and* hoi polloi. I was quickly introduced to Alan Vega, from Suicide, who was stood talking with Andrew. Loud, gregarious, and ebullient, he was everything I expected my Americans to be. He had a huge full head of jet-black hair, dyed I'd guess, which didn't move one iota in the outdoor evening breeze. Made me wonder whether it was actually a peruke.

"Here, Alan, I know I've only just met you an' all but is your hair real or is that a wig?" I inquired, a tad insensitively.

"Ah, Wayne, my son. You're wondering why my hair don't move, right? I have four words of advice for you. Aquanet Extra Super Hold!"

"Uh? What the fuck you on about?" was all I could utter in reply.

"It's the strongest hairspray in the world and it's American and you should go out and buy yourself a large can of it tomorrow. It's a life-changer. Here, feel this."

And with that he grabbed my hand and put it to his hair. It was like stone, an immoveable object. Magic. And yeah, I did go out and buy some the next day and every other time I was in the States until I stopped back-combing my hair later in the decade.

Craig and I both started to use Aquanet Extra Super Hold all the time, as evidenced by the photos of us on the inner sleeve of TSOM's *First And Last And Always* album released less than a year later.

That stuff was highly bloody flammable as well. I remember being stood side stage once waiting to make my grand entrance after our intro music, 'Kashmir' by Led Zeppelin, had finished. A pyro (yeah, I know, not my idea) on top of the PA went off and a spark fell into my hair, quickly setting it ablaze. I wasn't immediately aware what was happening but Stevie Sex Pistol, who was stood next to me, thinking quickly on his feet and with nary a thought for his own and, particularly, *my* safety started whacking my flaming head with the 18-inch-long metal-cased Maglite torch that he had in his hand.

"What are you doing, you fucking madman?"

"Your hair's on fire!"

"What? Hit fucking harder then. Quick!"

Despite a few bumps and a slight headache the next morning Stevie's quick thinking had extinguished the fire and averted a potential catastrophic hair loss. Though a few ends were singed and I had the smell of burning in my nostrils for the next few days, there were no bald patches and the show went on.

By this time I had been introduced to a group of people that Craig and Andrew had dallied with on their previous East Coast visit. Three of them lived together in an apartment near Washington Square. There was Lisa who was Craig's friend, and Jenny with her bangles and her reference, and Debbie, the lairyest mouthed girl I had ever met after Courtney Love. Debs was great, took no prisoners, she still doesn't, she's been married to Simon Hinkler for the last 20 years. She'd arrive home and Lisa would say, "Oh, Greg called for you."

And in broad New Jersey like Janice from *The Sopranos*, Debbie would respond: "Oh, fuck that guy, he's like a leech up my ass."

The only time I ever saw Debs dumbstruck was when Craig and I had met Lenny Kaye from the Patti Smith Group for an afternoon booze and, being in the area, decided to call around to the girls' apartment. We were sat there with Lisa and Jenny and Lenny supping on beers when Debs arrived blustering through the door,

"Some asshole on the subway touched my fanny*, I fucking knee'd the jerk in the balls and then as he went down I smacked the... fuck, it's Lenny Kaye in my apartment..."

And then she just stood there with her mouth open wide in stunned silence.

Now, Debs, who worked at Right Track Recording Studios on 54th Street, right next door to the world-famous Manny's

---

* The first time I ever heard a girl refer to her fanny in America I automatically assumed she was talking about her front lady parts as they do they in Britain. In actual fact fanny in America relates to the derriere.

Guitar Shop, was the *biggest* Patti Smith fan in the world and had met Patti one time when she, Debs, was 15 years old. According to Debs, without her divine intervention the world would be shy of the classic much loved and covered 'Dancing Barefoot'.*
The legend apparently goes something like this. Growing up very close to Patti's familial home in Mantua, NJ, Debs had befriended Patti's mum and would regularly visit, as any besotted slightly encouraged 15-year-old fan would do, to share Angel Food Cake and sift through Patti's fan mail with her. This particular Christmas Debs took over a few presents for Patti and was invited to return on Christmas Eve when Patti would be visiting. As a fan availed of all the facts of Patti's life and art, Debs knew that Patti used to carry a picture of Modigliani's *Mistress* around with her but had recently lost it. Debs found another in a book and gave this to Patti who then confided to Debs, "I have been writing a song about her and you have inspired me to finish it", and the song was 'Dancing Barefoot'. The photo that Debs gave Patti is featured on the inner sleeve of the album, *Wave*.

At the time Debs had a boyfriend named Brian whom we affectionately rechristened Brain Damage (BBD). Wanna know why? I'll tell you. BBD was the only person we knew in NYC who could get us the specific drugs we craved. One time he needed to drive downtown to pick up some more 'party favours' as the night was still young and our supplies were getting perilously low. I decided to go along for the ride. The only problem was that we were both completely out of our heads tripping on acid and amped up on the ol' sniff-sniff. BBD installed himself behind the wheel of his automobile while I took the passenger seat.

---

* Even I was to cover 'Dancing Barefoot' as an extra track on a Mission 12-inch single.

The lights of the city were dazzling, flaring like fireworks, the colours merging into an ever-changing kaleidoscopic mess as we pulled out into the late evening Manhattan traffic flow. After a short navigation through side streets we hit one of the big avenues that ran the length of the island and, for a laugh, I suggested to BBD, "Just put your foot down and go through all the lights without stopping and let's see what happens." And with that he did and we careened full pelt through red lights, green lights, screaming and giggling maniacally, slowing for nothing, miraculously avoiding hitting and being hit by any other vehicle. It was crazed, drug-induced madness, and we could easily have been killed, or worse caused an horrific accident involving other people. But the angels were on our side and we didn't.

When we reached our destination we fell out onto the sidewalk, exhilarated, adrenalised, laughing with realisation at the magnitude of what we'd just gotten away with. Once we'd made the pick-up we headed, in a more law-abiding manner, back to the hotel and the waiting party in my room. On arrival I regaled the others with the tale of our "playing chicken in the NYC traffic" and Brian was henceforth forever known, and deservedly so, as Brian Brain Damage.

After our Danceteria show we played in Trenton, NJ, the next day and then flew onto Chicago to play the Exit Club on Sunday the 15th. The Exit was packed to the rafters, as they say, and the night was memorable for me as I'd caught the eye (and she mine) of Terri, a very cute waitress working at the club. After the show there was the by now regular dressing room gathering of freeloaders and sycophantic well-wishers but I made my excuses and my way to the bar to sit, drink and talk with Terri while waiting for her to finish her shift for the night.

Once she had she invited me back to her apartment where we sat on the veranda talking, drinking, and smoking, until it was time to make our way to the bedroom. We came together, our bodies engaged, we kissed, and kissed some more, our clothes soon discarded and strewn to the floor, naked we clasped each other, and fell onto the bed… and then my whole world went wibbly-wobbly. It was a waterbed and we were undulating up and down on the waves caused by the movement of our bodies.

Way-hey, I'd never been on a waterbed before and I have to say that once the novelty and giggles subsided it was actually a very fun place to spend a couple of hours with a paramour. Every motion would make a swell in the water and we'd be surfing and hanging onto each other for dear life lest we be carried away by the waves. I enjoyed myself so much poppling* about on Terri's waterbed that I did look into purchasing my own when I arrived home but aqua-filled mattresses weren't very fashionable in Leeds at the time and proved impossible to find. The waterbed episode reminds me of the time I tried to have sex on a trampoline in Gary Numan's back garden. Now, that was really hysterical, trying to stay 'inside' while bouncing up and down proved to be fair impossible. And when, on one particular bounce, I landed awkwardly and painfully on my knackers I had to retire from the fray with my dignity and erection in a state of collapse, much to the hilarity of my partner who, I hasten to add, wasn't Gary Numan.

With the sun rising and peeking through the drawn curtains of her bedroom it was time for me to leave and join the rest of the band back at the hotel as we had a morning flight to Detroit. I left Terri floating on the waves of her waterbed and the afterglow of our night together and bade my farewell with

---

* Popple – to tumble around like bubbles in a boiling liquid.

the promise of staying in touch by letter and by phone (this was years before the internet) and walked out blearily into the morning sun to hail a cab.

During this tour we'd been playing a couple of new songs in the set, 'Body And Soul' and 'Walk Away', two tunes I had penned with words by Andrew, alongside venerable faves such as 'Alice' and 'Floorshow' and our classic rendition of Hot Chocolate's 'Emma'. Each night there would be a few pitiable calls from the audience for 'Temple Of Love', the Sisters' biggest song thus far, which were summarily and inimically dismissed by Andrew. In all the time I was in the band we never played it, the reason being that we couldn't play it very well. We did attempt it in rehearsal but could never get it to sound any good. So rather than persist with it, the unilateral decision was made not to play the song at all. Word soon spread that we never played 'Temple Of Love' and requests for it soon died out while the popular perception of Andrew being a contrarian flourished. It was true he could be a stroppy bugger but on this occasion the decision was pragmatic as opposed to being one designed to enhance the myth.

Our last show on this, my first, jaunt to the US was in Detroit, birthplace of Iggy & The Stooges, MC5 and Motown, at St Andrew's Hall. By the early Eighties Detroit was and had been in decline for a good few years, its boom period of pre and postwar motor car productivity now in steep descent with much of the inner city in decay and disarray. The biggest selling t-shirt on sale at the airport on arrival was emblazoned with the legend, 'Detroit – The Murder Capital Of America'. Yeah, that was something to be proud of. I do seem to remember Craig buying himself one of those t-shirts.

All the shops, businesses, and buildings around the area of St Andrew's Hall were empty, boarded up and derelict. It was grim. We were driven past the old Motown building that was, at the time, also boarded up. It would, thankfully, re-open a year later as The Motown Museum. We were advised not to walk the streets near the venue or the hotel, advice which of course we ignored but no harm came to us with the locals. Considering our dishevelled Limey rock band appearance, they were probably more wary of us than we were of them. It was on our walkabout in Detroit that Ruth Polsky took the photograph of us that ended up on the inner sleeve of our 1985 album *First And Last And Always*.

At the show that evening, in lieu of being given bottles on our rider, two large plastic bins full to the brim with beer were deposited in our dressing room. With none of us being huge beer drinkers and certainly not from a plastic pail, it was decided that one bin would be for band consumption exclusively with the other saved for the after-gig liggers. With us starting to resent the buggers coming into our dressing room uninvited (we hadn't yet heard of security) at every show in the US and drinking our booze, Craig and I hatched a dastardly plan. We decided that we would flavour the beer with our own special ingredient for the after-show soiree. We informed Andrew and Mark of our intention but, funnily enough, both declined to join in, though Andrew did counsel us, judiciously, to make sure we were certain to label both bins correctly. "It wouldn't do, now, to drink from the wrong one, would it?"

With that piece of sage advice ringing in our ears Craig and I whipped out our dicks and pissed in the pail marked 'After-Show'. We could barely contain ourselves when the unsuspecting throng descended on our dressing room. I had barely put my guitar down when they arrived.

"Anyone wanna beer? It's our own special brand of 'pail' ale. Help yourselves!" I invited our after show invaders.

It seemingly went down a treat as evidenced by the fact that there were only frothy dregs left at the bottom of the bin by the time we were ready to leave for our hotel. Evil Children indeed.

Bye-bye America, see you all again next time.

The following day we flew back to London.

CHAPTER 15

One Day We'll Look Back At This & Laugh & Laugh & We'll Die Laughing

PLAYLIST:
1. Damage Done – TSOM   2. Watch – TSOM   3. Body Electric – TSOM
4. Anaconda – TSOM   5. Immigrant Song – Led Zeppelin
6. The Needle & The Damage Done – Neil Young   7. Dreams – Fleetwood Mac
8. Stop Dragging My Heart Around – Stevie Nicks & Tom Petty
9. Purple Haze – Jimi Hendrix   10. Knocking On Heaven's Door – Bob Dylan
11. Careless Whisper – George Michael
12. Sister Ray – The Velvet Underground   13. Poison Door – TSOM.
14. Black Planet – TSOM 15. Marian – TSOM
16. First & Last & Always – TSOM   17. Some Kind Of Stranger – TSOM
18. A Rock & A Hard Place – TSOM   19. Nine While Nine – TSOM

When I joined the Sisters in October 1983 I had little interest in their past. I was really only concerned with the present and, to a slightly lesser extent, the future. That's not to say I didn't respect what they had achieved from their very humble beginnings but I wasn't part of their story to date so why should I be interested? Nonetheless I began to piece together a potted history of the band from small tidbits of information gleaned from very casual conversations with Andrew, Craig, and Mark. It goes something like this.

Mark Pearman and Andrew Taylor had formed The Sisters Of Mercy in 1980. The first thing they did was change their names to the more rock-star sounding monikers of, respectively, Gary Marx and Andrew Eldritch.* Andrew was originally the drummer but, realising he couldn't keep a beat, traded in his drum kit for a microphone and a cheap drum machine affectionately christened Doktor Avalanche. Mark knew a few rudimentary guitar chords and managed to scrounge some money together to buy himself a very cheap guitar and amplifier. Their early attempts at writing songs and making records were charmingly inept at best but they persevered and somewhere along the line they enlisted the services of Craig Adams to play bass and Ben Gunn, not his real name, to play second guitar.

Sporadically they began playing shows, and slowly but surely developed and built up a healthy live following. They also started to write and record better songs, making improved and bigger selling records with each successive release, culminating with the thunderous 'Temple Of Love' that hit number one in the UK alternative chart just weeks after I had joined their ranks. From what I could ascertain, when they started the division of responsibility, decision making and artistic input was shared fairly equally between Mark and Andrew but over the course of the three years or so, depending on who I spoke with, Andrew had wrested – or Mark had relinquished – more and more control. By the time I joined Andrew was managing the band, designing the artwork, writing the majority of the songs thus far, producing the records, running the band's label Merciful Release (which also released singles by The March Violets and

---

* The dictionary definition of eldritch is weird and sinister, strange and frightening. It's a bit like the chicken and the egg conundrum, what came first, the name or the persona? Pitch-black humour or pretentiousness? I'll let you decide.

Salvation during this period), controlling the band's purse strings and recording and tour schedules. Pretty much in complete control. And a huge workload by anybody's standards. This was the dynamic that I came into.

In the early months of my tenure with the band Andrew negotiated a record deal with WEA that allowed us to keep the Merciful Release identity while utilising their worldwide corporate structure for manufacture, distribution and promotion. He had also set up Candelmaesse through RCA Music to handle the publishing of the band's songs. All of this took an inordinate amount of energy, attention, and most importantly, time. Administering all of this from the living room of the house in Leeds he shared with Claire and Danny was proving impractical and so Andrew took the lease on an office located on the first floor of 19 All Saints Road in the Ladbroke Grove area of London which was helmed by former *Melody Maker* journalist Nick Jones.

I had met Nick previously when he had been working at Rough Trade. He was planning to distribute the Mogodon's single that I had played on before my friend, Kris, sold the tapes to facilitate his heroin habit. Nick was a few years older than the rest of us and was one of those typical Sixties hippies that had cleaned himself up and, the smoking of joints notwithstanding, had *kind of* gone straight. He had been on the periphery of the music business for years without ever taking it, or himself, seriously. I liked Nick a lot, he was always laughing (stoned, maybe?) and never got stressed no matter what duress Andrew would put him under. In fact, in many ways Nick was the antithesis of Andrew and certainly a calming influence in the office when things sometimes got fraught.

Nick's job was to basically answer the phone and do Andrew's bidding while keeping the wheels of the machine greased and rolling in Andrew's absence when we were away on tour or in the studio. Saying that though, Nick wasn't just a 'yes' man and he would make his feelings known if there was something he didn't agree with. I'm not sure that Andrew always appreciated Nick's forthright candour but then, in my experience, Andrew very rarely invited opinion. Nick lasted maybe a year before he was replaced by a university colleague of Andrew's, Boyd Steemson, with Andrew claiming he sacked Nick because "I couldn't trust a hippie". The story I heard later from Nick himself was he resigned because he could no longer stand to work with Andrew. Whatever the truth is will probably depend on which side of the line you're on. Nick later eventually left the music business for good when he came into a substantial inheritance and retired to the south coast. Good for him.

Andrew had painted the walls of the office black, of course, and furnished it with a telephone, a desk, a few chairs, a couch, and a couple of framed Sisters posters for the walls; The Spider's Lair, a title bequeathed by Dave Allen a few months later. Unable to afford London hotels, or rather Andrew being unwilling to cough up for our accommodation while 'down in the smoke', Craig and I spent many nights camped out in the office drinking ourselves into a stupor after an evening out on the tiles. With Andrew entrusting us with the keys he would mosey off to stay the night with his mate, Tony James of Generation X and Sigue Sigue Sputnik fame. I'm guessing their evenings were largely spent patting each other on the back as clever manipulators of the media and the music business.

Next door, sharing the same floor, was Trinifold, a company run by Reg Halsall and ably assisted by Trina and VeeGee, that specialised in tour management for bands; itineraries, booking hotels, flights, ferries, van hire, hiring crew, procuring visas and carnets, that sort of thing. It was through Trinifold that we were introduced to Dave Kentish and The Flying Turd.

Dave, like Nick, was a good few years older than us although it'd be safe to assume that, unlike Nick, he'd never been a hippie. More likely a member of some London East End gangster mob. To call him portly would've been kind. He had a penchant for brown leather jackets, sometimes worn with black leather pants and open-necked shirts that exposed a hairy chest adorned with gaudy gold chains. He was the jolly sort who liked a nip of brandy, Marlboro Reds and the company of young girls. In an act of entrepreneurial prescience, Dave had bought himself a red-and-white Dodge minibus in which he could cart around bands, of which the Sisters were one, that couldn't yet afford the big sleeper coaches that 'proper' bands used on tour.

The inside of Dave's van was veritable luxury compared to what we'd known previously: two plush reclining pilot seats in the front, two more in the spacious rear along with a cushioned bench that we could pull out into a bed to accommodate two. With curtains across all the windows in the back to shut out prying eyes, the interior was tastefully carpeted from floor to ceiling in a lovely shade of shit brown, hence the appellation, The Flying Turd. It was a bordello on wheels, a shagging wagon, and this became our home from home for the next few tours. Dave, whose official title was tour manager, took the driver's seat while Andrew, with his natural proclivity to be in control, claimed the front passenger seat so he could map-read and navigate, and also select the music we heard en route to wherever we were going. The remaining three of us took our places in the back with Craig and I more often than not sprawled out on the bed suffering from hangovers.

Having by now signed to WEA, each time we visited their offices in Soho we were invited to help ourselves to records that we might want, along with the contents of their well-stocked fridges. It was the mid-Eighties and excess in the music business was perhaps at its zenith. These days, if there are any fridges at all, then they're all under lock and key and strictly supervised. And probably full of health concoctions anyway. Oh, how times have changed and not for the better...

Anyway, rooting through the cupboards there was very little that WEA was releasing at the time that interested me. I mean, come on, Matt Bianco? But I did find, hidden away, all Led Zeppelin's albums along with a bunch by Neil Young. By 1984 both Zeppelin and Young had fallen from grace in the eyes of the British media and were disdainfully dismissed as old farts. I'd been a big Zeppelin fan as a kid but over the course of the intervening years, and with the advent of punk, I'd sold or lost their albums as well as the couple of Neil Young LPs that I'd also owned. With very little new music exciting me at the time I started playing Zeppelin and Young constantly and even made myself cassettes to take on tour. These tapes ended up being played in our minibus and became firm faves. I started mentioning how great Zeppelin were in interviews and Andrew and Craig, particularly, followed suit. Now, I'm not claiming to be responsible for the critical renaissance of Zeppelin and Young, they were both due a reappraisal anyway certainly by the UK press, but I, specifically, and we, generally, were lauding them at a time when no one else seemed to be. Little by little I started to read others singing their praises and within a year or two both Led Zeppelin and Neil Young were enjoying a favourable re-evaluation.

One consequence of our re-found love for Zeppelin was that we started using their epic, 'Kashmir', as our walk-on music at live shows.

Andrew, by this time, was also getting into Fleetwood Mac. Not the cool early Peter Green records but the more recent albums made with Stevie Nicks and Lindsey Buckingham aboard, the 'clean as a freshly minted one pound note' Fleetwood Mac. To be fair I also harboured a fondness for *Rumours* though I don't remember Craig and Mark being overly enamoured with it. A particular fave of Andrew's was actually a solo Stevie Nicks' track she had recorded with Tom Petty, 'Stop Dragging My Heart Around'. Again, I have to concur that it is a mighty fine song. So much so that we would mess around with it in soundchecks along with Hendrix's 'Purple Haze' and, heaven help us, 'Stairway To Heaven'. Another classic we started playing in soundchecks was Dylan's evergreen 'Knocking On Heaven's Door' which we soon dropped into the live set as an encore. One of the very few instances I remember where Andrew and I were in accord was our fondness for George Michael's 'Careless Whisper', a top, top song, and whenever it came on the radio Andrew would turn the volume knob to full and he and I would sing along with gusto much to the bemusement of the others.

In the late morning on Wednesday, May 2, 1984, we all piled into The Flying Turd and headed out of Leeds to Nottingham where we were starting a 30-date UK and European tour at the legendary Rock City, a venue I would come to know and love over the ensuing years. As we were hitting the M1 on-ramp in Leeds city centre we spied two soon-to-be-familiar figures with their thumbs out trying to hitch a ride. We knew where they were going. They were part of the ever-growing legion that were following the band from show to show. We'd sometimes stop and pick them up and give them a ride. They became known to us as Hard Shoulder Beverley and Red Adair, the latter because she, obviously, had red hair. We were nothing if not imaginative, eh? They were both recent converts to the cause as were a fair proportion of the regular faces we began to see in the audience every night.

On these early tours we would fraternise with the audience post show and as a result came to know a fair number of them quite well, some in the biblical sense, with many post-show parties in the hotel room occupied by me and Craig. By this time the powers that be, namely Andrew, had given up trying to keep Craig and I apart and just booked us a room to share on the nights we were staying in hotels and not driving back to Leeds. Mark and Andrew both enjoyed single rooms.

The tour passed in a haze of alcohol and white powders and I have very little memory of any of the specific shows. We played exactly the same set as we'd played in the US except we dropped 'Gimme, Gimme, Gimme (A Man After Midnight)' because we knew the audience would appreciate the irony and we, ironically, preferred it when they didn't. We replaced it with my favourite, 'Gimme Shelter'. The main set wouldn't change from night to night, but as an encore we varied between Suicide's 'Ghost Rider' or the Velvet's 'Sister Ray' or a combination of the two.

Unbeknownst to me at the time was that a small coterie of Sisters fans didn't like the more expansive direction the band was taking with me in its ranks, preferring the previous incarnation with Ben Gunn strumming his barre chords. But would I have cared if I had known? Nah. As far as I was concerned we were moving forward, we were now more musical, more dynamic and I considered myself an integral component in what was fast becoming a brilliant live band with a fanatical audience. Rightly or wrongly, there are always casualties in the pursuit of progress. As any government will have you believe.

Early in the tour, third show in to be precise, at Manchester University there was a delay in soundchecking due to a PA malfunction so, to alleviate the boredom, Craig and I drank the bottle of vodka demanded on our rider. And just carried on drinking until it was time to hit the stage by which time we could barely stand up. During the show Craig climbed up on top of his huge Ampeg stack and at a particularly dramatic moment jumped in the air. As his feet hit the stage the impact made him throw up all over the front row of the audience. He didn't miss a beat.

Another amusing moment, for everybody else if not for me, was when I was playing the rock star by standing on the wedge monitor at the lip of the stage, leaning over the audience thrashing away at my guitar. Craig came up behind me, gently nudged me on my backside with the point of his winkle-picker and I toppled into the audience, guitar an' all. Mayhem. Of course there was a postmortem after the show and it was decreed by management, Andrew, that from now on the spirits and wine on the rider would not be delivered to the dressing room until an hour before stage time. That taught us.

On Sunday, May 13, we had a night off and as we'd played Glasgow the previous night and were on our way to Norwich the following day we stopped off for a quiet night at home. Except I didn't have a quiet night at home, did I? The Cult were playing in Leeds at the Bierkeller so Craig and I donned our glad rags and caught the bus into town to go see 'em. With introductions made we shared a few drinks with them after the show and that was the start of a long association with The Cult for Craig and I. Billy Duffy, in particular, became a very good friend of mine over the next few years. Typically, the 'Dritch absolutely deplored the fact that we were fraternising with a band he considered the enemy.

In Plymouth there was an incident with a sadist that got her kicks inflicting pain with a beer bottle that left me walking bloodied and bow-legged. Much to the rest of the band's mirth it was salt baths and sanitary pads for me for a week.

In Birmingham Craig and I had a bit of a shindig in our hotel room after the show and started showing off to our guests with acts of mindless vandalism. The next morning Dave, our tour manager, went down to reception and asked to speak with the hotel manager.

"I'm sorry but we seemed to have had a bit of an incident with a wardrobe," he explained.

"Oh, that's okay, I'll take a look at it. Which room is it in, sir?"

"Well, actually, it's not in a room. It's in a tree outside."

Craig and I had our wages docked to pay for the damage. That taught us as well.

At the Hunky Dory in Detmold there was an after-show party in our honour. Most of the audience were invited. Consumption was rampant, everyone was having fun. Then Andrew and I got into a squabble, about what I have no memory but it wasn't particularly unusual, and that evening's bacchanalia was over. I woke up the next morning on the floor under a table in the club. The club was dark and empty. I spied a light peaking under a door so I knocked.

A voice from within: "Hello?"

I entered the room. It was an office, and there sat last night's promoter. "Where is everybody?"

"Oh, they've all gone. You left the band last night, you don't remember?"

"Shit, no."

I had just a few minutes to get to our hotel before The Flying Turd was due to leave for the next town. I borrowed a few Deutschmarks, caught a cab and made it with seconds to spare. They were already in their seats waiting for Dave to settle the hotel bill and they'd be off. And they were gonna leave without me, the bastards. I grabbed my bag from my room and joined 'em on the Turd with no one saying a word during the whole journey from Detmold to Bochum. No 'Careless Whisper' that day.

It was on this tour that I first played the Zeche in Bochum, Germany, perhaps my favourite venue on the continent. Depeche Mode were in town with a night off so they came down to see us and after the show I went out with Daryl Bamonte, Depeche's right-hand man, who was celebrating his 21st birthday. Somehow the evening ended with just him and I, deserted by our compadres. A few years later Daryl informed me that he woke up the next morning in the gutter. He'd lost his memory of the night before, his jacket and his new, expensive watch that his mum had given him for his birthday.

Despite this unfortunate beginning Daryl and I would become very good friends to the extent that I would give away his bride, Alison, at their wedding on a boat in Newport Beach during a lull in a US tour by The Cure with whom he was working at the time. Daryl, incidentally, is the younger brother of Perry who played guitar with The Cure for years in the Nineties and beyond. More of Daryl another time.

See, these are the things that I remember from touring, not whether we played 'Sister Ray' or 'Ghost Rider'. I think it's the same for every touring musician. We remember the really great shows and the truly rotten ones but everything in between is a blur and it's generally the incidents offstage that distinguish one day from another.

Flushed with the advance from WEA we'd gone out and bought ourselves a new Dr Avalanche, our drum machine to the uninformed, and it was on this tour we started using it in place of the less reliable cassette porta-studio that we'd used until now to run the drum tracks. The Oberheim DMX was the instrument that Dead Or Alive had purchased when we had made the move from human to machine providing rhythm for us. Because of my previous experience in programming the DMX it was thought prudent that we, the Sisters, furnish ourselves with the same so as to avoid any steep learning curves and endless hours perusing indecipherable manuals. It became part of my job to programme all the old songs, and the new, into the new Doktor and to press the start and stop buttons on stage. In practical terms this meant that it freed up Craig to drink more between songs which, of course, he did, a habit he persists with to this day.

Dave Allen, with whom I had worked with Dead Or Alive, was flown out to Amsterdam on Saturday, June 2, by WEA to see the band at the legendary Melkweg venue. On a rare occasion when I was asked my opinion I vouched for Dave, who had just produced The Cure, as being a more than suitable candidate to produce the Sisters album we were due to start recording once the tour had ended.

During the show Dave was perched atop the PA stack smoking freshly acquired hash from a local head shop. I had clambered onto the shoulders of Jez, one of our guitar techs, who walked out into the audience with me still playing guitar without dropping a note. Dave also remembers yours truly manually kicking up the tempo and changing drum patterns live on the DMX while playing guitar. Clever boy. "A perfect singer performance" was how he describes Andrew on stage that evening, and I'm sure it was, what with Andrew being in particularly good form on that tour.

After the show Dave took us all for a wander, my first, around the red light district of Amsterdam where we ended up drinking Chimay Blue in Big John's Fat City, a hostel previously known to Dave. The next day, while we travelled onto Groningen, Dave flew back to Heathrow and was busted for dope possession on re-entry into the UK. That same day WEA received a fax from us stating, "The Sisters say yes to Dave Allen". Dave had got the job but what a poisoned chalice it proved to be.

With the tour ending early June we made our way back to Leeds and, apart from a brief sojourn to the London BBC Maida Vale studios to record a John Peel session on the 19th, we spent our time honing the new songs we were planning to record for the album. Scheduled for an autumn release and with a working title of *Black October* we had maybe ten to 12 tunes, mostly written by myself and Mark. Craig contributed a little here and there but the biggest surprise of all was the lack of songs that Andrew put forward for consideration.

Now, Andrew could hardly be considered prolific, sometimes taking up to six months to finesse a set of lyrics to finality and he was not unknown to spend two weeks on a single note of feedback in the studio, but his contribution thus far to the band's recorded output had been huge and masterful. The biggest problem for Andrew was a distinct lack of time to work on new songs as he'd been so caught up, mostly by choice I hasten to add what with his natural disinclination to delegate, with the business end of things for the previous six months and more.

By the time we went into Strawberry Studios at the end of June to begin work on the album Andrew had only two partially completed sets of lyrics, 'Walk Away' and 'No Time To Cry', two of the four songs we had recorded for Peelie. In the absence of lyrics for the other songs Andrew encouraged Mark and I to try and put words to the tunes we had written. Having had only limited experience of writing lyrics it didn't come easy to me and I struggled to come up with anything meaningful. 'Dance On Glass' was a set of words I did manage but they were eventually replaced by Andrew and so became 'Black Planet', and that was my solitary lyrical contribution at the time. Mark was more adept than me at writing words, as evidenced by the very pointed lyric of his song, 'Poison Door', which strongly indicated his disenchantment with the way things were between himself and Andrew. At least that's how I read it.

During our time in Stockport, five weeks in all, we were billeted in a boarding house just a short taxi ride from the studio. I was sharing a room with Craig and Mark, although I have very little recollection of Mark actually being there during the recording of the album. He must've been though because I can hear his guitar playing on the record so I'm going to assume that, for the duration, Mark commuted between Wakefield and Stockport on a regular basis. It's fair to say that by this point tension between Mark and Andrew had reached a critical level and an already challenging situation was exacerbated with Andrew isolating himself from all of us more and more as time passed and Mark largely absenting himself from proceedings.

Andrew was supposed to be sharing with Dave Allen. According to Dave he and Andrew, "Got totally monged on grass and blue label vodka" on the first night in their room together. "It was very uncomfortable, we already didn't get on," added the producer. So much so it seems that the very next morning Andrew moved out of the boarding house and into a tiny office in the basement of the studio, with one gold disc on the wall, St Winifred's Choir's 'There's No One Quite Like Grandma'. Andrew didn't see the light of day for the next five weeks.

When he saw us play live in Amsterdam Dave was mightily impressed by the power of Dr Avalanche through a large sound system and he came up with the novel idea of hiring in a PA and setting it up in the studio so he could run the drums through it and mic it up. Good idea, right? Dave and the engineer, Chris Nagle, spent three days wiring, setting up microphones, patching everything through to the studio and getting a workable sound to start the sessions. Towards the end of the third day we took a break and went to the pub for a quick pint and a packet of crisps. During our absence Chris suffered a diabetic meltdown and, zeroing the desk, un-patched the whole studio and piled all the cables on the floor in a massive heap. On his return from the pub Dave freaked. We had just lost three day's work.

From then on we went 24/7 with two assistants on call, Chris working the night shift and young tape-op Nigel Beverley the day. Alas, the PA idea was dumped. We soon settled into a routine of me and Craig and, I assume, Mark working during the daytime hours while Andrew would beaver away through the night, with poor ol' Dave having to straddle both shifts. Typically I would start work at around 11am and continue until 8pm when Andrew would surface with Dave coming in at, say, 2pm having been working with the 'Dritch until maybe 4 or 5am. Seven days a week, no days off. It was a tough schedule, more so for Dave than anyone else.

We were allowed a per diem* of £2 which barely paid for a packet of fags let alone being able to eat. We did manage to get by with Craig and I pooling our resources and subsidising our PDs with our wages, £20 per week, and living off whizz,

---

* Per diems, also known as PDs, are a daily allowance paid to the individual to cover daily expenses such as eating, drinking and entertainment.

ciggies and a cheap bottle of wine a night. A trip to the local Chinese or Indian was a luxury once or twice a week. With insufficient funds to go out of an evening, after finishing work Craig and I, unwilling to return to the dismal boarding house, spent our time working our way through the video library in the downstairs lounge area. A firm favourite we'd watch regularly was Cheech & Chong's hilarious *Up In Smoke*. I watched it again just a couple of years ago and while I giggled like a stoned teenager at certain scenes I would have to concede that it's not aged very well. At the time we thought it was the best thing we'd ever seen.

As most of the tunes were already written and previously demoed we just got on with recording them as best we could, not knowing what Andrew would be singing and where. It's sometimes difficult to work like that as where I thought a chorus would be Andrew might think of it as a verse, or what I thought of as an intro and instrumental interlude Andrew would use as a chorus. Still, it ultimately worked but we did have to go through purgatory to get there.

Originally released only on vinyl and cassette, the final album is more or less divided into my tunes on side one with Mark's on side two. I know that I ended up playing much of the guitar on Mark's tunes because of his sporadic presence in the studio, basically copying his guitar lines from his demos. There are some brilliant guitar riffs in among Mark's tunes; 'First And Last And Always', 'Some Kind Of Stranger' and 'Nine While Nine' coming to mind in particular.* In a technical sense, Mark was not as good a player as I was, probably not even as good as

---

* While *FALAA* is, in my not-so-humble opinion, a great guitar record I do have to concede that there is no guitar riff on the album that is as monstrously brilliant as Andrew's guitar riff on 'Alice', an earlier TSOM single. I *loved* playing that guitar part live.

Andrew, but he had a style, and energy, that was uniquely his and he came up with some great songs. I did get on well with Mark and, unlike most bands that have two guitarists, there was no clash of egos between us. I believe there was a healthy respect from both of us for what the other could bring to the table. I think the only competition between us was to see who could come up with the better songs and that… was healthy.

One morning I recorded the backing track for what we'd been calling 'Dance On Glass', adding a few extra guitar and piano parts that weren't on the demo. Finishing the track early and finding myself alone in the studio I started working on a new simple bass line that I had just come up with. I set the DMX to play a very straight-forward bum-twat-bum-twat rhythm and recorded the bass line adding additional sections as I went along. With the bass completed I started overdubbing guitar parts, six and 12-string electric, and e-bow, a little piano and very soon had this glorious sounding backing track. It was alchemy at work, I was in the flow and inspired. It's rare but it's wonderful and you have no choice but to surrender yourself to it when it happens. The whole song was written and recorded within the space of, maybe, a couple of hours. Neither Mark or Craig played on it as neither of them were around at the time.

Dave came in later and loved what I had done with both songs and helped me to tidy up the tracks and bung down rough mixes to tape. When Andrew surfaced in the early evening he asked what we'd done that day and so we played him the two tracks. Firstly, the one with the working title of 'Dance On Glass'. He sat in the producers chair in front of the desk and listened. When it finished he swivelled his chair around and said, "Don't like it. You've added too many new guitar parts and I hate that piano. Next."

Whatever.

Dave played the new song. Again, Andrew listened intently. When the song had finished he was quiet for a moment and then, leaning back, he remarked, "Nah, it sounds like the Banshees. Anything else?"

"Nope, that's all I've done today, just the two backing tracks," I replied. "Sorry. I'll try to do better tomorrow," I added, dripping sarcasm.

As I was leaving the studio Dave followed me out and tried to cheer me up by telling me the songs were brilliant and not to be too disheartened about Andrew's reaction as he was not liking anything any of us was doing at the time. Absolutely nothing. In hindsight I think Andrew's attitude was fuelled by a feeling that he was not in control of all that was going on, compounded by his amphetamine use, his increasing isolation, and, maybe most severely of all, lack of daylight.

Feeling deflated and wondering why I bothered I went back to the boarding house early that night to lick my wounds and watch some crappy TV on my own. Craig wasn't there, he must've popped back to Leeds for a few days, so I didn't even have my mate to bitch to about soddin' Von and his disdain for *everything and everyone.*

Next morning I woke up and had breakfast at Mrs Miggin's boarding house, tea and toast more than likely, dreading going into the studio that day. I felt like doing what Mark and Craig had done and just fuck off back to Leeds for a few days to get away from the bugger and the oppressive black cloud that was hanging over the studio. But I knew we still had a lot of work to do if we were to make the scheduled October release date. Plus I didn't think it'd be fair to leave Dave alone with our paranoid, maudlin, misery-guts of a singer.

Walking into the studio that morning all was quiet. Nigel, the engineer, was sat reading a newspaper. I asked him to put up the multitrack of the song with the working title of 'Dance On Glass'. We hit play and lo and behold there were finished vocals on the track and the song was now evidently called 'Black Planet'. Astonished at this turn of events and overjoyed with, at last, some progress being made I asked Nigel to thread up the new song. Andrew's deep baritone began, "In a sea of faces…" and I nearly cried at how beautiful it was. Again, I was flabbergasted. Another finished vocal. The song, of course, was now called 'Marian'.

Not bad for a day's work, eh? 'Black Planet' and 'Marian'. And it's a perfect example of synergy, of how artistic tension, conflict, can provoke stunning results. When 'Black Planet' was eventually mixed to Andrew's liking all the extra guitar parts and the piano I recorded were all included, with the piano actually the very first thing you hear at the start of the album. Apart from one extra guitar overdub that Andrew played towards the end of the song, 'Marian' was as I had recorded it in that gush of inspiration.

Of writing the lyrics for 'Marian' Andrew was quoted as saying, "'Marian' is a very special song. It's not like any of the other songs. I wrote it in ten minutes. Usually the lyrics take me up to half a year."

And therein that sentence lies the crux of our biggest problem with finishing the album.

With the recording of the music left in the capable hands of myself, Craig and Mark, it was assumed that Andrew would use the quiet, night-time hours to write the lyrics and record his vocals. Except he didn't. Procrastinating, he would, driving Dave insane, spend all night obsessively working on the eq of a bass drum or the reverb for a snare. Stuff that didn't really need to be addressed until we were ready to mix and that was still a long way off. A lovely wry comment attributed to Mark perhaps best sums up the situation: "We could've recorded a double album in the time it took Eldritch to get a headphone balance he was happy with."

We encountered a couple of technical problems along the way, one of which was Dave blowing up most of the outboard effects attempting to make a sound that would weave through the whole of 'Some Kind Of Stranger'. In the end he only managed to record enough for the intro before the gear went kaput. Andrew didn't like the sound anyway, of course, but Dave put his producer's foot down and kept it in when the track was eventually mixed. Another problem we had with 'Some Kind Of Stranger' was that because the tempo of the song was so slow the Doktor wouldn't lock to the time code that had been recorded to tape so I had to spend a day re-programming the drums at double speed. That was an interesting brain exercise.

One thing I introduced to the proceedings was essentially the same thing that I had introduced to Dead Or Alive. On the song that came to be known as 'A Rock And A Hard Place' I played the bass with a triggered gate over it to give it that clean, sequenced duh-duh-duh, duh-duh-duh which propels the song in a very mechanical way. This time though, introducing the sequencer effect into the equation didn't ultimately lose me my job. 'ARAAHP' heavily featured an acoustic guitar that I was playing at the time, an El Rio. The El Rio was Fender's budget acoustic but it was one of the first on the market to boast in-built pick-ups. It wasn't particularly good sounding as an acoustic but it had this unique crystalline brittleness to it that was perfect for the Sisters' album. You can hear it on 'Black Planet' too as well as 'Marian' and 'Possession'. I wish I still had it.

The other guitars I was using on *FALAA* were the Aria electric 12-string, a black Fender Telecaster and Andrew's pride and joy, a vintage black Gibson Les Paul, all put through a Roland JC120 amp. The effects would've been the standard Boss compressor, phaser, distortion with my Memory Man Deluxe. I would've used the studio effects, such as the MXR flanger/ phaser, and Eventide and AMS boxes that Strawberry had in their racks. I also used an autoharp on the album but not in the conventional way, i.e. chords. I'd work out the notes of guitar lines and tune the strings of the autoharp to those specific notes and double the guitar part. Tucked in behind the guitar in the mix it gives the part a shimmer, an open resonance that the guitar alone wouldn't. It's probably most evident on the title track and 'Possession' and a neat studio trick that I have employed time and time again.

As the studio also boasted a beautiful grand piano I ended up playing that on a few tracks too, most notably as far as I'm concerned, on the wonderful 'Nine While Nine'. Mark's guitar playing on this song is superlative and I was proud to be able to add a few additional guitar parts as well as the piano to what is arguably Andrew's finest lyric and vocal on the album.

We also recorded a basic version of live favourite 'Emma' as a potential future B-side. WEA were trying to persuade us to release our version of Hot Chocolate's classic as a single but our feeling was that it was too obvious and a bit of a cheap trick just to secure a hit. We'd prefer to break the Top 40 with one of our own songs. 'Emma' was to remain unfinished until we came back to it almost a year later.

By the time it came for us to leave Strawberry at the very end of July we were still a long way from the album being finished. Andrew had maybe finalised the lyrics and completed vocals for three or four songs, as well as 'Emma' and Mark's 'Poison Door'. It was a slow and painful process and in the meantime it seemed as though the band was quietly disintegrating in an atmosphere of isolation, paranoia, and mistrust.

Craig and, even more so, Mark were both absent from the studio for long stretches of time. Andrew was hidden away in his bunker in the basement, some days never appearing until we had all disappeared for the night. Even though I was the new boy, I sometimes felt like I was holding the whole thing together in the face of a seemingly inevitable collapse.

We needed to get out, get some air, play some shows and remember we were a band. Fortunately for us we were due back in NYC at the beginning of August to play a couple of shows, a much needed respite from the insularity of being locked away in the studio for weeks on end.

CHAPTER 16

Treasure The Moments Touched With Joy (But Remember The Moments Tarnished & Stained)

PLAYLIST:

1. 2000 Light Years From Home – Danse Society

2. Second Skin – The Chameleons   3. Purple Rain – Prince

4. Big New Prinz – The Fall   5. Amphetamine Logic – TSOM

6. Walk Away – TSOM   7. No Time To Cry – TSOM

8. Blood Money – TSOM   9. Bury Me Deep – TSOM   10. Freedom – Wham!

11. You Spin Me Round (Like A Record) – Dead Or Alive

12. Possession – TSOM

Escaping from the studio, on the first weekend of August 1984, we flew back to NYC. We were due to play the Irving Plaza as part of the New Music Seminar. First launched in 1980 the NMS was an annual music conference and festival, gathering together record label bosses and personnel, producers and musicians, for daily lectures, debates, Q&As and quorums, which became ostensibly a week long piss-up in the Big Apple.

In the evenings, the NMS put on showcase gigs throughout the city by up-and-coming bands for its attendees. That's what we were there for. We were sharing the bill with two other bands from the north of England – The Chameleons from Manchester, and Barnsley's Danse Society. The organisers wanted the iridescent Chameleons to open the show followed by Barnsley's finest with us to close it. But Danse Society took umbrage at this suggestion, claiming that as they were bigger than TSOM they should close the show. They may well have been bigger at the time but, if this was indeed the case, it was largely because they had an unfeasibly pretty frontman in Steve Rawlings, as opposed to the quality of their music. Anyway, we didn't care, it was fine with us. Go ahead, lads, fill yer boots. If we go on earlier it means we finish earlier and can get to the party that's going on at the Danceteria afterwards. As it happens, the place was rammed when we were on stage and then the weirdest thing occurred. As soon as we finished our show everyone left to go to the parties that were going on elsewhere around town. Danse Society ended up playing to just a handful of people. I'm not one to gloat so I'll just leave it there.

Now... in researching this book I came across a lot of apocryphal bunkum written about my time in TSOM, from know-it-alls purporting to, ahem, know it all. I applaud them for their endeavour and zealousness but how anyone can state as fact what went on is beyond me. I'm not attempting to rewrite history here or recast myself as anything other than the villain of the piece that certain factions of the Sisters audience still see me. I couldn't care less what that bigoted, sour bunch think.

But I will say this. None of the protagonists involved can remember the exact sequence of events. We all have *our* own truths and somewhere in the middle of it all is the *real* truth. A little bit of enthusiastic online sleuthing by a fan does not a fact make. Just as I'd advise the reader not to take what I've written as fact. It's just *my* truth. None of us had any idea of the future significance that the recording of *FALAA* would hold for the legion so no one attempted to chronicle at the time its making and attendant tour dates. In the absence of diaries we rely on memory as best we can and that is nebulous for sure.

So, while I wouldn't swear on the bible I am fairly certain that we had another show the following weekend at the Ritz in NYC.* The outcome was that, while Andrew donned his metaphorical record-company-owners' hat and attended various NMS lectures and seminars, the rest of us had the best part of a week off in the city to entertain ourselves.

Once again we were at the Iroquois Hotel replete with its malfunctioning ACs and armies of cockroaches. During those few days I made my first pilgrimage to the Dakota building where John Lennon was gunned down at the front entrance in December 1980. It was a sobering and quasi-mystical experience for such an avowed Lennon devotee as I. Mark and I went to the cinema in Times Square to see the newly released Prince film, *Purple Rain*. The audience were up and dancing around and singing along to all the songs, just like a gig, and there was an extended ovation at the film's conclusion with everyone on their feet a'clappin' and a'whoopin' and a'hollerin'. I've never witnessed anything like it before or since.

---

* Further research after finishing this particular chapter proved that, yes indeed, we did play a second show in NYC this week at the Ritz; a support slot to Black Flag. And I have to say that I found Henry Rollins to be perhaps the most obnoxious, belligerent oaf I've ever had the misfortune to come across in all the years of sharing the bill with other bands. Our paths crossed again a few years later when he was low on the bill at The Mission's headline Finsbury Park show in 1991 and he was, again, needlessly bellicose and offensive. Maybe he considers his boorishness as funny but I've never really believed or seen merit in his graceless shtick. He'll probably duff me up now the next time he sees me.

272

My 'special' friend Terri flew in from Chicago to spend a few days. You remember, she with the waterbed. I guess by this point you could say that Terri and I were an 'item' although I would have to make it clear that the relationship wasn't exactly exclusive, certainly not on my part at least.

At my invitation Terri would come to England later in the year to visit me in Leeds. During her stay we went to Manchester to visit her best friend, Brix, who was married at the time to the iconoclastic Mark E. Smith, singer of The Fall. We traveled by train and were met at the station by Brix and Mark who then drove us to their small terraced home. Immediately on arrival lines of speed were chopped out and it was decreed that us two boys would go down the pub so the girls could have a little time to themselves for a natter. Fine with us.

Suitably chemically refreshed we ambled down the street to Mark's local. Mark was good company, his world view hysterical if not a little curmudgeonly, but that just added to his singular charm. Between laughs and pints we snuck off to the toilets for a white line top up every now and then. He had heard *of* the Sisters but professed to have not heard us. I, of course, had heard of and listened to The Fall but unlike most of my peers I was no great fan. While I could understand their esoteric appeal I never really got it myself. I think that says more about me and my more populist tastes than it does The Fall.

Anyway, pint after pint and I eventually had to concede defeat. Despite being no slouch in the drinking department Mark E. Smith drank me under the table. With Terri on my arm I left for Leeds the next morning laden down with Fall records and a blinding hangover. Weirdly, I never bumped into Mark again despite later being on the same record label for a number of years and occasionally appearing at the same festivals. And

273

things between Terri and I quickly fizzled out, one of those "we should have just left it as a good bounce about on a waterbed" scenarios, and she returned to Chicago never to be seen or heard from again.

Back in the UK after our NY trip and we were really up against it to get the album finished in time for its scheduled October release. We had a huge UK and European tour announced to coincide, with tickets already on sale. It was unthinkable that the album wouldn't be ready in time. With that in mind we were booked into Genetic Studios in the bucolic Berkshire countryside. I'd worked there previously while with Dead Or Alive. It was where I'd first met Dave Allen, the house engineer. Craig and I were booked into a picturesque riverside B&B pub in nearby Goring-On-Thames. Again, Mark was largely conspicuous by his absence while Andrew once more found a cupboard in the studio to nightly lay his hat.

With pretty much all the backing tracks already completed the plan was for Andrew to finish writing the lyrics and record the vocals while Dave would get on with mixing the tracks as and when they were finished. Again, progress was painfully slow.

Highlights were few and far between. The only thing I remember recording at Genetic was the slashing guitar chords of 'Amphetamine Logic' for which I put my telecaster through a huge Leslie speaker that was in the studio.* A couple of blissful sultry, sunny afternoons were spent laying in the verdant tall grass of the riverbank smoking joints and supping cider from

---

* More typically used in conjunction with a Hammond organ, the Leslie is an amplifier-loudspeaker system that modifies the sound by rotating the speakers, the speed of which is selected by the user from a front panel switch, typically either chorale or tremolo.

plastic bottles with Craig and a most-becoming barmaid we'd befriended at the pub where we were staying.

One lyric and vocal that Andrew did finish at Genetic was 'Some Kind Of Stranger'. According to Dave it took two whole days to record that vocal. And then, while Andrew slunk away to hibernate in his lair, Dave mixed the song. After a few hours Dave had a mix with which he was happy. He called Craig and I into the studio and made us sit on the couch at the back of the control room. He turned off the lights, hit play on the tape machine and, with the track playing back at full volume, lit a match and set the SSL mixing desk ablaze. It was an awesome immersive sonic and visual experience that left Craig and I giggling on the couch while we gave Dave the thumbs up. Of course the SSL was undamaged, the blaze being superficial. He had dowsed the desk with lighter fluid and once the flames had burnt off the liquid then the fire extinguished itself. It was obviously a trick that Dave had employed before to entertain easily impressed simpleton clients such as Craig and I. It's not a trick I'd suggest trying at home though, kids... Not averse to moments of wackiness, this crowning achievement earned Dave the new nickname of Trolley, as in "He's off his..."

Jill Furmanovsky, the renowned photographer of rock stars, came to the studio one afternoon to take photos of us for the album sleeve. There was a wooded area adjacent to the studio and Jill managed to persuade the vampiric Eldritch (he wouldn't have done it for us) to venture out into the daylight and together the four of us struck some moody poses amidst the trees.* We also posed for individual portraits in the studio that were eventually used on the inner sleeve. There was obviously a competition going on between Craig and I to see who could

---

* It's one of Jill's photos from this session that adorns the front cover of this book.

erect the biggest hair. I think I won courtesy of Aquanet Extra Super Hold. Another competition was for the gaudiest shirt for which Craig surely took the prize with Mark running him a close second.

These minor diversions aside all was evidently not well with Andrew in the studio. He was falling increasingly ill and spending long hours hiding away and sleeping. Obviously the impending deadline was making him sick. He had taken on an enormous workload over the previous 12 months and now it was finally taking its toll. Dave remembers that on the last night in Genetic we were all booked into one room at the B&B with Andrew curled up on the floor, shivering and blue, wrapped in a curtain. Dave went to the studio and called for a doctor.

Mark remembers the situation differently. Mark claims that he made the decision to pull the sessions at Genetic before the completion of the vocals and mixing, causing the now inevitable delay in the album's release. The reason was that on a visit to the studio, perhaps for the Furmanovsky photo shoot, he was alarmed at the physical deterioration in his erstwhile friend and former housemate. Mark, in a throwback to earlier days when he was Andrew's equal partner, would've been the only one, apart from Andrew himself, that could make that call. A brave one it was too, putting the October–November tour in jeopardy as well as postponing the album release date to the new year and thereby throwing WEA's carefully planned promotion campaign into disarray. Of course Andrew didn't thank him but, as Mark remarked, "I wouldn't expect it of him anyway." I suspect there is some truth in both Mark's and Dave's retelling of events. Me? I can't bloody remember, I was no doubt too out of it.

We had another pressing concern to consider. We were due to play a couple of festivals in Germany at the beginning of September, low on the bill to Frank Zappa and Rory Gallagher.

Could Andrew recover in time, and enough, to perform? No one was sure, least of all Andrew himself. Andrew suggested that maybe we could find another singer for the shows. Not ideal but something we considered. Mark suggested that maybe he and I could share the vocals. We even had a rehearsal where we tried out the idea but, if truth be known, it was useless. Most of the guitar lines were too intricate to play while singing as well. Plus neither of us were anywhere nearly good enough. We aborted the idea. As it happened, Andrew rallied and we played the two festivals without incident or relapse.

We then had a couple of weeks, during which Andrew recuperated somewhat, before we joined Echo & The Bunnymen, Spear Of Destiny and The Chameleons at York Racecourse on a windy, damp Saturday, memorable for three incidents.

Firstly, gremlins were afoot during our show and the Doktor threw a few wobblers. Maybe, like his lord & master Eldritch, he didn't like being out in the daylight. Anyway, we coaxed him into staying on his metaphorical drum stool with the promise of a shiny new flight case for future touring and, with a reboot or two, he muddled through the show. As did we.

It's fair to say we weren't at our best that day and our misery was compounded by a whipping wind that played havoc with our carefully coiffured hair despite the Aquanet. Playing in the daytime was not our forte and we wouldn't do it again.

Secondly, Ian McCulloch got beaten up by the security after the Bunnymen set for deservedly twatting one of them with his mic stand during their show for being overly aggressive with members of the audience.

And lastly and least of all, on our way back to Leeds that evening in The Flying Turd Andrew ceremoniously handed us a fiver (£5) each as a bonus with the instruction, "Here you are, boys, go out and enjoy yourselves tonight."

"Thanks," we replied in unison, but not in earnest. His generosity was and always would be spectacularly underwhelming.

With Andrew returning to, if not rude health, then certainly health good enough to embark on a 35-date tour, we set off on Thursday, October 4, to Edinburgh Caley Palais, the first night of the Black October tour. There was never really any serious consideration to cancel the tour with the postponement of the release of the album. The dates had been announced months before and tickets had been sold – a lot of tickets.

Again, the tour passed in a blizzard of amphetamine and an ocean of booze. By this time I had well and truly bought into the lifestyle of debauched hedonism. After years and years of living with repression and religious guilt, I had finally shaken off those shackles to become the clichéd licentious, degenerate, promiscuous rock star – everything my mother had feared I'd become. And I can honestly say that the time I was playing guitar with The Sisters Of Mercy is the only time in my life I have truly felt 'cool'.

Being cool is a weird one though because to *try* and be cool is seriously uncool. Being cool has to be natural and not contrived. There is the 'studied' cool though that sometimes works, studied in this case meaning nicking little bits of other people's cool to assimilate into a persona that appears cool but is in actual fact just a cover-up designed to conceal the lack of a strong personality. A bit like method acting. Just like Robert De Niro, say. A brilliant actor who, I suspect, in real life to be a little bit dreary. I could be wrong of course.

Let's look at it like this: Ian McCulloch is cool, Julian Cope is not. Jim Reid of JAMC is cool, Bobby Gillespie, nope. The Cure's Robert Smith is cutely cool while Dave Gahan of Depeche Mode tries so hard he comes across as American – not cool. Ian Brown of Stone Roses is cool, Liam Gallagher, nah. Bowie was cool, Iggy not so. I'd say that Mac, Reid, Smithy, Brown, Bowie, are all 'studied cool' to varying degrees while Copey, Bobby, Gahan, Liam, and Iggy are open, flawed, human and not afraid to make an ass out of themselves. And that in itself is the pinnacle of coolness.

There are some that have absolutely no hope in my book (and this *is* my book): Jim Kerr, Chris Martin, Bono, Mark King... to name just a few. And then there are those that transcend "to be cool or not to be cool": Thom Yorke, Nick Cave, Morrissey, Johnny Marr, Mark Hollis, PJ Harvey, Robert Del Naja, Siouxsie, Bjork, ah, you know who they are.

Where I fall on this spectrum of cool I have no idea. I long ago gave up trying to work it out, but when I was a guitarist in TSOM I was definitely cool and I *knew* it. Before TSOM being cool was something I aspired to. I craved to be invited to sit at the head table; the table at the bottom of the stairs at Eric's on a raised dais where the local self-appointed royalty sat and held court, a table to which I was never invited. Instead of being Steve McQueen-like I was more Woody Allen. When I later became singer with The Mission I lost my cool. I became too self-conscious, a caricature of who I thought I had to be; a persona I adopted to cover up my insecurities (and there were plenty); a mask I wore to preserve a little of my true self for myself. Anyway, it's all bollocks really, isn't it? As with beauty, 'cool' is all in the eye of the beholder, right?

'Walk Away', the first single from the album, was one of my tunes we'd been playing live since my first show with the band back in April. The song was one of the very few that was completed at Strawberry earlier in the summer and mixed early during our time at Genetic. Coupled with Mark's 'Poison Door' on the B-side, it was released in early October to coincide with the tour. Like its predecessor, 'Body And Soul', it failed to breach the UK Top 40 singles chart, peaking at number 45 the same week that Wham! hit number one with 'Freedom'.

On the Black October tour Craig and I caught crabs. Horrible little fuckers, those things are. They really are tiny little crabs and a nightmare to get rid of. Where and how we caught them neither of us know. We were sharing hotel rooms again and so I've always contended that I caught the buggers from Craig while he's positive that I passed 'em onto him. We shall never know. The upside of this unfortunate state of affairs was that Andrew refused to travel with us. And really, who could blame him? No longer subjected to endless hours of Stevie Nicks and Foreigner, Craig, Mark, and I revelled in the new found freedom of being able to listen to Motörhead, The Stooges, Hendrix and Zeppelin.

Mark took over the navigation in Andrew's absence while Craig and I sat in the back in our underpants slathered with crab, and self-esteem, destroying ointment all over the areas of our bodies where we had hair. Sound guy Pete Turner, whose wife Sue was a nurse, advised us to wear shower caps on our heads all day so as to trap any of the little buggers that attempted to escape their grisly fate. Weeks later Pete admitted he had made that up so as to give the crew a laugh when we turned up for soundcheck wearing shower caps. Bastard. After about a week we'd managed to get rid of the blighters. Andrew rejoined us in The Flying Turd and it was back to Fleetwood Mac.

It was during this tour that the Victims Of Circumstance were born. Minor mishaps would happen to me, just things like being late for the Turd, guests emptying the mini-bar in my room, losing my itinerary and AAA pass, being caught in flagrante, that kind of thing, and during chastisement I would plead my innocence by claiming to be a victim of circumstance. It stuck and became the tour's catch-phrase and whenever anyone was caught doing something they shouldn't they simply recited, "I'm just a victim of circumstance". When later compiling cassettes of new songs, rough mixes and various covers we'd recorded I'd label the tapes *The Victims Of Circumstance* and these became a much sought after series of bootlegs. I just thought you might like to know how we got the name.

In Bremen, Germany, we were playing a squat little club on a piece of wasteland near a development of high-rise tenements. While on stage we heard loud banging on the roof, as if it was a particularly heavy hail storm. We were seemingly under attack from a large group of neo-Nazis throwing rocks, bottles and whatever they could get their hands on, at the club. Apparently they were mighty irked at their turf being invaded by an army of black-clad weirdos and decided that we and our audience needed to be taught a lesson. The Polizei were summoned, the neo-Nazis ran off like the cowards they were. When the show ended we got the hell out of there as fast as we could like the cowards *we* were.

After the show in Cologne Craig and I met two American girls whose fathers were in the military and stationed in Germany. They were inseparable. Literally. Hand-cuffed together they were. The one talking with Craig had painted an alluring spider web on her face. They didn't need much persuading to come back with us to our hotel, silver-tongued devils that we were. However, once in our room they refused to unlock their handcuffs so Craig and I had to push our tiny little beds together with the two girls in the middle while Craig and I climbed on from either side. When business was concluded the girls, still hand-cuffed together, got up to leave.

"Why are you leaving so soon?" I asked.

Spider Web Face replied, "Oh, my parents are waiting for us in their car outside."

Gulp.

"Okay, see you then," Craig responded as he hurried them out of the door.

When it came time to check out in the morning we made our way down to the hotel lobby where the crew were sat waiting for their bus to pick them up. All of them had painted a spider's web on their face. "Oh, shut up," was all our bass player could muster in riposte.

With the tour ending in Germany on November 18, Andrew found himself back in the studio a few days later, this time Livingston Studios in Wood Green, London, for one final push to finish the album. As well as relations with Mark having gone up the Swanee, Andrew's relationship with Dave Allen had by now also become very strained and fractious. There were clashes between Andrew and Dave about the mixing and the sound of the album. Some mixes had been completed at Genetic, 'Marian', 'Walk Away', 'Poison Door' and maybe one or two others, but the bulk of the album *still* needed completed vocals. Dave, fearing WEA would hold him culpable for the ongoing delay in the album's completion, began to withdraw to, in his words, "save my career". As a consequence he would never work with WEA again anyway. The house engineer for these sessions was Tony Harris who established a decent working relationship with Andrew and managed to coax finished lyrics and vocals from him.

Rather than spend my nights on the couch at Merciful Release, during this period I would stay with my new best mate, Billy Duffy and his girlfriend, Mitch, in their first floor flat at 28 Dealtry Road, Putney, at least when he was around. Billy had just been awarded a silver disc* for the recently released Cult album *Dreamtime* and, being the Manc that he is, was prone to rubbing my face in his success. Still does.

"Look at this, Hussey, when're you gonna get yerself one of these little beauties then, eh?"

"It won't be long now, mate, just you wait and see," was my pithy retort. (30 bloody years I had to wait, actually, for *FALAA* – see below).

Of course I'd seen silver, gold, and platinum discs adorn the walls of record companies and studios but this was the first time one of my friends had been bestowed the honour and I was mightily impressed although I, of course, didn't let on to my host.

One evening Billy, pitying my lowly financial state, took me out to a new Mexican restaurant in Covent Garden. This was the first time I had ever eaten Mexican and it was to become my favourite food, Billy breaking my cherry so to speak. It was also the first time I saw one of my mates use a credit card, an AMEX, none of us ever having enough money before to qualify for one. When I got my own AMEX a couple of years later in The Mission, the next time I saw Billy I extracted it from my wallet (now that's what a wallet is for!), proudly showing it off to him. He responded by opening his own wallet and showing me his gold AMEX. When I later got to gold he was platinum. Always been playing catch-up to the bugger. Which reminds me. When we were first issued with our AMEX cards in the early years of The Mission, Mick (Brown, the drummer) wryly

---

* The award of a silver disc in the UK is for sales of 60,000 or more. For gold 100,000 or more. For platinum I have no idea as I've never even come close.

observed: "It's bleedin' useless, can't use it anywhere. All I can do is buy petrol and pay for phone sex."

With Andrew having now more or less finished his vocals I'd make the trek up to Wood Green regularly to see how things were progressing in the studio. R.E.M. were in the adjacent room mixing their *Fables Of Reconstruction* album with Joe Boyd a lot faster than we were mixing ours, and I'd spend most of my time hanging around the lounge area. Being in the control room and listening to Von tinker interminably with drum EQs is both very, very tedious and potentially damaging to your mental health. Poor Dave and Tony had to sit there twiddling their thumbs growing increasingly frustrated at the apparent lack of progress while Joe Boyd would bounce in every few hours and say, "That's another mix done."

I do recall that Dave had tried to re-instigate his idea of using a PA to put the drums through while mixing. Andrew had other ideas and the PA was left set up in the studio but unused for the duration at a cost of more than £100 per day. That money could've been spent a lot more wisely. On the occasional hotel room, or an extra gramme or two, for example.

We eventually finished in Livingston sometime in early December. Then there was an issue with the final mix. Having listened to it away from the studio Andrew decided that certain songs needed remixing. Here we bloody well go again. At this point Dave Allen bowed out with the conversation going something like this:

AE: "I don't wanna fight a battle I can't win, Dave."

DA: "No problem."

In truth, and in hindsight, Dave got a rough deal working with us on *FALAA* and wasn't treated very respectfully by certain parties who shall remain nameless. Oh, go on then, by Andrew. Dave would go onto enjoy a long and a varied career as a record producer, his biggest success with The Cure. I kept in touch with him through the years and we later worked together again a few times with The Mission. He remains a good friend of mine and one of my very favourite people, certainly within the duplicitous music business.

Before Christmas Andrew travelled to Munich to remix a couple of the tracks with Reinhold Mack, renowned for his work with Queen and ELO, but, again, the two didn't get on and the sessions proved fruitless. So, with the season of goodwill to all men having just passed it was back into the studio in London, Good Earth on Dean Street, just around the corner from WEA in Soho to be exact. More mixing, more tinkering and tweaking, and with the choice of 'No Time To Cry' as the next single from the album having been made by Andrew, an errant choice in my opinion, mine being either 'Marian' or 'First And Last And Always', B-sides were needed for the release.

Two new songs, 'Blood Money' and 'Bury Me Deep', were written by Andrew for the purpose. As I was around I helped Andrew to record the tracks, playing guitar and helping to programme the drum machine. On the record I was credited as having written the music for 'Blood Money' but I didn't. I was credited as part of the earlier pact between Andrew and myself when I had written the music for 'Body And Soul' but due to extenuating circumstances I agreed to forego the writing credit in lieu of credit on a later song, and 'Blood Money' was that song. I bet 'Body And Soul' has earned Andrew a whole pile more than 'Blood Money' earned me.

While in Good Earth Craig, attempting to broker a peace between Andrew and Mark, paid a visit with Mark in tow. They didn't stay long and little progress was made despite Craig's best diplomatic efforts. It was apparent that Mark didn't really want to be there. I have read that he has since claimed there was some kind of weird bromance going on between Andrew and myself during his visit. I don't know about that but this was the time when Andrew and I probably got on the best we ever did. Maybe it was because I was the only member of the band besides Andrew that was taking any interest in what was going on in the studio and as a result spent most of my time there. While he wasn't always inclusive, I do believe Andrew welcomed the moral support. I know I unrequitedly craved it myself in later years with The Mission at times when I felt I was solely carrying the band. And the can.

It was during this period that Andrew started to develop alopecia, no doubt through a mixture of stress, overwork, lack of sleep, daylight and nutritional sustenance. He was not well. He took to constantly wearing his wide-brimmed black hat, similar to the one I'd been wearing. While I took to wearing mine to "cover up the sick", Andrew started wearing his to cover up his temporary hair loss. It was a look that was to become iconic, much loved and much copied (hello, Fields Of The Nephilim!) and, for both of the protagonists, it was a look born out of pragmatism rather than for sartorial effect.

Sadly, Andrew's hair loss got worse before it got better. On one occasion we were in WEA doing some promo, and we'd been allocated a small office in which to do so. We'd been at it for a few hours and then there was a break scheduled. Taryn, who was looking after us for the day, took Craig and I out for lunch – Japanese, the first time for both of us, we couldn't believe how delicious teriyaki chicken was – while Andrew, still not feeling too good, opted to stay in the office for a little shut eye. He closed the door and curled up on the couch. His hat fell off during his nap, exposing his bald patch.

While Craig, Taryn and myself were still at lunch the next scheduled journalist and photographer arrived early. Knocking on the office door and receiving no reply, they quietly entered the room, only to spot Andrew asleep on the couch with his baldness exposed. The scumbag of a journalist apparently insisted that the arsehole photographer take photos of our comatose singer. At the sound of a clicking camera Andrew awoke and, with total justification, went ballistic at the two despicable interlopers. It was at that moment as we arrived back from lunch, a little bit sake'd up, that we were confronted with the commotion. Taryn demanded the roll of film from the photographer and then promptly had them both ejected from the building empty-handed – no interview and no photos.

Meanwhile Andrew had started to berate Craig and I for leaving him unguarded, the whole unsavoury episode apparently being our fault (victims of circumstance, you see) rather than the fault of the two reprehensible members of the Great British media. Nevertheless, Andrew's castigation proved to be a rallying, a clarion call, as thereafter, particularly on the next tour, when anyone got sufficiently close to Andrew that there was a chance they might snatch his hat we thought nothing of kicking them offstage or even taking off our guitars and swinging them at the head of the potential offender. Andrew himself wasn't averse to battering someone's head with his mic stand either. Blood was spilt protecting our brother.

On Friday, March 8, 1984, 'No Time To Cry' was released as a single. In the week that my previous band, Dead Or Alive, reached number one in the UK chart with 'You Spin Me Round (Like A Record)', 'No Time To Cry' sneaked in unnoticed at number 63. That was as high as it would go.

The following day we opened our next UK tour – the Tune In, Turn On, Burn Out tour – at Strathclyde Uni in Glasgow. On Monday 11 *First And Last And Always* was released, reaching number 14 in the UK album chart and eventually, in May 1989, attaining gold status. It took almost 30 years for Craig and I to eventually receive our much-deserved gold discs for *FALAA* and not without much detective work and jiggery pokery from our manager, George Allen (thanks, George). We were eventually presented with them while on tour opening for Alice Cooper in the arenas of the UK in November 2017.

In many ways *First And Last And Always* was a defining moment in my life. At the end of its recording I felt I'd poured every ounce of my energy, every idea I'd ever had and every trick I'd ever learnt into its making. I felt exhausted at its completion, not in the same physical way as Andrew, but in terms of my creativity. I now realise, many years later, having gone through similar trials and tribulations with various Mission albums, how much of himself Andrew sacrificed for the album.

As my health and sanity suffered with recording Mission albums so did Andrew's with *FALAA*. I've been left spiritually and emotionally bereft after recording albums as I'm sure Andrew was with *FALAA*. Rightly or wrongly *FALAA* is perhaps a work that has been held up to scrutiny much more than anything else I have done before or since. Everything I *have done* since has been judged against it. It's a long, long time, more than 30 years since its release, to live with the nagging notion that maybe, just maybe, *FALAA* has been my life's best work.

Obviously in my more reflective moments I don't think so and I certainly don't admit to it when I am so often confronted with that question in interviews and by fans. But there is a consensus out there among the zealots and fanatics that it is the best ever work by all four of us, a synergy involved in its creation. It's perhaps not for me to claim it as a seminal album but certainly nobody can argue about its far-reaching eventual influence, as evidenced by the plethora of mostly piss-poor imitators.

CHAPTER 17

Living On The Edge, The Razor Edge

PLAYLIST:

1. First & Last & Always – The Sisters Of Mercy (OGWT on YouTube)
2. Marian – TSOM (OGWT on YouTube)   3. Mambo Sun – T. Rex
4. Slaughter On 10th Avenue – Mick Ronson   5. The Rain Song – Led Zeppelin
6. Shine On You Crazy Diamond – Pink Floyd
7. Down By The River – Neil Young   8. Leaf And Stream – Wishbone Ash
9. Elevation – Television   10. Nightshift – Siouxsie & The Banshees
11. Show Of Strength – Echo & The Bunnymen
12. The Drowning Man – The Cure   13. Paranoid Android – Radiohead
14. City's Full – Savages   15. Keep On Loving You – Cigarettes After Sex
16. Let It Happen – Tame Impala 17. Angels – The XX
18. Living With Ghosts – Smoke Fairies   19. Jessica's Crime – Salvation

The Tune In, Turn On, Burn Out tour of March 1985, with the tagline of 'Armageddon Will Be Held Indoors This Year', commenced in Glasgow on Saturday, March 9, and ended in Brighton on Monday, April 1, All Fool's Day. How very apt. It was the third full UK tour we had played in less than 12 months and our star was on the rise as evidenced by the healthy ticket sales in larger venues. But I look at that tour itinerary now and I have absolutely no recollection of any of the shows, nor of any incidents of note occurring throughout its duration.

Undoubtedly my dissolute appetites were accelerating which would account somewhat for my blurriness. I'm sure I left the band again several times during its duration but regretted and reversed the decision in the clarity of the next morning. As I'm equally positive Craig, Mark, and Andrew, as well as several crew members, did also. Someone was always leaving by this point. While we were getting stronger in performance we were coming apart at the seams internally and the tour was largely joyless. A situation exacerbated by all of us seeking solace in the bottle and/or the ingestion of various narcotics. Even Mark was hitting the sauce on this tour such was his palpable unhappiness. To all intents and purposes he was already more than half way over the threshold of the out door.

Was our heavy use of booze and drugs a symptom or the disease itself? I think for Craig and I it was always more about enjoying the altered state. I can't really speak for Andrew and Mark but if I had to hazard a guess then I'd say that Mark was so disillusioned with the way things were he felt he had no recourse but to try and numb himself to get through each day. Andrew Taylor, and this is just my theory, was so innately insecure that he used whatever means he had at his disposal to help him become Andrew Eldritch, the impenetrable rock star.

I never really met Andrew Taylor. By the time I'd joined the band the Eldritch persona was already firmly in place; the metamorphosis from Taylor to Eldritch was complete. Very occasionally though, the mask would slip slightly and I would catch a glimmer of vulnerability or glimpse a surprising sensitivity. I believe this possession of Taylor by the incubus Eldritch was another factor in the deterioration of the relationship between Andrew and Mark. After all, Mark had known Andrew as a geeky student for years before his mutation into Rock God and could see right through Eldritch's contrivance. And maybe Andrew resented this as much as Mark resented the change. Of course this is all just hindsight conjecture on my part but, knowing them both as I did, in the absence of anybody telling me otherwise, it's as good a hypothesis as any. As it transpired the final show in Brighton on the UK leg of the tour was to be Mark's last with the band. But none of us, excepting maybe Eldritch, knew it at the time.

The following day, Tuesday, April 2, we found ourselves at the BBC TV studios in London to film a live appearance on the long running *Old Grey Whistle Test*. And when I say live I mean *live*. This was no taped performance; as we played it went out directly into the living rooms of Britain. The rehearsals were fine. Having brought in our own sound and lights people it sounded good, and with the extra smoke machines, as was our wont, it also looked good. Not for us the glaringly unflattering studio lights normally employed on such TV shows. The *OGWT* had never seen the like and one or two of the studio crew had a grumble about how "dark and smoky" it was for television. Sod 'em.

I had recently heard about a new designer drug coming out of California that was purported to aid and heighten sexual pleasure. Ecstasy. I couldn't wait to get back to America to try it. In the meantime I was broadcasting my intent on national TV. Pre-show, using an indelible white marker pen I had scrawled 'SEX DRUG' on my guitar. Oh, how rebellious was I.

We were to open the show with the title track from our *First And Last And Always* album. The studio floor manager shouts, "Alright, boys, are you ready? Here we go. 10, 9, 8..." Blind panic. Mark's guitar isn't working. "...4, 3, 2, 1, go!" And I hit play on Dr Avalanche and we are live on air. With Mark's guitar still not working and roadies scrabbling around changing leads and looking puzzled at his amp we had to ad-lib, so I started playing the opening guitar riff that Mark normally played. Craig came in with my counter melody guitar line on the bass and switched to his normal bass line half way through the intro before it all dropped down into the groove of the song, by which time Mark's guitar was working again and he came in with the main riff. It was seamless and inspired improvisation. Despite being wired to the hilt.

I may be imagining this but, watching the video clip on YouTube, there's a point just after we all kick into the song where Eldritch turns towards Mark and seems to give him 'the stare' as if to say, "What the fuck happened there?" That moment could well have been the final straw that broke the camel's back.

After being introduced by the smarmy presenter Mark Ellen with a glib quip along the lines of "Throw another log on the fire, boys" we played the second song 'Marian'* and that went off without a hitch.

It's been assumed by some of our following that it was machination on my part to get rid of Mark and that I, ultimately, was responsible for the demise of this particular line-up. That's not true in the slightest. I believe that without my presence the band would've split up *before* they'd even recorded *First And Last And Always*. As it was it was disintegrating before my very eyes from the moment I joined. I just didn't recognise it as such at the time. Let me now set the

---

* As the co-writer, over the years I have been asked many times who 'Marian' was written about. I wrote the music not the words. But, without ever asking him directly, my understanding is that 'Marian' was a girl that Andrew had met and fell for in Hamburg while on tour, one of the primary reasons he moved to that same city later in 1985. Apparently, once there 'Marian' didn't want anything to do with Von despite the sincerity and brilliance of the song written for her. A case of unrequited love. This, of course, could all be tittle-tattle as this story was related to me with some glee by Craig Adams. Ho-hum.

record straight with regard to the events that abetted this fallacious and long-held belief that the more unforgiving of the Sisters' audience have since harboured.

After our *OGWT* performance Mark travelled back to Wakefield that very same evening while the remaining three of us were holed up in a hotel in London for a few days. Andrew called a band meeting with Craig and I and issued us with an ultimatum. Either Mark goes or he does. We had a long European tour starting in just over a week, closely followed by an American jaunt. This spate of touring would climax with a show at the Royal Albert Hall on Tuesday, June 18.

So what choice did Craig and I genuinely have? Go with Mark and form a new band as he had suggested the previous year on the top deck of a double-decker bus, or stay with Andrew and finish the tour? It was a no-brainer really and without much debate Craig and I decided to stay put.

"Okay, but I'm not telling him," said Andrew. "It was your decision so one of you two have to do it."

Craig looked at me and, shrugging his shoulders, said, "I ain't doing it either. We've known him longer than you so it'll be easier for you to tell him and he'll take it better from you."

"Really?" was my response. "You bloody cowards. Okay, I'll do it but let it be noted that I think Mark deserves better than to be informed by the new boy."

As our Royal Albert Hall show was scheduled for June 18, that date being Mark's birthday, it was decided that, as a blow softener, I could suggest to him that he rejoin us for that one show as a chance for him to say farewell to the Sisters' audience. I retired to my hotel room and after a stiff drink I summoned the courage to call Mark at home in Wakefield. I dialled his number, the phone rang a few times and then I heard his voice.

"Hello?"

"Hi, Mark, it's Wayne. I've got some bad news, I'm afraid. Andrew doesn't want you in the band anymore. He gave us an ultimatum, either you or him. I'm sorry but we decided we're gonna stay with Andrew."

A brief silence.

"Okay. I thought this was coming. I'm really quite relieved, to be honest," said Mark stoically.

"But we'd like you to come back and play the Albert Hall show with us as your send-off. Would you be up for that?" I asked.

"Yeah, maybe. I'll let you know."

And with a couple more sorries on my part he wished us good luck in our future endeavours without him. Mark and I then said our goodbyes.

Mark, Gary Marx to the legion, was a founding member of the band alongside Eldritch. He was as central to its story as Von was in the early days, as committed to the cause as anyone else, and he brought unique energy to the party. Neither Mark, or Ben Gunn for that matter, were what you could call guitar virtuosos but their playing was as integral, as essential, to the sound of the Sisters as Andrew's voice, Craig's bass, or Doktor Avalanche. That early run of records they released were what made people sit up and take notice of the Sisters in the first place.

When Ben left the band his departure changed the sound. It wasn't my joining that changed it. The process of change was already in play before I even set foot in Leeds. I came into the ranks at a time when the band, collectively, wanted more commercial success and, being the person I am, I implicitly insisted on creative input. And it was tacitly welcomed. I was the guitarist that could help them facilitate their aim at that particular point in time. I brought the pop to their snap and crackle. But, in hindsight, it's now apparent that Ben's exit only deepened the fault lines that already existed and nothing I could do would ever fix 'em again.* And as he came to realise that no amount of success could compensate for the betrayal he felt of the original concept and ideals that he and Andrew had conceived together for the band, Mark had, to all intents and purposes, expedited his own departure.

Mark went onto form Ghost Dance with Anne-Marie Hurst who had been the singer in The Skeletal Family, a band that had supported us on occasion. They enjoyed a modicum of success before splitting up in 1989. Mark then worked for a good few years as a teacher at Paul McCartney's Liverpool School Of Performing Arts while also keeping his hand in writing and recording and releasing the occasional solo record.

With Mark finally gone we flew out to Germany to film a performance of 'No Time To Cry' for the TV show *Formal Eins* that was broadcast less than two weeks later on April 16. We were back in England the very same day and straight into Strawberry Studios in Stockport again for a few days to continue work started almost a year previously on 'Emma', and to record our version of 'Knocking On Heaven's Door'. I can't remember quite why but we had some dead time in the studio during this period so I used it to write and record demo versions of two new word-less songs that ended up, ultimately, being early Mission songs: 'Serpent's Kiss' and 'Wake (RSV)'. Another tune of mine I recorded and for which I had managed to scrabble some lyrics together was 'Garden Of Delight'. Andrew had a go at singing it, but his heart wasn't in it, he

---

* One contentious issue I discovered when I first joined the band was the question of authorship of 'Temple Of Love'. When the record had been manufactured Andrew had listed himself as the sole composer of the work which was contested by Craig. This situation, as far as I know, still remains legally unresolved to this day.

bemoaning the fact that the lyrics meant nothing to him. Fair enough. I ended up singing it much better than him anyway.

Once we finished in Strawberry, Craig and I had only a few days to adapt the songs to a single guitar and bass, so we spent our scheduled days off in the rehearsal room. To be honest it was good to hear space in the music that wasn't there previously but there were definitely places where we missed Mark's guitar and, more pointedly, his spirit and energy. We had to adjust the set to take Mark's absence into consideration so most of the older pre-*FALAA* songs were dropped, the exceptions being 'Alice', 'Floorshow' and 'Body Electric', to be replaced with album tracks and more recent single B-sides. Our first show as a three-piece band was on Friday, April 12, in Gent, Belgium, and was memorable only for the fact that no one in the audience apart from a few weekending Brits seemed to notice or care that Mark wasn't there.

I guess now might be a good time to talk about guitarists and their various styles and who I feel have been an influence on the way I play. I had started using an electric 12-string guitar on stage because I loved the sound; the double octave on the lower strings and the slightly chorused effect on the two higher strings that were tuned to the same pitch but were never quite in perfect tune with each other. It's a great sound for arpeggios and for ringing, open chords. Having 12 strings on your guitar makes you think differently about how you play. It inclines me to take the less obvious route. As a rule, chugging, big power chords, and bending solo notes don't really work on a 12-string, certainly not for me. I'll leave that up to the Gibson Les Paul six-string bully boys. Another reason is that, being the only guitarist in the band and reluctant to just hit clichéd big chords, it stems the flow of a show if and when I break a string on a six-string guitar. At least with a 12-string guitar I have 11 other strings to play if that happens and I can still play everything that I need to.

The guitarists that inspired me to play in the first place, as mentioned elsewhere, were glamsters Marc Bolan and Mick Ronson. Then Jimmy Page, Dave Gilmour, the ragged glory of Neil Young, the twin guitars of Andy Powell and Ted Turner in Wishbone Ash, and later the cold, remote, acardiac guitars of Television's Tom Verlaine and Richard Lloyd all served as beacons to the fledgling guitar hero I aspired to be. Later still the flair of the brilliant John McGeoch with the Banshees – *Juju* is *the best* guitar album – Will Sergeant of the Bunnymen, Robert Smith of The Cure, and Radiohead's genius plank spanker in residence, Jonny Greenwood, have all been fave raves. I have a lot of affection for James Honeyman-Scott of The Pretenders, Dave Gregory of XTC, David Byrne and Jerry Harrison of early Talking Heads, the B52's tragic Ricky Wilson, and utmost respect if not awe for Johnny Marr, Noel Gallagher, Keith Levene and a host of others who ply their trade with a six-string razor in their hands.

Of the modern-day guitarists I adore the angularity in Savages Gemma Thompson's playing; the simple serenity and lack of dynamism in Greg Gonzalez's navigation of the fret board in Cigarettes After Sex; Tame Impala's Kevin Parker's pushing of the envelope and mastery of making a guitar sound unlike a conventional guitar; the choice notes of spare beauty that Romy Madley Croft brings to The XX along with that fabulous voice of hers; the history-soaked Delta Blues guitars of Katherine Blamire and Jessica Davies conjoined with the most English of English folk voices in The Smoke Fairies. So many great guitar players, the best being those that serve the song rather than their ego. I've surely missed some that really should also be mentioned. We all have our own particular favourites, don't we?

Ⓐ My first The Sisters Of Mercy show, Birmingham Tin Can Club, April 1984.
Ⓑ My first promo shoot with TSOM in the cold, dank cellar where we used to rehearse, circa 1983/84.
(L to R) Craig Adams, Andrew Eldritch, me and Gary Marx. (Credit: Terry Cryer)

C 'Dazed and confused.' Craig in the Iroquois Hotel, NYC, April/May 1984.

D Aquanet Extra Super Hold, circa 1984. (Credit: Craig Adams)

E Before the roach attack. Gary Marx, Iroquois Hotel, NYC, April 1984.

F TSOM with Alan Vega. (Credit: Howard Thompson)

G Post-show shebang, Leeds, 1984.
(Standing L to R) Gillie, Claire, Grape, Stevie 'Sex Pistol',
Von, (sitting) me.
H The Flying Turd.
I As rake thin and translucent as a dry dead autumn lea
Sound checking in Manchester, 1985.

J Dave 'Trolley' Allen.
K The four of us struck some moody poses amidst the trees, August 1984. (Credit: Jill Furmanovsky)

And then there were three. Belgium, April 1985. (Credit: Patrick De Spiegelaere)

🄻 On the 'Black Planet' video shoot in the Monkeemobile, July 1985. (Credit: Craig Adams)
🄼 This is, as far as I know, the last known photo of me and Eldritch together before I drive off in the Batmobile into a widescreen future, July 1985. (Credit: Craig Adams)

Billy Corgan told me a year or two ago that, for him, the guitar was dead. I couldn't disagree more. For me it's been the one true lifelong abiding unconditional love that has seen me through all the ups I've been blessed with and downs that life has had the temerity to throw at me. It's been the shoulder to cry on when my heart has been shattered; redemption when my soul has been blackened; the guiding light when there's been darkness surrounding me; the encouragement to soar when my spirit has felt tethered; the ever-present faithful companion that has travelled every road with me. True, there have been times when we've gotten bored with each other's company, as happens in any long-standing relationship, and annoyance and irritation that we sometimes haven't quite done the other's bidding, but when I am laid out finally in my coffin and ready to be sent into the fiery furnace then I would like a favoured guitar to take with me to keep me company along that very last leg of my journey. And just in case I'm wrong and there is a heaven. How could it be heaven if there is no guitar there for me in the hereafter?

With yours truly now handling all the guitar chores in the Sisters live show as well as the operation of our redoubtable Doktor, we marauded our way through mainland Europe on the Armageddon tour. Spirits among the three of us were raised for a while and we actually felt like a band again, albeit temporarily. The general toil and excess of the tour began to take its toll and soon fractures began to reappear.

As exemplified by this morality tale. One after show shebang in a German city, Munster or Hannover or some such nondescript großstadt, Craig and I were running around the club carousing and fraternising and generally being loud and garrulous, no doubt fuelled by certain white powders that we'd shovelled up our noses. Knocking back the drinks at the bar, the disco playing the dark hits of the day trying to tempt us onto its dance floor, and surrounded by a crowd of boys that wanted to be us and girls that wanted to shag us. Or maybe it was the other way around?

Either way Craig and I were the King and Queen at this particular infernal prom and loving every second of it. I needed a pee but rather than share the urinal in the public restroom and have prying eyes peeking to see how big my dick was (paranoia or what?) I went back to the sanctuary of our dressing room to use our own private facilities. Opening the door I was confronted with Andrew sitting there with maybe five or six people sat around him like an emperor with court jesters – except no one was laughing or even saying a word. No conversation going on here. What kind of party is this? Not one I'd want to go to, that's for sure. Certainly the 'Dritch was not playing the part of genial host as he should but then he was the 'Dritch and being party host was never part of Andrew's shtick; way too cool for that.

"Bloody 'ell, it's like a morgue in here, who's died?" asked I, breaking the silence.

No answer. No one even looked at me.

"Come on, it's supposed to be a celebration, what're you all moping about for?" I pressed.

Again, no reply, no acknowledgement.

"What's up with you all, ya soddin' stiffs?" persisted I.

Andrew slowly raised his head and with naked contempt in his voice admonished, "We're all stoned, Wayne."

"Since when did you start smoking spliff? You hate dope smokers. Ah, fuck that, ya bunch of hippies," and off I flounced to relieve myself.

Bands are okay when we're all using the same drugs at the same time but when one or more starts using different drugs then that's when divisions can occur. It happened with The Mission in later years and ultimately split us up, I reckon. I was on the white powders and acid, Simon was on the spliff, Craig was off the drugs altogether but heavily into the booze, and Mick just did it all. We were very rarely in the same headspace anymore and consequently we were rent asunder and ended up galaxies apart. But that's for later.

On the morning after we'd played Bielefeld I woke up in a strange bed with a strange person in a strange house with rabbits bouncing on the bed and all around the room. Nah, I wasn't hallucinating as I found out to my dismay when I stepped out of bed and straight into a pile of bunny poo with a bare foot. I hopped one legged to the bathroom and washed my dirtied hoof and then got dressed and tiptoed quietly out of the house leaving my dowsabel* sleeping beauty alone in the bed with her floppy-eared bunny buddies. Later in the tour the same minx extended to Andrew the same hospitalities that she'd shown me, replete with rabbit droppings. Oh, how we laughed hares, hounds, and horses when we compared notes in the back of The Flying Turd.

During the tour we had a few days off in Switzerland. The country that has bequeathed the world cuckoo clocks and second-rate chocolate; that harbours the hoarding of stolen wealth and ill-gotten gains within their bank vaults; that maintained their neutrality throughout the Second World War and the formation of a European Union. And even today they still see themselves as apart from Europe even though Switzerland is slap bang in the middle. (Actually, it is Slovakia

---

*   Lady-love, sweetheart

that is physically slap bang in the middle of Europe but you know what I mean.) They don't even have their own language, for Chrissake, speaking French, German and Italian depending on which part of the country you find yourself in. You could say they are hedging their bets, eh? *And* they were the last European republic to grant women the right to vote – as late as 1971.

I dunno if you've ever been stuck in the suburbs of Zürich on a bank holiday but it's far more tedious than being in Hull or Milton Keynes on a wet, windy, winter's day. To help ease our boredom Craig and I invited a group of Italian-speaking Swiss girls we'd previously gotten cosy with to visit us in our hotel. There were maybe four or five of them and along for the ride they had brought a male friend, an annoying flibbertigibbet of a thing, who just wouldn't, couldn't, keep quiet.

We were all hanging out around the hotel's rooftop pool and working our way through the various bottles we had accumulated over the previous few weeks from gig riders that hadn't been polished off on the night. We were, however, getting low on smokes so Craig uncharacteristically but very kindly offered to traipse to the nearest supermarket to purchase fags for us all. Big Pete Turner, our sound guy, went with him to keep him company and out of trouble. Being a bank holiday it took them a little longer than it should have to find a place open that sold ciggies.

In the meantime, Jez Webb, our guitar tech, and I were close to the end of our rouzy-bouzy* tether with the constant twittering of the male of our visiting party. In tandem with Nipper, our other backline tech, Jez held the poor ditz down and I, holding the bridge of his nose to force his mouth open, poured the contents of an almost full bottle of vodka down his

---

* Boisterously drunk

throat. I know, I know, what a waste *and* not a very nice thing to do. You know, I have no defence except to say that like every other musician in the world once even a small degree of success has been achieved it's very easy to feel that you have impunity and behave like a complete dick-head, impervious to being held responsible for your actions. We exist largely in a cocoon, cosseted and indulged by those around us. I literally felt I could get away with murder at times and this is one occasion where I was actually close to it.

The poor kid was soon staggering around and being violently sick everywhere before passing out. He really wasn't in a good way so it was thought prudent to call for an ambulance and get him taken to hospital to have his stomach pumped. As we were sat there by the pool waiting for the ambulance to arrive, nursing our victim and making sure he wasn't choking on his own vomit, Craig and Pete were on their way back to the hotel with the ciggies. Just before they reached the turning to the street where the hotel was, an ambulance came roaring past them with its sirens blaring. Pete turned to Adams, apparently, and said, "I bet that's on its way to our hotel. What's that idiot Hussey done now?"

And lo and behold as they turned the corner they saw the ambulance pull up to the doors of our hostelry. The kid was stretchered into the waiting conveyance and, with a couple of his girlfriends as companions, taken off to hospital. A few hours later they returned and he was as happy and bright as the first lark of the morning and even started drinking again although in moderation. It has to be said he was thankfully a lot quieter than he was earlier; almost killing him had done the trick. Apparently he was asked in the hospital whether he wanted to press charges against us but, being a fan, declined to do so. Thank fuck for that. In return for the favour I put him on the guest list for the following day's show. I've got some bad karma coming back at me, I reckon, or, maybe, it's already been and gone.

Jez Webb is on the short side in stature but more than makes up for it by having a heart as big as a blue whale, a wicked sense of humour, and an innate ability to get on with anyone in any social situation. He was also nicknamed Tripod. Think about it.

In Milan a few days later it was Jez's 21st birthday. There was cake and a few drinks and consumables backstage after the show in his honour and then a small group of us wanted to continue the soiree elsewhere after we'd been kicked out of the venue. We found an open bar but stumbling distance from the hotel and continued our drinking. One by one each of our party staggered back to their beds eventually leaving, surprise surprise, just Jez and I. Anxious to mark his momentous day with a memorable act of senseless vandalism we decided to try and blow up a car. Lurching about the quiet and deserted streets we tried the petrol caps on several cars until we found one that we could open without a key. Having found a newspaper from somewhere we stuffed a few pages of Italian newsprint into the opening of the petrol tank. Using my fag lighter we set it ablaze and ran and, giggling like two hyenas on helium, hid behind a nearby car to watch the impending result of our handiwork. We waited for a good two minutes and nada. The fire had just fizzled out without any huge explosion.

Stifling our disappointment we tried the same on a few other cars with, fortuitously for us, the same result. In desperation we even tried a couple of mopeds. Hmmm, this wasn't working. What else could we do?

"I know, let's set a shop awning on fire!" exclaimed I in a moment of unbridled inspiration.

Many years previously on holiday in Barcelona with my family I had set a rubbish bin on fire and we'd been ejected from the campsite where we were staying. In an attempt to stave off a potential career as an arsonist my parents had bought me a guitar. And now it was that guitar, in a very roundabout way, that was leading me back to arson.

We lit up a sheet of newspaper and using it as a fire-lighter tried to set aflame a few awnings but again to no avail. Disappointed at our failure we trudged our way back to the hotel. On arrival we spied an awning over the front door. A-ha! Looking around to make sure no one was looking and no one was on reception in the hotel we took our last chance to set something afire. That thing went up this time and lit up the darkened street like fireworks on New Year's Eve on the Copacabana.

Jez and I, by this point sobering up a little, ran into the hotel as fast as we could and made it to my room without, seemingly, anyone seeing us. After dispensing with my ever-present hat and having only one bed in the room Jez and I jumped into it fully clothed and pulled the sheets up to our necks still giggling like lunkheads at a loud fart. It wasn't long before we heard sirens approaching which stymied our cackle to a more nervous titter. Hearing Italiano basso profundo agitato fortissimo in the street I'd like to say that we began to feel guilty but I can't remember guilt being part of our encroaching fear. Isn't conscience really no more than the fear of being caught anyway?

Before long we heard heavy footsteps stomping down the corridor outside our room and then three very loud raps on the door.

"Hussey, are you in there?" It was Pete Turner.

"Who is it? What do you want? I'm in bed," I replied, trying to sound like I'd just woken up.

"Is Jez with you?" inquired our giant sound man.

"Yeah, he's sleeping here. Why, what's up?"

"There's police downstairs looking for someone with long, dark hair dressed in black wearing sunglasses and a black hat. There was a fire outside and two lads were seen running into the hotel by a neighbour."

"It wun't us, we've been asleep for ages. It must've been Eldritch, he's gotta black hat and sunglasses as well, you know. Go and bleedin' accuse him instead of me every time something goes wrong."

"Well, alright, you two stay there and don't answer your door to anyone, okay?" instructed Turner knowingly.

We heard no more about it that night and eventually the fire engine and police car drove away from the scene of our crime with us believing that we'd gotten away with it. But we bloody well got it the next morning from Pete who threatened to send Jez home as punishment until I chimed in and took all the blame by claiming it was all my idea and doing. See? I am just a victim of circumstance.

This particular leg of the tour ended in Stockholm on May 17 with a rather tetchy, fractious show at the Kolinsborg, our undisguised loathing for each other by then even manifesting itself on stage and in full view of the audience. It was only the music and the knowledge that we were by then one of the best live bands in the world that kept us together. Craig and I had reached the point where we couldn't stand the sight of Von and I'm certain the feeling was mutual. What we needed was a few days off and away from each other.

Back in England, with the best part of two weeks in which we didn't have to see or speak to each other, I spent a few days in the company of Danny Mass and his band, Salvation, at

Slaughterhouse Studios in Great Driffield, West Yorkshire, producing their single, 'Jessica's Crime'. It was a cracking little song elevated by Danny's fine lyric and some rather mournful fiddle playing.

I hung out with Danny quite a bit during the brief periods of downtime I enjoyed during that summer and it was Danny that introduced me to heroin. Danny's girlfriend, Debs, was from Manchester and so for a couple of weekends I went along with them to drug parties in a squalid flat in the concrete high-rise monstrosity of Hulme.

Smack was particularly frowned upon by the 'Dritch who threatened to sack anyone, band or crew, that used it. I had seen my good friend, Kris Guidio, lose his family, friends, talents, and dignity to his junk habit and had heard of others that had lost even more to theirs. Despite these misgivings and making a pact to never let Andrew know, my natural curiosity to experience any, every, and all drugs took over and I was easily persuaded by Danny and Debs to chase the dragon with them.

Danny lit me up and I smoked heroin. It was unlike anything I'd ever experienced before, initially making me sweat profusely from every pore in my body and then violently throw up before being enveloped by clouds of fluffy cotton wool and floating off into a dreamland where everything was seemingly a various shade of blue. I made slow languorous love with a girl I had just met and every touch felt like the caress of a feather and every kiss felt like the breath of a sigh. We went down on each other and it could've been for five minutes or five hours, I had no concept of time. I couldn't hold a thought, I felt no pain, no paranoia, no worry, no need to impress or be impressed, I was lost to the moment. It was quite honestly the furthest I've ever felt from reality, and that's saying something, and even though I was with company I had never felt so alone. Not lonely, just isolated and removed, a being adrift from the world. And I loved it.

Eventually we both fell asleep entwined in each other's arms and I awoke the next morning with an aching jaw and a blushing shyness as I formally introduced myself to my fellow traveller into the blue. Paula was her name. In the cold light of day we had nothing to say to each other but goodbye. I could certainly see how easily it would be to become addicted to riding the White Horse.

I smoked it a couple more times with Danny in Hulme and enjoyed a very similar experience each time but without the sweating and vomiting. Ultimately though, knowing how destructive heroin could be, I made a vow to myself to never touch it again and I never knowingly have. I preferred my drugs to stimulate me into action and creativity rather than lie around floating about in space a million miles from terra firma.

Towards the end of May we flew out for my first ever visit to the West Coast. Before commencing our US tour with a chaotic show at Fenders Ballroom in Long Beach, we shot a video for 'Black Planet' in LA, more of which next chapter. On the flight over from Heathrow we were again sat at the back of the plane in the smokers' seats. With Andrew still suffering with alopecia his hat was ever-present to spare his blushes.

In the seat in front of Andrew was a little kid of maybe three or four years old sat between his American mother and father. This little brat thought it was great fun to stand on his seat and try to grab Andrew's hat or the sunglasses from his face. With great relish Von would light up and blow smoke from his Marlboro Red directly into the face of the 'orrible tyke who would no doubt grow up to one day be a Trump supporter. But the kid was persistent and Andrew was now getting mightily vexed with the blighter, after all it's a long flight from Heathrow to LA. Andrew stood up and leaning over the seats, malevolently threatened the parents.

"If you don't control your devil's spawn then I will kill him. Understood?"

Both parents were too shocked at the lookalike Evil Child Catcher from *Chitty Chitty Bang Bang* sitting behind them to register any response apart from dragging their little holy terror down and strapping him into his seat. It did the job, the whippersnapper didn't bother Andrew again all flight.

After Long Beach we embarked on a gruelling schedule of late nights and early morning flights with five shows in five days taking in San Francisco, LA, Chicago, Detroit, and Boston before ending up in NYC for a very welcome evening free. How did we spend our night off? Not by resting, I can tell you, no sir-ee. With Andrew and I attired in our best glad rags and donning our black hats and dark glasses we travelled the short distance by limousine from the Gramercy Hotel to the famous Radio City Music Hall.*

As she was on the same label as us, WEA, we'd managed to blag a couple of spots on Madonna's guest list for the first night of a short run of NY shows that she was playing as part of The Virgin Tour, her first ever. Fighting our way through the hordes of 12-year-old Madonna wannabes we found our seats about half way back in the middle of the stalls. Already in the seats next to us was Joey Ramone and a female companion. A nod of recognition passed between us but no words. There we were, sat

---

* By this time we'd been upgraded from the flea-pit that was the Iroquois to the slightly posher flea-pit that was the Gramercy, located at Lexington and Gramercy Park North, a more salubrious neighbourhood. An historic, bohemian NYC establishment that still exists today although it's been extensively refurbished since we stayed there, as has the Iroquois.

in a row, three long-haired blokes in our mid to late twenties, scruffily dressed in black and wearing sunglasses, surrounded by teenage and pre-pubescent girls all screaming for Madonna. Talk about feeling like a pork sausage at a Jewish wedding... Being the pop connoisseurs that we were though, remembering our mutual fondness for 'Careless Whisper', Andrew and I remained in the auditorium until the end of the show and thrilling it was too. Mr Ramone, however, took his leave about three quarters of the way through, around the time that Madonna was sitting astride a huge ghetto-blaster simulating masturbation. What's not to love about that, uh?

Our final show on this particular jaunt was at the Ritz in NY on Friday, June 7, but we were to stay on in the city for a few days after because WEA had lined up a bunch of promo for us to do, you know, TV, radio and print interviews. The last thing we were scheduled to do was an interview for a cable TV sex show. Conducted in mine and Craig's room at the Gramercy, we hatched this brilliant idea to do it in bed apparently naked with a blow-up sex doll laying between us. We found a local sex shop and persuaded the record company rep to flash the cash and buy us the Miss Dee Lite model, with the guarantee, printed on the box, of her being your most pliable girlfriend ever. Complete satisfaction or your money refunded.

Back at the hotel Craig and I stripped down to our underpants and climbed into bed with Miss Dee, now full of hot air, sat between us. I, of course, was still wearing my dark glasses and hat. Andrew was supposed to join Craig and I for the interview but on entering the room he took one look at us both, tutted loudly and, rolling his eyes, immediately turned around and walked back out. We did the interview without him.

Once it was over and the cameras were being packed up I bagsied Miss Dee for my mate back in Leeds, Grape, who collected blow-up dolls along with various other odd sex toys. Deflating her as gently as I could I packed Miss Dee Lite into the bottom of my suitcase for the journey back across the Atlantic to Blighty. Of course, on arrival at Heathrow I'd forgotten all about the contents of my suitcase due to a slight case of in-flight inebriation, and I got stopped by a young female customs officer who insisted on rooting through my suitcase.

Standing in the customs hall with all the other passengers passing by she reached into my case and pulled out the blow-up doll. Holding it up for all to see and snigger at, she asked loudly, "So, sir, what is it we have here, then?"

"Um," I mumbled, "It's a present for a friend."

I'm sure she didn't believe a word of it and enjoyed every moment of my discomfort.

CHAPTER 18

Wake, Wake For You, My Precious

PLAYLIST:

1. In Every Dream Home A Heartache – Roxy Music
2. A Day In The Life – The Beatles
3. Knocking On Heaven's Door – TSOM
(YouTube Clip from The Royal Albert Hall)
4. Man Of The World – Fleetwood Mac
5. I Need Your Love So Bad – Fleetwood Mac
6. Arpeggios From Hell – Yngwie Malmsteen   7. Emma – TSOM
8. Body & Soul – TSOM (YouTube video)
9. Walk Away – TSOM (YouTube video)
10. No Time To Cry – TSOM (YouTube video)
11. Black Planet – TSOM (YouTube video)

Returning to Leeds I gave Grape his present and most grateful he was, too. I saw him a few days later and asked after Miss Dee Lite and he told me that she had a puncture and would deflate every time he blew her up. He had attempted to repair her with a bicycle tyre repair kit but to no avail. "Blimey, Grape, what have you been doing to the poor girl?" I asked. Despite the humiliation I endured in getting her into the country Miss Dee Lite ended her short life in the rubbish bin without, I presume (Grape?), ever fulfilling the role she was made for. And how many of us can the same be said for?

Just over a week later we were back down in London staying at a hotel just off Kensington High Street. Tomorrow, Tuesday, June 18, 1985, we were playing the Royal Albert Hall. Our Altamont: A Festival Of Remembrance, and it was being filmed and recorded for future video release. Best get some beauty sleep then, eh? Well, Andrew and Craig did but I didn't need any. And anyway I'd received a call from my mate, Ian Astbury of The Cult, asking if I fancied going out that evening to the Hammersmith Palais to see Killing Joke. He arranged to pick me up later in a cab and asked if it was alright if he brought a friend.

"Of course," I replied, fully expecting his friend to be female.

A couple of hours later the phone rang in my room, "Wayne, it's Ian. I'm downstairs in reception."

"Alright, mate, I'll be right down."

Downstairs I saw Ian waving to me from the waiting cab outside the hotel. I could spy another shadowy figure with long hair sat in the back next to him. Ah, that'll be his girlfriend then, I thought to myself. I opened the door of the Hackney and climbed in, sat down on the pull down seat and then looked up. Bloody hell, it wasn't a girl, it was Lemmy.

Ian introduced us, not that any introduction was needed for Lemmy, who immediately pulled out a wrap and asked if I wanted some. "It'd be rude not to," I replied, and with that Lemmy conjured up a knife and, shovelling a small pile of the white powder onto its flat edge, held it up to my nostril. One big snort later and my pulse was racing. As was the taxi as it wound its way from Kenny High Street down to Hammersmith roundabout, by which time Lemmy had commandeered the other pull down seat and wound down the window so as to shout abuse at pedestrians as we drove by. A bottle of brandy was passed around from which we three slugged. A couple more blade-fulls each of the white stuff and we had arrived at the door of the Palais.

I must admit that being with Lemmy and Ian and jumping the queue waiting to get into the venue felt pretty fucking cool. "I'm on the guest list and these are my two mates," said Lemmy. And straight in we were, no messing. The girl on the door didn't even bother looking to see if Lemmy's name was on the list. I was impressed, still am if truth be known.

Once inside, following Lemmy, we headed straight for the bar. Lemmy started talking to someone who was leaning against the bar whom I couldn't quite see over his shoulder. Lemmy turned around and pulled me into the conversation.

"Wayne, meet Jimmy."

Holy roaring schnikes, it was only Jimmy bloody Page, with whom, in 1985, I was obsessed. Good job I wasn't wearing my 'four symbols' t-shirt that particular night, that would have been embarrassing. It was my first encounter with a Zeppelin. Jimmy didn't offer to shake my hand as both his arms were wrapped around the shoulders of two very young scantily clad nubiles, one on each side, evidently holding him upright.

I danced the stagger in front of him. "Good to meet you, will you produce our next album?" I ventured.

"Fuck off," was Jimmy's considered reply, and with that he turned away from me and began talking with one of the girls.

To be fair it was neither the time nor the place and Jimmy was obviously pretty messed up so I've never held it against him that he dismissed my proposition with such haste. And anyway, while I would've loved to have worked with Jimmy, I did get to later work with the two other surviving ex-members of Led Zeppelin so two out of three ain't bad.

I don't know what time or how I got back to the hotel that night but I awoke the next morning, the day of our big RAH show, with the most ferocious hangover. I couldn't stand up without throwing up, not that throwing up was such a rare occurrence for me. I spent most of the morning curled around the toilet bowl, retching up the lining of my stomach until it was time to leave for soundcheck. Just making it downstairs to the hotel reception was a huge feat of endurance. At any moment I feared I'd unleash another stream of projectile puke. Climbing into the back of The Flying Turd that conveyed us to the RAH both Andrew and Craig could see what state I was in.

Looking all fresh-faced and rested, the bastards, Craig just raised an eyebrow whilst Von scolded me for my lack of responsibility.

"You do realise, young Wayne, that today is a mightily important day, don't you? You need to look and play your best."

"I'll be alright once I've had a toot and a hair of the dog," was my less than confident response.

Once within the hallowed walls and backstage of the RAH I began to make good on that promise and bit by bit during the course of the afternoon I started to feel *marginally* human again. Soundcheck took longer than usual due to The Rolling Stones Mobile Recording unit parked outside checking mic lines, EQs, recording levels, etc, as well as our usual sound guy, Big Pete, taking his time with the front-of-house sound. Everybody was a little bit on tenterhooks, nervous that the show should go well. We also had the video director, Mike Mansfield, he of *Supersonic* fame, flitting about directing his cameramen to go hither and thither while we were playing. It was all go – apart from me. All I wanted to do was lie down and die. I had a sick bucket installed at the side of the stage, maybe for the first time but certainly not for the last. Later, in The Mission, we had them on both sides of the stage for years because, as well as yours truly, Craig was also pre-disposed to a little heave-ho on occasion. Vomit was to feature heavily in the forging of our legend.

John Lennon lied when he sang "4,000 holes in Blackburn, Lancashire", followed by "now they know how many holes it takes to fill the Albert Hall". The official seating capacity is 5,272 but because we took the seating out in the stalls for our show we had sold close to 6,000 tickets.

As showtime approached my ingestion of white powder accelerated in concert with my nerves. Funny that. One hour before stage time was, and still is, wine o'clock. That's when I allow myself the first sip. Other drinks don't count although nowadays I have come to discipline myself to drinking *only* wine pre-show. Blue Nun was my favoured tipple back in 1985, copious amounts as it was as easy to guzzle as Ribena and probably boasted a very similar alcohol content. I have since acquired more refined tastes. Black Tower became my preferred vintage for a good few years but these days, and it's been this way for a while now, I prefer a red pre-show, a Cabernet or a Shiraz. Yeah, a lot more refined, eh?

Because I am very often seen with a bottle in hand, and it has certainly become a stage prop for me, people tend to presume that I am either an alcoholic or a sommelier. I am neither. Drinking is merely a means to an end for me, a conduit to get me to my preferred state of mind for going on stage. I have so very rarely tread the boards stone cold sober. It frightens me to death to do so. The only times I've done it is when I've been ill and I'm taking antibiotics but even then a full-bodied *vinho tinto* can be a good, healing tonic.

Because some do believe I'm a connoisseur of fine wines I'm very often given presents of very rare and expensive bottles while I'm on tour and I now have quite the collection stored in a lock-up in Bristol. I try to take a bottle or two back with me to Brazil whenever I fly home but baggage allowances being what they are these days I can barely get my wife's shopping list in let alone any of my things – hence the lock-up. Whilst it's true that I have been known to like a drink my habits have somewhat been tempered with age. The hangovers have gotten more severe and grown exponentially in length with each passing year. I am no longer convinced that an evening's revelry is worth three days or more of shivers and shakes and nausea and headaches. And while I do occasionally enjoy a decent red at home with the wife of an evening it is a snifter of brandy that has become my favoured bedtime drink before hitting the wooden, or in my case, the iron stairs. So, if you're coming to a Mission show and want to bring me a gift, then a bottle of Courvoisier or Rémy Martin would be very much appreciated. Or a good book. I already have a storage unit full of good wines, thank you very much.

We didn't have a support act at the RAH show. Firstly we screened the 1982 cult film, *Koyaanisqatsi*. And for the interlude we'd employed an organist to perform Lynyrd Skynyrd's 'Freebird' on the Grand Organ that is a huge central feature of the Royal Albert Hall. That was Andrew's idea and certainly set the tone for the evening. It was an event, a ceremony, not *just* a gig. And as it happened it was to become our last ever show together, immortalised on film. Our In Memoriam. None of us knew that at the time though, not even Eldritch despite his later claims to the contrary. How could he? We started working on a second album shortly afterwards and had a tour of Japan lined up for very early 1986 that was ultimately cancelled when Craig and I left the band. Anyway, I'm giving the ending of the book away prematurely here, so let's rewind.

Despite trying several times beforehand to call Mark, he was a no-show. There was some conjecture that he may just turn up on the day but, nah, he obviously had more pride than he was given credit for and decided not to appear. He didn't even let us know one way or the other. Fair play to him, I would've done the same. Stick that in yer eye. As it was, though, I was relieved in a way because we had played more than 30 shows without him and by then Craig and I were making a pretty good racket on our own; and we would've had to adapt what we'd been playing for the last two months without any rehearsal and in front of 6,000 people just to accommodate Mark. And, of course, we ran the risk of him purposely sabotaging the show to exact some kind of revenge. Maybe that's just the cynic in *me* talking as I really don't believe Mark had that much malice in *him* but we were, in my opinion, courting a potential disaster if Mark had turned up to play.

I wore a poncho for the occasion… yes, I know, a bloody poncho. Who did I think I was, Clint Eastwood? Well, yeah, actually. Of all the items of attire and accessories I unwittingly or otherwise introduced into the lexicon of gothic fashion, the poncho was perhaps my least successful. Although I do have to insist that it did actually look quite rakish on film. It made me perspire like a bastard though, which was alright as I quickly sweated all the alcohol from the night before out of my system.

If Eldritch thought I was gonna let the team down he should've known better. The show was fine, we played well, Andrew was singing great, and the audience were well up for it. We played the same set we had been playing since Mark's departure so we were tight, a well-oiled machine. Take that how you want. We were called back for an encore and Craig and Andrew performed a menacing reading of 'Fix', just drums, bass, and voice, before I joined 'em and we finished with perhaps our best ever rendition of Dylan's 'Knocking On Heaven's Door'. I am a huge Bob Dylan fan. He is one of the very few Americans whose music I love, and I love *his* version of *his* song but I have to say that of all the very many others that have covered this song I think the Sisters' version is maybe the best I have heard. From the monotony of the very simple drum machine, to the Neanderthal monolithic quality of Craig's phased bass, to the brooding malevolence of Andrew's vocal, and all topped off by quite possibly my finest ever guitar solo* – one of the very few times I actually played it well; and thankfully the cameras were there to capture it.

It's such a simple song but so many bands play it and it becomes hoary old pub rock. We've even played it with The Mission a few times and never even came close to the magnificence of the Sisters' rendering. The problem being, in my opinion, too many musicians playing too much. Bad musicians are afraid to leave silence and space, good ones keep it simple. The Sisters version is stripped right out and all the better for it. I'd like to think that Dylan himself has heard our rendition and given his nod of approval whilst I'm also pretty damn sure that Guns N' Roses used our version as the starting

---

* As you've probably guessed by now I am not a big fan of guitar solos per se unless they serve the song or are musical interludes that say something a little different to me. Anybody, and I mean anybody, can learn and practise to play notes very fast on the guitar. You know the kind of playing I mean, the shredding five hundred notes per second performed without any discerning taste that is usually associated more with heavy metal than other genres of music. What can't be taught and practised is the 'right' choice of notes. That is an innate ability. One note played by Peter Green, for example, can say a whole galaxy more than five hundred notes played by Yngwie Malmsteen, again for example. Just compare Malmsteen's 'Arpeggios From Hell' (aptly titled in my humble...) with Fleetwood Mac's 'I Need Your Love So Bad' or 'Man Of The World' or 'Albatross'. Go on, have a listen and then tell me which you prefer. I won't believe you if you say Malmsteen.

point for theirs, which ended up being pretty horrendous, it has to be said.

We left the stage and made our way back to the dressing room after Andrew decided that was it, we were done for the night. The house lights came up but the audience wouldn't leave. There were insistent calls for more. Lemmy was in the dressing room giving Eldritch hell, "Come on you miserable git, get back out there and give 'em what they want."

After much cajoling and the flash of Lemmy's blade under each of our noses Andrew relented and we went back out to play 'Louie Louie' and 'Sister Ray', neither of which made it onto the final video release. Our film, and quite rightly so, ended with our majestic version of 'Knocking On Heaven's Door'. And the film, when it was finally released in 1986, was entitled *Wake*. Hmm.

We had an idea to release a covers EP featuring the two tracks we'd began recording earlier, 'Emma' and 'Knocking On Heaven's Door', and so booked back into Strawberry yet again to finish and mix the two songs. We were planning to record Abba's 'Gimme, Gimme, Gimme (A Man After Midnight)' and Stevie Nicks' 'Stop Dragging My Heart Around' as the other two tracks for the EP but, sadly, didn't get around to doing so before we disbanded. Obviously, what with Mark not being with us anymore it was left up to me to finish recording all the guitars. Neither song saw the light of day while Craig and I were still in the band though I do believe they became available on bootleg shortly after our departure. How and by whom the recordings were leaked I can only speculate. I will say this though, bootlegs are a good way to raise extra revenue for bands that possess a willing and fanatical fan base who will search out everything and anything to do with their favoured musicians.

And both TSOM and, to a slightly lesser degree, The Mission enjoy more than their fair share.

'Emma' was eventually officially released with a newly recorded vocal by the 'Dritch as an extra track on the later TSOM 12-inch single, 'Dominion'. The story I heard may be apocryphal but I love it, it's so Diva-like. Evidently Andrew, having vocal'ed the song several times previously in the studio, was not happy with the results, feeling that it lacked the intensity of a live performance. So the Kilburn National Ballroom was duly hired along with a full PA and lighting rig, everything needed to invoke the atmosphere of a live show. Except there was no audience. Andrew was alone on stage performing to an empty venue. With the instrumental backing track blaring through the PA and monitors and the dry ice machines turned up to eleven Andrew sang the song with the required amount of vigour and vim and his vocal was recorded on the Rolling Stones Mobile truck parked outside the venue. That's the vocal you hear on the official release of 'Emma'. A typically extravagant, very Eighties indulgence of which we were all guilty of in one way or another. I certainly had my Diva moments too but we'll keep shtum about that for the time being, shall we?

I mentioned earlier that we had shot a video for 'Black Planet' while we were out in LA just before our US tour had started. Alas, calamity struck and the film was ruined and rendered unusable in the processing stage so we had to re-shoot. I say calamity, well, it was for the production company but not for us. It meant another all-expenses paid trip out to LA. This time, with no pressing commitments to follow the shoot, we all decided to stay on for a few days to top up our tans. Ha, that's a joke.

We'd already made three previous videos. Early in my tenure with the band 'Body And Soul' was filmed at Pinewood Film Studios, if memory serves, on the outskirts of London. A post-apocalyptic vision of an ancient city in ruins, pillars aflame, and amongst the rubble and dry ice lays, symbolically, a smashed up drum kit. And we stand in this desolate, windswept, landscape with our instruments miming to the song. What it's all supposed to mean I have no idea, it's just hokum to my mind. As are most music videos.

Whilst I'd done a few things on TV previously, to my knowledge this was the first time the rest of the band had been in front of the cameras. For a novice, or even a seasoned hand, it can be very difficult to take filming seriously, although both Andrew and Mark did a fairly good job of pulling it off straight-faced. Craig and I exhibited less reverence for the form, and the process, with me taking my Jimmy Page obsession *possibly* a step too far by wielding a violin bow to my guitar. And this was a year or more before I'd met Page. Thinking about it now, maybe that's why he'd told me to fuck off; he'd seen the Sisters video and thought I was taking the piss. Well I was. But out of the situation, and out of the po-faced posturing of myself and my comrades.

The next video we shot was for 'Walk Away'. Filmed in an empty warehouse in Central London again, this was another exercise in strutting our stuff along a cat walk. Highly coiffured and reminding me slightly of a gothic Les Gray from Mud, Andrew mimed to camera while scattering stardust all over the place. As you do. Mind you I can't talk, by now I had perfected my bird-nest-hair Robert Smith wannabe look. In fact there was an awful lot of hair all around in that video. Unlike how it'd be today (smirks). No instruments this time, just our buffoonery accentuated by shadows, lights and dry ice. One truth proven beyond any reasonable doubt is that, while we may have been lovers we certainly weren't dancers.

'No Time To Cry' we filmed at the Electric Ballroom in Camden. By this time we were perfecting the moody lighting, dry ice and miming, throwing shapes, hats and capes, look. It is considered by far the best of the three by those in the know – namely me. No story line though, not that there has to be a story line for a music video but it is a medium that has been used to great affect by some... and not so much by most, including us.

Most musicians I know feel the making of videos can be a very alien, unnatural experience. Very few of us feel entirely comfortable in this arena. Miming is tantamount to acting which is something that we all have to learn to do convincingly if we want our videos to be credible. And having to contend with vidiots; video directors who fuss and flap when you just can't quite invest the right amount of gravitas into your performance to camera that they are demanding. Vidiots inbloodydeed.

That's why, apart from making videos where I didn't have to appear at all, 'Black Planet' was the easiest video to make that I have ever been involved in. The lyric to the song is a stroke of prescient genius on Andrew's part, a damning environmental indictment that is as pertinent today as it was back in 1985 when the song was written. It is also genius because, knowing Andrew's tendency to be calculating, the lyric mentions riding down the Highway 101 by the side of the ocean heading for Sunset. Now, you couldn't do that in Leeds, could you? Or Skegness? Only in Southern California would that make sense.

Why didn't we make a video for 'Marian', for example, which was a far more popular song, rather than 'Black Planet'? Because Andrew knew it would entail an all-expenses paid trip out to LA for us to shoot it. And, once we had Elektra, our American record label, on board, it was always inevitable that this was going to happen. More prosaically it might be argued that 'Black Planet' stood more chance of airplay on American radio than the darker 'Marian'. Either way, Andrew was a clever boy and both Craig and I were very grateful to be invited along for the ride.

All I had to do for the 'Black Planet' video shoot was essentially lie out in the back of the Monkeemobile – the car in which the Monkees used to drive around LA in their late-Sixties TV show – and pretend to be asleep for a couple of days in the Southern California sunshine. For most of the shots the car was fixed on a trailer that was pulled by a flat-bed truck, with a camera and crew on the back of it filming, along the streets and the PCH around LAX, LA harbour, and Redondo Beach. It was a good way to see parts of LA that we didn't normally get to see.

Andrew was *pretending* to drive. For the shots where the car was off the trailer, as Andrew couldn't drive and didn't have a license, we had a stand-in driver donning Andrew's hat, shades and jacket. Quite comical really as he was at least a head taller than Andrew and as broad as the three of us put together. When Andrew's jacket was returned to him it was a slightly looser fit than it was when he loaned it to the stand-in.

There was one shot, though, where Andrew *did* have to drive the car on the street. I'm assuming the Monkeemobile was an automatic otherwise I'm certain he couldn't have done it. A quick driving lesson ensued and Andrew declared himself ready to take mine, Craig's and his own life in his hands. It was a scene that, as a passenger, made me wish I hadn't drank quite as much the previous evening, or rather, had kept on drinking through the night and into the day. I asked for a stand-in for me for that shot but was just laughed at.

At speed and following the camera truck in front, Andrew had to accelerate right up to their back bumper, brake inches away from it and then stay at the same speed as the camera truck. A hairy scary stunt even for an experienced driver. Remember, he couldn't bloody well drive! I made sure I kept at least one eye open while he was executing the manoeuvre, not trusting him at the wheel one iota. But credit where credit's due, Andrew managed it in one take and we could all breathe easy again. There's more to that Eldritch fella than meets the eye, you know.

I had to do one small bit of acting during the shoot. Towards the end of the journey I had to wake up from my prone position in the back seat and look around as if I wasn't sure where I was. There was a degree of truth in my acting but not enough to earn me an Equity card. Actually my movement makes it look more like I'd escaped from one of the zombie films that my friend, Kris Guidio, so loved. We're all dressed in black and pasty white faced as if we hadn't seen daylight in years which, again, held an element of truth. The make-up girl certainly had her work cut out for her that day, being out in the sun for hours on end ensured that more sunblock than foundation and blusher was used on us. Careful there, we don't want a healthy complexion now, do we?

As a dash of colour I decided to wear a pretty little yellow patterned head scarf as a bandana (yeah, I know, shush). At the end of the first day of shooting we climbed into the back of the mini-bus that was our mode of transport between the location and our hotel and the first thing I did was remove my bandana.

"Ah, that's better," said I, giving my forehead a good scratching.

Craig started laughing at me. Andrew and John Hanti, who was in LA at the time looking after us, both turned around from their seats in the front and joined in the mirth.

"Whatcha fucking laughing at, ya twats?" I demanded.

"Have a look in the mirror, Wayne," replied Von trying to suppress a grin as wide as the brim of his black hat.

I stood up and leaned over the front two seats and looked at my face in the rear view mirror. "Ah, bollocks."

Of course being exposed to the sun all day had left me a little red-faced, in more ways than one. Where the bandana had been tied there was a white stripe across my forehead. I couldn't go anywhere for the next two weeks without either wearing the bandana or my hat until my skin had returned to its more normal pallid pallor.

At the end of the second day of shooting we were invited back to the George Barris Celebrity Cars showroom from whence we'd hired the Monkeemobile. They also owned the original Batmobile from the Sixties TV show as well as the Knight Rider car and various others not quite as celebrated. Typical bloody Hollywood really, they revere the celebrity car yet will pull down historical buildings as easily as a kid tears apart his lego. I made sure I got to sit behind the wheel of the Batmobile and had my photograph taken for posterity. Using the Monkeemobile for the 'Black Planet' shoot was quite the coup and made for a good press story. It didn't help the record become a hit though and neither did the video achieve heavy rotation on MTV. It is, however, by far my favourite of the four that we made while I was in The Sisters Of Mercy.

For the duration of the shoot we were ensconced in the legendary Tropicana Hotel on Santa Monica Boulevard, just a stone's throw from the Troubadour and Barney's Beanery, and a short blurry-eyed stumble from the Whiskey A Go Go on

Sunset. And as the music scene of the late Sixties and into the · Seventies grew up around these venues, then the Tropicana became its unofficial HQ and flophouse. Janis Joplin, Bob Marley, Alice Cooper, Iggy Pop, The Runaways and Ramones, Blondie, The New York Dolls, The Clash, Television, William Burroughs and many more all slept in the beds at the Trop. Even Jim Morrison would pass out here when he couldn't book his preferred room at the Alta Cienega Motel just around the corner. It was cheap and very liberal about what was allowed to go on within its walls. Also on the premises was Dukes Coffee Shop, a diner where you might see Shelley Winters breakfasting on pancakes or permanent resident Tom Waits noshing on a burger. This was where Craig and I ate when we had both money and hunger. It boasted quite the rock'n'roll heritage. Of course, what with Americans having no respect for history, it was all torn down in 1987 and replaced by a modern, generic, character-free hotel.

With our work finished it was then time for us to have fun. As I mentioned, we decided to stay on for a few days at the record company's expense. Craig and I were sharing a room again while Andrew and John shared another. Now, I've read that the 'Dritch has since claimed that we, Craig and I, decided to go to Disneyland rather than accompany him and John to Tijuana just over the border in Mexico. Well, yeah. Having never been to either place before, Disneyland was one place that was totally synonymous with SoCal and just had to be visited at least once.* In many ways it sums up the whole Californian

---

* I ended up going to Disneyland several times and loved it. Until I was living in Orange County less than five miles away, that is, in the late Nineties. My daughter, Dylan, was five or six years old at the time, so I bought annual passes for her and I. I'd very often pick her up after school and take her to Disneyland for a couple of hours. The only ride she ever wanted to go on though was It's A

culture for me; that and the Hollywood sign and Griffith Observatory atop the Hollywood Hills. And besides, *we weren't even invited* to go with you to Mexico, ya twat. Whilst relations between us were cordial at this time I certainly wouldn't lay claim to being friends and saying that we wanted to spend time together socially would be like saying we wanted a urethra swab.

Andrew and John rented a convertible and off to Tijuana* they went while Craig and I were left the keys to the rented minibus. I couldn't drive** and while Craig possessed a driving license he hadn't driven since he'd passed his test five or six years earlier. But he decided he'd have a go and drive us from Hollywood to Disneyland. We asked for directions at the hotel reception.

"Take the on-ramp for the 10 East, go straight until you hit the 5. Go south and exit in Anaheim, there'll be signs. Should take you about forty minutes," we were told.

Small World. It's like a bad acid trip, that ride. It's a water-based ride that features over 300 audio-animatronic children dressed in traditional costumes from cultures all around the world, frolicking in a spirit of international unity, and singing the attraction's title song in their own native languages. Its theme of global peace is to be commended but the tune is as catchy as gonorrhoea and almost as unhealthy for you. It's a nightmare... unless you're five years old. That was enough to put me off Disneyland for the rest of my God-given days.

* The Mission played in Tijuana once. It's a party town in Mexico just across the border from San Diego. In the US the legal drinking age is 21 in most states, including California. It is 18 in Tijuana. Hordes of rich white American kids are lured there each weekend with the promise of dirt cheap tequila, drugs, both illegal and prescription, and hookers. I don't know what it's like today but back in the Eighties the town was squalid and sordid. And great fun. The complete antithesis of Disneyland. When I lived in Orange County I went across border a couple of times with white American friends but was appalled by the disgraceful and abusive way they treated the Mexicans, as the inferior race they believe 'em to be. The Mexicans, along with other minority races, are the ones that work all the menial jobs in SoCal. Without them Southern California would grind to a halt.

** I didn't learn to drive until I was well into my thirties. I never felt the need for it while living in cities with decent public transport.

Sounded easy-peasy, didn't it? Thinking we could easily remember that we didn't write it down. Instead we had a quick stiff drink before we hit the road, a bit of Dutch courage for Craig – and I didn't need an excuse. We found *an* on-ramp so we took that and because Craig was a little nervous of driving we stayed in the nearside lane, the slow lane, and in second gear. When the minibus started to pick up a bit of speed the engine started screaming.

"Hey, mate. What's that noise?" I asked.

"It's the gearbox, I think, or it could be the engine. I should change up to a higher gear, really," replied Sterling Moss from the seat next to me.

"Well, why don't you?" I said, asking the obvious.

"I'm not really sure how to and I don't want to stall the car in this traffic," was Craig's sage reply.

"Alright mate, just keep it in second then," was my equally judicious response. After about two hours driving on the same freeway we began to think we'd gone wrong somewhere. It can't have been a wrong turn as we hadn't taken *any* turns. I was sure we were heading south by the position of the sun in the sky. Yeah, right. Nah, it just felt south to me, dunno why. We thought it best to pull off and find, using the local vernacular, a gas station to ask for directions again.

Next exit, we came off, found a garage, and while Craig was filling up I went to ask the way to Disneyland. Now that's not a question you ask every day, is it? Anyway, we were indeed heading south on the 5 but we were almost in San bloody Diego, near the border to Mexico. We'd obviously missed the Anaheim turn-off miles back. Being given new directions and writing them down this time on the back of the petrol receipt with a borrowed pen we got back on the 5 but headed north this time. Our new directions were good and we arrived at Disneyland only three hours later than we should've.

We parked up, paid our entrance fee, and wandered around Disneyland for a few hours, taking rides on as many attractions as we could. I don't remember there being long queues, as there were on subsequent visits. We even did It's A Small World, both of us feeling like we were on some nightmarish acid trip. But my favourite rides on my first visit were The Matterhorn, Space Mountain and The Pirates Of The Caribbean. Being of the gothic persuasion we also did The Haunted House and Craig and I were mistaken by some Midwesterners as part of the exhibit. Boo. Got ya.

With the sun starting to set to the west we decided to leave The Happiest Place On Earth and try to make our way back to the Tropicana in Hollywood before it got too dark. We found the on-ramp for the 5 North, pulled onto it and straight into the biggest traffic jam I'd ever seen. Rush hour in LA. We crawled all the way back to Hollywood, taking hours.

At one point we decided that we should turn on the car's headlights as it was now dark and every other car had their lights on. Except Craig didn't know how to and I was no help, I didn't even know where the ignition was. The next time the traffic came to a halt Craig jumped out and ran to the car in front and asked the gentleman driving if he could help us turn on our lights. Stepping out of his car he was laughing his head off at us, these weird-looking limeys that didn't know how to turn their headlights on. Anyway, he found the switch immediately, turned them on for us and showed Craig the difference between low and high beam. He was laughing all the way back to his car too. Eventually we made it back to the Trop and in one piece.

Being away from home for as long as we had, we'd not had the opportunity to do any clothes washing and the term 'a change of underpants' meant something different to us than actually changing into a clean pair. It meant turning them inside out. Of course you could only do this so many times before they became disgusting. So, that evening, after some quick scran in Dukes and a shower and 'a change of underpants', Craig and I visited the nearby Whiskey A Go Go.

I can't remember who was playing or even if there was a band on but we found ourselves a corner and soon struck up conversation with a couple of friendly honeys dressed to kill. I do remember there being a lot of those LA-band poodle-hair types, Mötley Crüe, Poison, Skid Row, LA Guns, those types, peacockising* around. They all looked the bloody same to me, like baby male chicks on a conveyor belt all bound for maceration.** We didn't talk to them though, and they seemed to be suspicious of us. The girls, being as forward as most other American girls I'd met, invited themselves back to the hotel with us and ended up staying and keeping us entertained until the 'Dritch returned a day or so later, bleary eyed and walking funny from his 'Lost Weekend' in Tijuana.

The next day we flew to New York City.

---

* To behave like a peacock, to pose or strut ostentatiously.

** A particularly heinous and barbaric practice employed in the chicken farming industry. Newborn, uncomprehending male chicks are sorted from females and then either thrown alive into giant electric mincers or gassed in their millions. It is a literal conveyor belt to death journeyed each year in Britain by 30 to 40 million animals, and all to bring the morning egg to our table.

CHAPTER 19

Let Sleeping Dogs Die

PLAYLIST:

1. Marlene On The Wall – Suzanne Vega   2. Friction – Television
3. Psycho Killer – Talking Heads   4. Gloria – Patti Smith
5. Rip Her To Shreds – Blondie   6. Blitzkrieg Bop – The Ramones
7. I Had Too Much To Dream (Last Night) – The Electric Prunes
8. You're Gonna Miss Me – The 13th Floor Elevators
9. Let's Talk About Girls – The Chocolate Watchband
10. Live At Live Aid 1985 YouTube clip – Madonna
11. Live At Live Aid 1985 YouTube clip –
Bob Dylan with Keith Richards and Ronnie Wood
12. Live At Live Aid 1985 YouTube clip – Led Zeppelin

As the trip was on Elektra's dime, rather than fly directly home to England after the 'Black Planet' video shoot the three of us decided to break the journey and stop off in NYC. There were no commitments for any of us to rush home for and if *you* had the choice of spending a few weeks off either in New York or in West Yorkshire, I'm damn sure you would've done the same as us.

Craig and I had arranged to stay with Lisa, Jenny and Debs, in their Mercer Street apartment between St Mark's Place and Washington Square. Andrew was elsewhere, possibly with his good friend Alan Vega. Craig was shacked up with Lisa in her room while I was sleeping on the couch in the living room.

Debs was with Brian Brain Damage and Jenny was nursing a broken, and betrayed, heart. Craig and I would either just hang out during the day while the girls were at work or we'd venture down to Bleecker Street to root through the record racks at Bleecker Bob's, or mosey on up to St Mark's Place to browse the alternative clothes shops. A couple of times we met up with our new mate, Lenny Kaye, who lived in a first-floor apartment just across the street from CBGB in the Bowery.

One afternoon we were in Lenny's place supping on beers. "Have a listen to this," he said. "I've just produced an album for this new girl on the scene. This is the first single, it's called 'Marlene On The Wall' and her name is Suzanne Vega."

When the song had finished we chorused, "Yeah, that's great that, Lenny," and it was. It became a huge hit.

"Hey, have you guys ever been to CBGB?" he asked.

"Nah," was our reply.

"Come on, let's go and see if Hilly* is there," said Lenny.

We walked out into the New York July afternoon humidity and crossed the street to CBGB. We were in luck, it was open. Walking in through the front door under that famous awning I remember the bar being on my right-hand side with the low stage at the far end of the room. Similar in dimension to a medium-sized British pub, I couldn't get over how much of a dive the place was. But musical history was seeping out of those walls, every inch of which was covered with band stickers, posters and graffiti. It reeked of disinfectant, stale beer and cigarettes, and urine. Authentic you might say. I'm sure there were some health and safety laws being broken at CBGB but this was the mid-Eighties before NYC became cleaned up and gentrified. Anything went.

---

* Hilly Kristal was the owner of the legendary CBGB.

There was a young lad working behind the bar. "Hey, man, is Hilly around?" asked Lenny.

"Nah, buddy, he'll be in this evening. You guys wanna beer?"

Looking at each other we all nodded. So, three beers ordered and we sat at a table taking in our surroundings. No one else was in the bar at the time, it being mid-afternoon. I sat there imagining the great bands that had started out playing here in CBGB – Television, Talking Heads, Patti Smith, Blondie, The Ramones and more. And how thrilling it was to be sat here with Lenny regaling us with tales about the early days when he and Patti used to open for Television here every Friday and Saturday and how The Ramones used to play four nights a week. How much Tom Verlaine despised David Byrne. Who shagged who and who used to shoot up downstairs in the toilets.

Lenny had stories about other luminaries too, Stiv Bators, Richard Hell, Johnny Thunders and Debbie Harry, the whole crew. It was brilliant to feel so close to that whole scene that I loved. I always preferred the NYC punk scene to the British one, Blondie to X-Ray Spex, Television to The Clash, Talking Heads to The Damned. By the way, if you are wondering who Lenny Kaye is then shame on you. However, just in case, Lenny plays guitar in the Patti Smith Group and has done so since the beginning of time. Just as impressive to me was the fact that he had curated the fabulous *Nuggets: Original Artyfacts From The First Psychedelic Era* compilation album that was originally released in 1972. Re-released in 1976 when it found favour, and influence, with the punk rock movement, it is a collection of classic garage band tracks from between 1965 and '68.

A year or so later Lenny would join us, The Mission, on stage at the Croydon Greyhound. He was wearing green dungarees and a work-shirt while we were all in our best black velvet finery. Our audience, predominantly aged between 15 and 18 at the time, had no idea who he was and probably thought he was just some old gimmer we'd pulled in off the street. It's hard to educate those that don't wanna be educated but we did try.

We were in NYC when Live Aid was broadcast on Saturday, July 13. Not being morning people and there being no one scheduled to perform that would warrant getting up early for, we missed most of the televised performances from Wembley Stadium. We did see highlights later and like everyone else in the world I was mightily impressed by my old faves, Queen. They rose to the occasion and then, off into the stratosphere. They were a killer live band. It was the first time we saw Bono and Co. in the role of 'Stadium U2' and it was novel to see a band of our peers become so instantly global. Maybe I'm stating the bleedin' obvious but it seems to me that playing Live Aid was the single biggest factor in breaking U2 on such a huge scale. Despite their undoubted best intentions it was a very good career move.

The only acts I was really interested in seeing though were all performing in Philadelphia. Madonna, whose genius has been to make the absolute best of an average talent, consolidated her position as queen of pop. She was fun and frivolous and brought some levity to the proceedings. Bob Dylan, with Ronnie Wood and Keith Richards, were, if I was being generous, shambolic.

Robert Plant, Jimmy Page, and John Paul Jones playing together publicly for the first time since Zeppelin disbanded after Bonham died was the one I was really looking forward to, and what a letdown it turned out to be. Jimmy Page, looking almost as dishevelled as he was when I'd met him just a few weeks earlier, his reputedly dissolute lifestyle beginning to take its toll on his once indisputable pulchritude, as it eventually does us all. Visibly dribbling down his front, he played the songs okay, if out of tune, until it came to the solos which he executed with a ham-fistedness that reminded me of mediocrely imaginative guitar players in any city centre rock pub on any given Saturday night. Sigh. Planty looked fine, tanned and healthy, although his threads were definitely of the disco-boy persuasion rather than the Rock God he undoubtedly is. Having early problems with his monitors, his voice was hoarse and scratchy throughout and he took a song or so to warm-up and find his pitch. As always live Robert didn't quite have the range he seemingly does in the studio. John Paul Jones we barely saw but he played the bass with his usual efficiency until he switched to keyboards for a startlingly grotesque version of 'Stairway To Heaven'. But worst of all was the fact that even with two supposedly top-class drummers, Tony Thompson and the reprehensible Pongo Collins who blamed *everyone* but himself for the debacle despite visibly not having learnt the songs, they could only muster a fraction of the power and finesse that the mighty John Bonham once brought to Zeppelin's infernal heat. Ah well, it did their legacy no real lasting harm and why should it? It was only a 20-minute festival performance, after all. To an estimated 1.9 billion viewers around the world. But for me it did dispel the myth somewhat seeing them perform so poorly... and in the daylight.*

Some evenings we'd get spruced up and go out and enjoy the cooling breeze at the rooftop bar of the Danceteria, scrounging drinks and lines from Ruth Polsky, our US promotor, and anyone else foolish enough to look our way. On occasion we'd also venture to the nearby Limelight where we'd sit in the roped-off area of the club terrified that someone more 'famous' than us would come in and we'd get bumped out of our VIP booth. Situated on Avenue of the Americas at West 20th and

---

* Led Zeppelin subsequently tried to block broadcasts of the performance and withheld permission for it to be included on the DVD release of Live Aid. Nevertheless, it can be found on YouTube.

housed in an old Gothic church, it was on the steps of the Limelight that Ruth was shockingly hit and slain by an out-of-control cab in 1986.

Brian Brain Damage would come through every few days with a cornucopia of drugs for us. Crystal meth was ever popular as was the occasional acid trip. One evening he burst into the apartment like a kid on Christmas morning with the exciting news that he could procure some ecstasy tabs, the new designer drug I'd heard so much about and was eager to try. Were we interested? Were we heck as like. So the following Friday evening he arrived with tabs enough for us all. With Jenny being away for the weekend, besides myself and Craig there was Lisa and Debs, BBD himself, and Frankie, an ex-pat friend of the girls, who had the kind of posh-school-educated plummy voice that BBC female newscasters used to have before colloquial dialects became all the rage. There's something inherently sexy about a woman that speaks with an accent of Received Pronunciation, probably something to do with the feeling that I'm batting way above my average. Frankie's regular beau, Steve Stevens (middle name Stephen?), the guitarist with Billy Idol's band, was away on tour at the time so Frankie was indeed slumming it a little by hanging out with me. But that's by the by.

Like a sacrament, BBD dispensed the tabs among his devout and zealous congregation. "Bless you, my child. May your trip be fervid," he'd minister to one and, "By the grace of heaven, let's fry your brain" to another.

As the X was kicking in everybody paired off. Craig was nestling with Lisa on the couch while Debs and BBD nuzzled up together in another quiet corner. So that left Frankie and I. With both of us a little uncomfortable at the intimacies going on around us we decided to go out for a walk. It was a warm, humid night accentuated by the chemicals that were flowing through our veins. We walked around the streets not really aware of where we were going while the X began to take full effect. I wanted to take all my clothes off, not for any carnal pleasure but to relieve some of the burning, itchy flush I was feeling on my skin. Frankie had to talk me out it. I wanted to lie down so we found a low wall that we both laid down on. But after what seemed like seconds I had to get up and walk around again. I neither wanted to stay still or to walk around, to lie down or stand up. I was very agitated. It wasn't the pleasurable experience that I was hoping for at all. Frankie was feeling the same.

Then we kind of realised that we were lost and didn't know how to get back to the apartment. The streets were dark and threatening. Neither of us could face asking a stranger for directions, not that we'd understand a word they'd say anyway. We just walked for a bit and then found a spot to lie down for a few minutes and then got up and walked some more. We held hands, not because of any feelings of amour but because we both needed to feel like we were connected and in the same predicament, that we weren't alone in this enveloping nightmare. Eventually, after what could've been an hour or five we found our way back to the apartment and let ourselves in. The other four had disappeared to the bedrooms so Frankie and I laid down on the couch finally stripped down to our underwear. We held each other but not a slither of sexual desire passed between us. We were just holding on for comfort, for dear life. We lay there whispering to each other as we waited for the come-down and, as the sky outside was touched by the first sigh of morning light that peaked through the blinds, we eventually fell into a feverish, disturbed sleep.

When we all started to surface later that day and compared experiences it seems that we'd all had bad trips, nothing like what had been promised on the packet. This ecstasy stuff was rubbish and nothing to rave about at all. Discussing it between us we decided that the tabs were a mixture of heroin and speed and some other ingredient none of us could quite identify. I wouldn't be touching it again, that's for sure. I'm gonna stick to acid and whizz from now on, I pledged.

Imagine my surprise when just a short three or four years later the whole acid house, rave thing blew up in Britain and the talk was of the new wonder drug, ecstasy. From the experience I'd had I couldn't understand it and so resisted doing E again until early in 1991 when Mick Brown, Mission drummer, brought some down to where I was staying at the time in the Herefordshire countryside on the border of England and Wales.

"Come on, Wayner, try this, you'll love it," Mick promised.

And I did and from then on I couldn't get enough of it. Mick's ecstasy was totally different to the dodgy tabs we'd had in NYC in '85.

Anyway, the upshot of our bewildering and not to say disappointing experience was that Craig and I both felt a little freaked out. We craved some normalcy so we decided that after four weeks of New York madness it was time for us to go home to Leeds. We called Andrew at wherever he was staying and told him we were going back to England and that we'd see him there when he got back later.

At home in Leeds I started writing new tunes for what I presumed would be the second Sisters album. I soon hit a rich vein of creativity and rattled off full demos for six to eight songs, complete with programmed drums, bass guitar and guitar parts. Along with the new stuff I'd demoed at Strawberry earlier that summer, I had more than enough as the basis for the new album. When Andrew arrived Blighty-side I went down to

London to visit him, taking a cassette of my new tunes. He was leaving for Hamburg in the next few days for the foreseeable. A friend of his had offered the use of an apartment so Andrew, who claimed to speak fluent German, thought it'd be a good place to go and start writing the next record. And, of course, Marian lived in Hamburg.

While in London on this particular sojourn, and feeling a little flush from a small publishing advance I'd just received, I visited one of the guitar shops on Denmark Street that specialised in rare and vintage guitars. Hanging on the wall I saw just the guitar to serve my Jimmy Page fixation. A Gibson cherry-red double-neck six and 12-string, just like the one Page had used on stage for years. I just had to have it. I think I paid £1,200 for it which was the most by far I had ever paid for a guitar up to that point. It might also have been more than its true value but, like anything else, it's worth it if you're willing to pay it.

What an albatross that beast became. I never got to use it on stage myself although Slink (Simon Hinkler) did in the early days of The Mission. We forced him to use it against his will and to compound his discomfort we affixed a stretchy, rubber strap on it so that the thing would bounce as he played it. He hated it with a venom and as soon as he felt secure enough in his position within the band he refused to use it anymore. In the studio we rarely used it as we had better both six and 12-string electric guitars. I later sold it and bought myself three 12-string Vox Teardrop guitars in various shades.

On the same afternoon I bought the Gibson double-neck I also bought myself a green Starcaster, a semi-hollow bodied guitar made by Fender that was so dark it looked black from a distance. Hambi had used one back in my days in Liverpool and I always loved the look of it. I had tried to persuade him to sell it me but he adored that beauty so much, as I came to love mine. Again, I later ended up with three Starcasters and although I've since sold two I still own the original dark green one. It has long since been retired from tours of duty and now resides peacefully at home in my studio. I have used it on every album I have ever recorded since. I paid £400 for it in August 1985. Both guitars are now, of course, worth thousands. For me, the first criterion in choosing a guitar is how it looks.

Of course we all have different tastes and aesthetics. I'm not a fan, generally, of modern-looking guitars, Flying Vs, or Stratocasters, my preference being for *big* guitars. Someone cruelly inclined may presume that big guitars are a substitute for a deficiency either bodily or mentally, much like sports cars are sometimes deemed as such. The next thing to consider is how it looks strapped on you and if it makes you look, and feel, more handsome and cool. Tall order, I know, for some guitarists. Next up would be its action, how it plays and feels. No point in having something that looks brilliant but you can't play it. Much like having the most beautiful girlfriend in the world who doesn't like shagging. What's the point?

And lastly, how it sounds, the noise it emits when you play it. A bit like David Beckham – looks great and would be an enviable trophy on anyone's arm and probably is very lovely to cuddle up to but, dear me, when he opens his gob all the allure is dispersed like dandelion seeds on a summer breeze. Even elocution lessons in David's case, or changing the pick-ups on a guitar, can't alter the basic inherent timbre. Mind you, I have owned a guitar or two like that and, in an attempt to salvage something from the relationship, have forlornly tried to change the way it sounds. Ultimately looks lose their lustre after a while and I have invariably ended up trading them in for a newer model. Guitars, eh? Can't live with 'em, can't live without 'em.

So a couple of weeks or so after Andrew had settled himself in Hamburg he called me and asked if I'd fly out there and join him for a while to work on the new tunes for the next album. Yeah, of course I would. I like Hamburg and a bit of time spent in the dens of iniquity in that fair city sounded to me like a fair swap for the now tired routine of the Faversham and Warehouse in Leeds. I had high hopes of Andrew and I bonding at last and finding *some* common ground while working on the music together during the day and cruising the more delinquent nightspots of Hamburg at night. I flew into Hamburg and caught a cab at the airport to the address I had been given.

As my journey commenced I noticed we were driving *away* from the city centre. Mmm, strange, I thought. Maybe the driver knows a quicker route or there's traffic going into the city. After all, it's not like a taxi driver to take an unwitting visitor the long way around just to put a few extra Deutschmarks on the meter now, is it? Nope, the taxi driver was going in the correct direction. After maybe a 20-minute drive we pulled up beside an apartment building on Hirsekamp, Bramfeld, on the outskirts of Hamburg, a residential area with no bars or restaurants evident anywhere close by. I rang the bell of the ground floor apartment and Andrew buzzed me in.

Seeing my compadre for the first time in a few weeks we bade each other a rather formal hello, no hugs or kisses, Andrew not being the kind to brook such displays of sentimentality. He showed me around the place like an estate agent on a soft sell. There was a couple of bedrooms, one each for him and I, a bathroom, and a long living room come dining area come kitchenette. At one end the porta-studio was set up along with Dr Avalanche and a few guitar pedals. At the other end of the room was a couch with a TV and video machine and a collection of films on video, all in bloody German, of course.

Off the lounge area was a small recessed kitchen. Surprisingly there were no dirty dishes in the sink. Andrew was either very tidy and clean or he had washed and tidied up before my arrival. Aw, bless. He explained that we were indeed about 10 kms from Hamburg city centre.

"So, what do you do of an evening then?" I asked.

"I just stay in and watch TV or do a bit of work," he replied.

"Really. So how often do you go into town and how d'you get there?" I enquired.

"Ah, once in a while, and by bus," he informed me.

Bloody hell, Andrew Eldritch on public transport? I couldn't imagine such a thing. He certainly wouldn't have done that in Leeds, God forbid. Taking stock of the situation and realising there was very little distraction to be had I resigned myself to knuckling down to the task that I'd actually come to Hamburg for, to work with Andrew on new songs. Over a cup of coffee I asked, "So, did you have a listen to the cassette I gave you?"

"Mmm, yes, I did."

"And?"

"I don't like it, it's not where I hear the next album going."

Disguising my bruised ego and feeling a little not unhurt, "Okay, fair enough. So where do you hear it going?"

"Let me play you some of the things I've been working on."

And with that he proceeded to playback five or six tracks on the porta-studio. Very skeletal in form, most of the tracks were basically one musical motif with seemingly no structure, no dynamic. The Doktor of course was ever-present; one song with just a sketch of a guitar line, a couple with just a bass line, another with a badly played keyboard, it was hard to see very much potential in any of this on first listen. But I bit my tongue and asked how Andrew saw my involvement with these tracks.

343

"Well, I thought you could flesh out the ideas with guitars and maybe some keyboard parts, and a bass line on the songs that don't already have one," he replied.

He handed me a piece of paper. "This is the album title and running order," he told me.

In Andrew's immaculate ornate calligraphy it read: *Left On Mission And Revenge*. This was followed by a list of ten or 12 song titles divided up into side one and side two. Some of the song titles I recall written on that paper were 'Torch', 'Giving Ground', 'Driven Like The Snow', 'Mission' and 'This Corrosion'. Andrew had yet to write any lyrics for these titles. He had *only* the titles. Strange then that 'This Corrosion' would eventually be written about me. Unless Andrew was being more Byzantine than usual, it took the initial success of The Mission a year later to ultimately provoke him into completing the lyrics of 'This Corrosion'. Andrew was never happier than when he had someone at whom to direct his ire.

And while we're about it let me put something straight here. I didn't steal the idea from Eldritch's proposed album title for naming our new band, The Mission, as has been presumed by the man himself. If I had been canny enough to use his title as inspiration then surely Revenge would've been the more apt choice. And as much as I'd love to take credit for scuppering his plans to use what is, indeed, a great album title and forcing him to use the more prosaic *Floodland*, I sadly can't. I'm not that ingenious or conniving.

My hopes for us bonding during our time together in Hamburg were quickly dashed. I soon realised that this work was less about collaboration and more about me being Andrew's musical lackey. It became clear that he was expecting me to fill in all the musical gaps on these unadorned tracks of his while he retained the full publishing credits. I'd been in this situation once before in Liverpool with Hambi and vowed to myself to never allow it to happen again. But here I was.

Rather than work together I would work alone while Von watched German TV and read newspapers. I was asked to use headphones while I worked so as not to disturb his viewing. Cheeky sod. I added guitar and bass lines to his bare bones songs and attempted to knock them into some kind of recognisable shape. The guitar line that eventually found its way onto the *Floodland* version of 'Dominion' certainly came about during these sessions. I nicked an approximation of it years later for 'Met-Amor-Phosis' on The Mission album, *Another Fall From Grace*. There were no guide vocals to work with, the songs being repetitious in the extreme, a form that was alien to me for its lack of musical movement. It was a dismal experience, four interminable weeks spent doing this.

I couldn't even watch TV with him as it was all in German, this being long before the advent of cable. And Andrew made no effort to be sociable any more than he'd ever been despite the fact that it was endless days of just the two us stuck in that Godforsaken place. Every conversation with him was a verbal tussle, it was so fucking wearing. My evenings were spent either working with headphones on or in my room with a bottle of Liebfraumilch and reading a book. I seem to remember even starting to scribble a lyric or two into a notebook for some of the songs I'd written that were being rejected. I had one entitled 'Wasteland', another called 'Sacrilege', 'Serpent's Kiss' another, and a Zeppelin pastiche I'd named 'Severina'.

I remember only two evenings out during the month that I was in Hamburg. One night I was picked up by my friend, Fiona, who played keyboards in the excellent German band, X-Mal Deutschland. We met up with her fellow band mates, Anya, Manuela and Wolfgang, in a bar just off the Reeperbahn for a rouzy-bouzy to-do. The other occasion I remember going into town was when our friends from Yorkshire, The Skeletal Family, were playing at the Markthalle on Sunday, September 29. Andrew and I caught the bus into the city centre and made our way to the venue. We were invited to join 'em on stage for the encore, a hammy version of 'Knocking On Heaven's Door'.

After the gig Andrew disappeared into the night with Karina, the singer, while I had bought the impoverished boys in the band a bottle of vodka to supplement their paltry rider. With none of us ready for bed we ended up strolling the Reeperbahn, as groups of lads in Hamburg are prone to do. All a bit sozzled by now we determined that if we pooled our meagre resources we'd have just about enough cash to pay for one of us to be entertained by a lady of the night. But how best to decide which one of the six or seven of us this dubious privilege would be conferred upon?

Taking the last gulp from his bottle of beer, Stan proclaimed, "Let's spin the bottle!"

"Great idea, that's a fair way to decide," exclaimed Trotwood lasciviously.

We found a quiet doorway and sat around in a circle. Martin, the Skels drummer, spun the bottle and when it eventually came to a stop it was pointing in my direction. Bloody hell, what's the chances of that, eh? Gathering up my ill-gotten gains from the others I made my way to the door of the harlot of my choice. I was in and out of there within two minutes and that included taking my clothes off and putting 'em back on again when the transaction was completed. What a waste of money. Ah well, it mostly wasn't mine.

When my prison sentence in Hamburg was up I couldn't wait to get out of there and leave the 'Dritch to his own morose company. I tried, I really did try to like him, to get on with him, but he and I were just two very different kinds of people and, while sometimes the work you do together is more valuable than any personal relationship you may have, it certainly doesn't make for a harmonious life. Andrew thrived on bile, and one-upmanship. He was a ferocious intellectual foe and I found it all too needless and exhausting. I arrived back in Leeds and went with Craig that night to the Fav to drown a few sorrows.

"So, how was it in Hamburg, mate?" he enquired.

"Don't ask."

So he didn't but he didn't need to. He fully understood.

A couple of weeks later Andrew arrived back in Leeds and we arranged to have a first rehearsal for the new album at Parkside Studios in Armley.

It was Monday, October 21. Craig and I arrived first and set up the backline and Doktor Avalanche. Andrew arrived and, after a coffee, a fag, and a line, we got down to work. Andrew played the demos he and I had worked on in Hamburg. I sneaked a peek at Craig during playback and knew him well enough to know that there was a dark cloud forming on his brow. We alighted on one of the songs to try first. 'Torch', I think it was.

Andrew had written a few snatches of lyrics that he mumbled into the microphone while Craig and I tried to inject a little colour, if not enthusiasm, into the rather pallid, etiolated chord sequence that Andrew had written. A storm was brewing and the atmosphere in the room was starting to feel toxic. Getting nowhere fast and attempting to keep the peace I suggested we have a go at something else.

Next up was an up-tempo bass line that Andrew had come up with which may or may not have eventually become 'Lucretia, My Reflection'. Essentially one bass loop for an undefined length of time and played at such a tempo that it was more like a guitar line rather than bass, this was the final drop of rain that broke the dam.

Craig simply didn't like it although, to be fair to him, it did have a different groove at that point and required him to play it at almost twice the speed it ended up being on *Floodland*. The words silk purse and sow's ear come to mind when I later heard the album version. Kudos to Von for that.

In the meantime, back in Armley, Craig was having none of it. After about ten minutes of this mindless repetition, Craig took his bass off and with a loud clatter it was flung it to the ground. I stopped playing guitar and shut the Doktor up. Andrew stopped moaning into the mic.

"That's it, I've had enough, it's fucking shit. These are shit songs and that's a shit bass line," ranted my best friend. "I'm leaving the group, fuck off, you twat."

That last remark was aimed at Andrew and not me, I hasten to add. And with his discordant open bass strings still resonating through his amp, Craig Adams stormed out of the rehearsal room and out of the band. A beat or two passed and Andrew turned to me

"Good. Now we've got rid of the driftwood maybe we can get down to some proper work."

If I wasn't speechless before then I certainly was now.

For an hour or two we played around despondently, certainly on my part if not Andrew's, with a couple more of the songs and then called it a day. As I left I said I'd see him on the morrow. That evening when I arrived home I called Craig and we arranged to meet in the pub. His mind was made up, he was definitely leaving the band, he declared. He hated Andrew's new material while loving mine, the songs that had been rejected. It was Andrew's intention at the time to curtail our touring activities anyway, and since being on the road is what Craig and I loved the most about being in a band, Craig suggested we form our own new band.

"Now, that's an idea," I replied.

Next morning I went to visit Andrew at home and informed him that I too was leaving The Sisters Of Mercy, and forming a new band with Craig. Andrew understood but asked me if I would play guitar on his new album anyway, to which I readily agreed. It was all very civil and amicable.

As I pondered the future I couldn't help feeling that the last two years had been merely a diversion, not a destination.

END OF PART ONE

Thanks & Acknowledgements to:

Chris Charlesworth, my editor, who navigated his way through my verbosity with sensitivity and empathy and pruned my words to a manageable and, hopefully, readable script.

David Barraclough for his support, encouragement, and guidance. Up the Mariners!

Imogen Gordon Clark for her diligence, organisational skills, and patience with my persnicketiness.

Debra Geddes and David Stock and all at Omnibus Press.

Eva Allen and Alex Jaworzyn for proofreading.

George Allen at Anger Management who has steered me through stormy seas and troubled waters and found me an island paradise on which to reside.

And in no particular order: Craig Adams, Gary Numan, Iggy Pop, Steve Power, David M. Allen, Kris Guidio, Brian Powell, Billy Duffy, David Knopov, Ambrose Reynolds, Denyze D'Arcy, Paul Barlow, Jonathan Moss, Doreen Allen, Jon Klein, Brian 'Nasher' Nash, Julie Irving, Nina Antonio, Rich Vernon, Jez Webb, Debbie Divell, Danny Horrigan, Hambi Haralambous, Tim Palmer, Chris Nagle, Bernardo Ribeiro, Alexander Reynolds, Mark Andrews, Trotwood, Mats Lernaby, Marcus Birro, Joey Musker, Pete Davis, Francesco Mellina, & Liverpool FC.